# AMC'S BEST DAY HIKES IN
# NEW JERSEY

## Four-Season Guide to 50 of the Best Trails
## in the Garden State, from the Skylands to the Shore

D0860932

**PRISCILLA ESTES**

Appalachian Mountain Club Books
Boston, Massachusetts

AMC is a nonprofit organization, and sales of AMC Books fund our mission of protecting the Northeast outdoors. If you appreciate our efforts and would like to become a member or make a donation to AMC, visit outdoors.org, call 800-372-1758, or contact us at Appalachian Mountain Club, 10 City Square, Boston, MA 02129.

outdoors.org/books-maps

Distributed by National Book Network.

Front cover photograph of the Delaware Water Gap National Recreation Area © Brady Robinson
Back cover photographs (left to right) of Mohican Outdoor Center © AMC/Paula Champagne and of the Appalachian Trail in New Jersey © Ryan Smith
Interior photographs © Priscilla Estes except where noted
Maps by Ken Dumas © Appalachian Mountain Club
Book design by Abigail Coyle

**Library of Congress Cataloging-in-Publication Data**
Names: Estes, Priscilla A., author.
Title: AMC's best day hikes in New Jersey : four-season guide to 50 of the best trails in the Garden State, from the Skylands to the shore / by Priscilla Estes.
Other titles: Appalachian Mountain Club's best day hikes in New Jersey
Description: Boston, Massachusetts : Appalachian Mountain Club Books, [2019] | "Distributed by National Book Network"--T.p. verso. | Includes index.
Identifiers: LCCN 2018051719 (print) | LCCN 2018054736 (ebook) | ISBN 9781628420821 (ePub) | ISBN 9781628420838 (Mobi) | ISBN 9781628420814 (paperback)
Subjects: LCSH: Hiking--New Jersey--Guidebooks. | Walking--New Jersey--Guidebooks. | Trails--New Jersey--Guidebooks. | New Jersey--Guidebooks.
Classification: LCC GV199.42.N5 (ebook) | LCC GV199.42.N5 E77 2019 (print) | DDC 796.5109749--dc23
LC record available at https://lccn.loc.gov/2018051719

The paper used in this publication meets the minimum requirements of the American National Standard for Information Sciences-Permanence of Paper for Printed Library Materials, ANSI Z39.48-1984. ∞

Outdoor recreation activities by their very nature are potentially hazardous. This book is not a substitute for good personal judgment and training in outdoor skills. Due to changes in conditions, use of the information in this book is at the sole risk of the user. The author and the Appalachian Mountain Club assume no liability for accidents happening to, or injuries sustained by, readers who engage in the activities described in this book.

Interior pages and cover are printed on responsibly harvested paper stock certified by The Forest Stewardship Council®, an independent auditor of responsible forestry practices.

Printed in the United States of America, using vegetable-based inks.

5 4 3 2 1    19 20 21 22 23

FSC
www.fsc.org
MIX
Paper from
responsible sources
FSC® C005010

*To Patricia and Steven Estes,*
*who loved nature and returned to it.*

# LOCATOR MAP

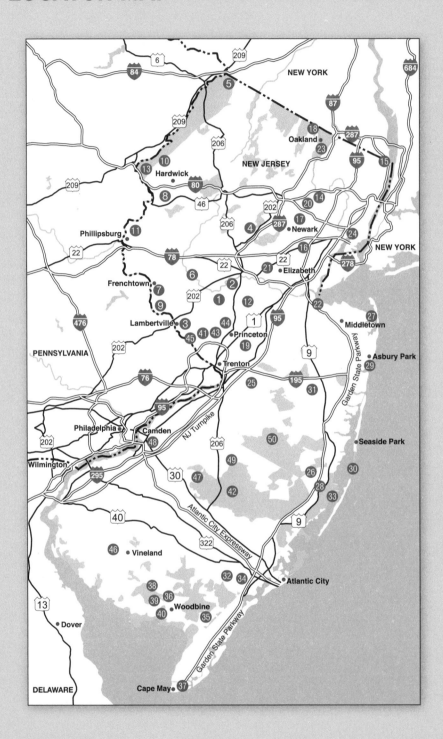

# CONTENTS

## ESSAYS

# AT-A-GLANCE TRIP PLANNER

| TRIP NUMBER | TRIP NAME | LOCATION | DIFFICULTY | DISTANCE | ELEVATION GAIN |
|---|---|---|---|---|---|
| **SKYLANDS** | | | | | |
| 1 | Sourland Mountain Preserve | Hillsborough | Moderate | 6.3 mi | 700 ft |
| 2 | Duke Farms | Hillsborough | Easy | 4.9 mi | 496 ft |
| 3 | Rockhopper and Dry Run Creek Trails | Lambertville | Moderate-Strenuous | 9.3 mi | 1,000 ft |
| 4 | Morristown National Historical Park: Jockey Hollow Section | Morristown | Strenuous | 10 mi | 1,250 ft |
| 5 | High Point State Park: Monument Trail to Appalachian Trail | Sussex | Strenuous | 7.9 mi | 1,250 ft |
| 6 | Deer Path Park: Round Mountain Section | Flemington | Easy-Moderate | 6.6 mi | 900 ft |
| 7 | Delaware and Raritan Canal and Horseshoe Bend Park | Frenchtown | Moderate-Strenuous | 10.6 mi | 900 ft |
| 8 | Jenny Jump State Forest | Hope | Moderate | 4.9 mi | 900 ft |
| 9 | White Oak Trail to Lockatong Creek | Stockton | Moderate | 5.8 mi | 725 ft |
| 10 | Delaware Water Gap National Recreation Area: Millbrook Village to Van Campens Glen Loop | Hardwick | Strenuous | 7.1 mi | 850 ft |
| 11 | Marble Hill Natural Resource Area | Phillipsburg | Easy | 4 mi | 900 ft |
| 12 | Six Mile Run Reservoir | Somerset | Easy | 6 mi | 400 ft |
| 13 | Mohican Outdoor Center: Coppermines-Kaiser-Appalachian Trails Loop | Blairstown | Moderate | 5.7 mi | 900 ft |
| **GATEWAY** | | | | | |
| 14 | Garret Mountain Reservation | Woodland Park | Easy | 2.8 mi | 400 ft |
| 15 | Palisades Interstate Park: State Line Lookout to Peanut Leap Cascade | Alpine | Moderate | 3 mi | 600 ft |
| 16 | Watchung Reservation: White Trail to Feltville | Scotch Plains | Easy | 3.9 mi | 550 ft |
| 17 | Branch Brook Park | Newark | Easy | 4.5 mi | 160 ft |
| 18 | Norvin Green State Forest (South) | Ringwood | Strenuous | 5.4 mi | 1,800 ft |
| 19 | Plainsboro Preserve | Cranbury | Easy | 4.9 mi | 200 ft |

| ESTIMATED TIME | TRIP HIGHLIGHTS | FEE | GOOD FOR KIDS | DOG-FRIENDLY | PUBLIC TRANSIT | X-C SKIING | SNOWSHOEING |
|---|---|---|---|---|---|---|---|
| 3 hrs | "Ringing rocks," boulder fields, a stream that roars | | ✓ | ✓ | | ✓ | ✓ |
| 2 hrs | Former Duke estate with lakes, fountains, statues, and orchids | | ✓ | | | ✓ | ✓ |
| 4.5 hrs | Boulder-hopping, cardio workout on Continental Army's route | | ✓ | ✓ | | ✓ | ✓ |
| 5-6 hrs | Rolling terrain on former farm past Continental Army encampments | | | ✓ | | ✓ | ✓ |
| 5 hrs | Panoramic views of three states from the highest point in New Jersey | | | ✓ | | ✓ | ✓ |
| 3.5 hrs | Woods, meadows, historic farms and barns, beehives | | ✓ | ✓ | | ✓ | ✓ |
| 5.5 hrs | Walk along the Delaware River then over ravines, streams, and rolling meadows | | ✓ | ✓ | | ✓ | ✓ |
| 3 hrs | Views of the Kittatinny Mountain Ridge and Valley; dramatic rock outcroppings | | | ✓ | | ✓ | ✓ |
| 3-4 hrs | Woodsy loop over wetlands and along a creek; stone ruins | | | ✓ | | ✓ | ✓ |
| 4 hrs | Waterfalls, wildflowers, wooded glens, and steep steps | | | | | ✓ | ✓ |
| 2 hrs | Views of Delaware River, rhododendrons, abandoned iron mine | | ✓ | ✓ | | | ✓ |
| 2.5 hrs | Zigzag between fields and woods, along a creek | | ✓ | ✓ | | | ✓ |
| 3 hrs | Ridge walk with views of Delaware Water Gap; waterfalls | | ✓ | ✓ | | | ✓ |
| 2 hrs | Excellent New York City views; climb Lambert Tower | | ✓ | ✓ | ✓ | ✓ | ✓ |
| 1.5-2 hrs | Hudson River vistas, steep stone steps to a waterfall | | ✓ | ✓ | ✓ | ✓ | ✓ |
| 2.5 hrs | Explore an abandoned village deep in the woods | | ✓ | ✓ | | ✓ | ✓ |
| 2 hrs | Largest collection of cherry blossom trees in the U.S.; hike the Lenape Trail | | ✓ | ✓ | ✓ | ✓ | ✓ |
| 4-5 hrs | 360-degree views of New York City and Wanaque Reservoir; rock scrambles | | | ✓ | | | ✓ |
| 2.5 hrs | Peaceful lake, secluded woods, nature center | | ✓ | | | | |

| TRIP NUMBER | TRIP NAME | LOCATION | DIFFICULTY | DISTANCE | ELEVATION GAIN |
|---|---|---|---|---|---|
| 20 | Mills Reservation | Cedar Grove | Easy-Moderate | 2.5 mi | 300 ft |
| 21 | Lenape Park | Cranford | Easy | 4.3 mi | 300 ft |
| 22 | Cheesequake State Park | Matawan | Moderate | 3.3 mi | 370 ft |
| 23 | Ramapo Mountain State Forest | Oakland | Strenuous | 5.4 mi | 650 ft |
| 24 | Liberty State Park | Jersey City | Easy | 5.2 mi | 20 ft |
| **JERSEY SHORE** | | | | | |
| 25 | Clayton Park | Imlaystown | Easy | 4.2 mi | 490 ft |
| 26 | Wells Mills County Park | Waretown | Moderate | 8.3 mi | 750 ft |
| 27 | Hartshorne Woods Park | Locust | Strenuous | 9.3 mi | 1,600 ft |
| 28 | Barnegat Branch Trail | Bayville | Easy | 6.2 mi | 100 ft |
| 29 | Manasquan to Asbury Park | Manasquan | Moderate | 9.8 mi | 50 ft |
| 30 | Island Beach State Park: Johnny Allen's Cove Trail and Barnegat Inlet Trail | Seaside Park | Johnny Allen's Cove Trail: Easy; Barnegat Inlet Trail: Moderate | Johnny Allen's Cove Trail: 1.2 mi; Barnegat Inlet Trail: 4.1 mi | Johnny Allen's Cove Trail: 100 ft; Barnegat Inlet Trail: 200 ft |
| 31 | Forest Resource Education Center | Jackson | Easy | 5.4 mi | 300 ft |
| **GREATER ATLANTIC CITY** | | | | | |
| 32 | Estell Manor Park | Mays Landing | Easy | 5.6 mi | 150 ft |
| 33 | Edwin B. Forsythe National Wildlife Refuge | Galloway | Easy | 5.3 mi | 300 ft |
| 34 | Egg Harbor Township Nature Reserve | Egg Harbor Township | Easy | 3 mi | 100 ft |
| **SOUTHERN SHORE** | | | | | |
| 35 | Belleplain State Forest | Woodbine | Moderate | 10.3 mi | 300 ft |
| 36 | Thompson's and Moore's Beaches | Heislerville | Easy | 2.4 mi and 1.4 mi | 20 ft |

| ESTIMATED TIME | TRIP HIGHLIGHTS | FEE | GOOD FOR KIDS | DOG-FRIENDLY | PUBLIC TRANSIT | X-C SKIING | SNOWSHOEING |
|---|---|---|---|---|---|---|---|
| 1.5 hrs | Rocky footing along edge of quarry; dramatic views of New York City | | | ● | | | ● |
| 2 hrs | Woods, streams, and a shopping mall; Lenape Pond on 1-mile extension | | ● | ● | | ● | ● |
| 2 hrs | Good beginner's hike with well-marked trails; boardwalk over Atlantic white cedar swamp | $ | ● | ● | | ● | ● |
| 3 hrs | Boulder scrambling, castle ruins, lakes, views of New York City | | ● | ● | ● | ● | ● |
| 2 hrs | Flat trail along the Hudson River; excellent New York City views; urban oasis | | ● | ● | ● | ● | ● |
| 2 hrs | Wildflowers; mountain laurels; and cozy, sparsely populated trails | | ● | ● | | ● | ● |
| 4 hrs | Scenic pine barrens primer but hilly; excellent nature center | | ● | ● | | | ● |
| 5 hrs | Excellent Navesink River views, deep woods, World War II bunkers | | | ● | | ● | ● |
| 2.5 hrs | Straight, flat trail is good for beginners; water, woods, and suburbs | | ● | ● | ● | ● | ● |
| 4 hrs | Walk the boardwalk and beach through popular shore towns | | ● | ● | ● | | |
| Johnny Allen's Cove Trail: 30 mins; Barnegat Inlet Trail: 3.5 hrs | Stroll the dunes of a barrier reef surrounded by water toward a lighthouse | $ | ● | ● | | | |
| 2.5 hrs | A flat Pine Barrens walk through a seedling nursery | | ● | ● | | ● | ● |
| 2.5 hrs | 1.8-mile boardwalk through a swamp; World War I munitions plant; South River views | | ● | ● | | ● | ● |
| 2.5 hrs | A birder's paradise with marshes and stunning views of Atlantic City | | ● | | | | |
| 1.5 hrs | An eerie world of water and pine trees through a former quarry; sledding hill | | ● | ● | | ● | ● |
| 5 hrs | Long woods walk past lakes, through wetlands and tunnels of mountain laurels | | ● | ● | | ● | ● |
| 2 hrs | Birds, butterflies, diamondback turtles, and spawning horseshoe crabs; secluded, non-crowded beaches | | ● | | | | |

| TRIP NUMBER | TRIP NAME | LOCATION | DIFFICULTY | DISTANCE | ELEVATION GAIN |
|---|---|---|---|---|---|
| 37 | Cape May Point State Park and South Cape May Meadows Preserve | Cape May Point | Easy | 3.4 mi | 100 ft |
| 38 | Maurice River Bluffs Preserve | Millville | Moderate | 5.5 mi | 400 ft |
| 39 | Glades Wildlife Refuge | Port Norris | Moderate | 5.2 mi | 200 ft |
| 40 | Bivalve Wetlands Walk | Port Norris | Easy | 3.8 mi | 50 ft |
| **DELAWARE RIVER** | | | | | |
| 41 | Ted Stiles Preserve at Baldpate Mountain | Titusville | Moderate | 9 mi | 450 ft |
| 42 | Mullica River Trail: Atsion to Quakerbridge | Shamong | Moderate | 9.9 mi | 320 ft |
| 43 | Jacob's Creek | Hopewell | Easy | 2.7 miles | 250 ft |
| 44 | Laurie Chauncey Trail | Princeton | Easy | 2.7 mi | 200 ft |
| 45 | Washington Crossing State Park | Titusville | Easy | 3.9 mi | 350 ft |
| 46 | Parvin State Park | Elmer | Moderate-Strenuous | 9.3 mi | 375 ft |
| 47 | Black Run Preserve | Marlton | Easy | 3.2 mi | 100 ft |
| 48 | Cooper River Park Loop | Cherry Hill | Easy | 7.8 mi | 200 ft |
| 49 | Carranza Memorial to Apple Pie Hill to Route 72 | Tabernacle | Moderate | 12.3 mi | 500 ft |
| 50 | Brendan T. Byrne State Forest | Browns Mills | Easy | 6.8 mi | 160 ft |

| Estimated Time | Trip Highlights | Fee | Good for Kids | Dog-Friendly | Public Transit | X-C Skiing | Snowshoeing |
|---|---|---|---|---|---|---|---|
| 1.5 hrs | A mix of sand, sea, woods, and marshes; prime hawk migration area; lighthouse | | ✓ | | | | |
| 3 hrs | Rugged trail through forests and along the bluff of Maurice River | | ✓ | | | | |
| 2.5 hrs | Old-growth forest, sugar-sand beach, bald eagles | | ✓ | | | | |
| 2 hrs | Boardwalk over coastal salt marsh; wildlife | | ✓ | | | | |
| 4.5 hrs | Aerobic workout through wildflower meadows and mature forest | | ✓ | ✓ | | ✓ | ✓ |
| 4.5 hrs | Quiet hike in the Pine Barrens along a river | | ✓ | ✓ | | ✓ | ✓ |
| 1.5 hrs | Secluded wildflower hike with easy stream crossings | | ✓ | ✓ | | | ✓ |
| 1.5 hrs | Green oasis along a creek; three-pony bridge | | ✓ | ✓ | | ✓ | ✓ |
| 2 hrs | See where George Washington crossed the Delaware; walk in his footsteps | | ✓ | ✓ | | ✓ | ✓ |
| 5 hrs | Wildflowers, lake, egrets, and a secluded swamp trail | | ✓ | ✓ | | ✓ | ✓ |
| 1.5 hrs | A pristine and calm corner of Pinelands National Reserve | | ✓ | ✓ | | ✓ | ✓ |
| 3.5 hrs | Urban and suburban adventure with water, woods, and hawks | | ✓ | ✓ | ✓ | ✓ | ✓ |
| 5-6 hrs | Pine Barrens wonderland: fire tower, blue lakes, cedar swamps | | | ✓ | | ✓ | ✓ |
| 3 hrs | Sandy paths through flooded cranberry bogs; tundra swans; Whitesbog Village | | ✓ | ✓ | | ✓ | ✓ |

# ACKNOWLEDGMENTS

The biggest thanks go to my husband of 39 years, Paul Wulfing, who in 1996 introduced me to the Appalachian Mountain Club as a connection to healthy activities we could do together. The AMC has been a big part of our lives ever since.

Much gratitude goes to my hiking companions who put up with my starts, stops, missteps, and general pokiness: Joan Aichele, Jim Bloom, Diane Chew, Geri Chmiel, Carol and Don Kluchinski, Lois Rothenberger, Lennie Steinmetz, and Paul Wulfing. Thanks go to the guidance and companionship of these hiking clubs: Outdoor Club of South Jersey, TriState Ramblers, and Appalachian Mountain Club (Delaware Valley Chapter and New York–North Jersey Chapter).

For pointing me to some of the best and least-understood hikes in New Jersey, kudos go to Mike Helbing, president of Metrotrails hiking club and chairman of the Warren County Board of Recreation Commissioners. His encyclopedic knowledge of the entire state is nothing short of amazing. (And thanks to Lennie Steinmetz for introducing us.)

Retired New Jersey game warden Greg Honachefsky introduced me to miraculous salt marshes and the horseshoe crab conservation program reTURN the Favor (returnthefavornj.org).

The cheerleading team gets a special shout-out. (Two months after signing the book contract, my father sickened and died; I was executor of his 110-acre farm in Georgia. I love you, brother Charlie!) Diane Chew pointed out that the book was not a marathon project, but a way to help others enjoy the outdoors. Candace Pedicord of Spirited Life Coaching encouraged me to make the process fun, because fun is essential to enjoying life. Barbara Celecz knew I could do it.

My extraordinary Pilates teachers, Barbara Blasko and Darlene Kalinowski, kept me in hiking shape.

Blogs and websites provided immense guidance, especially these: *Gone Hikin'*, *South Jersey Trails*, and the New Jersey Forests website.

My editors at AMC Books were great, and made the book better by improving readability: books editor Shannon Smith, editorial director Jennifer Wehunt, and copyeditor Lenore Howard. Map illustrator Ken Dumas worked his magic on the maps. I owe a debt to Lois Rothenberger, my unpaid literary "agent," for bringing the book opportunity to my attention.

Mostly, again, thanks go to my husband for his considerable map-reading skills, encouragement, understanding, hours of help, and unending love.

Gratefully,
Priscilla Estes
Writer, hiker, yoga teacher

# INTRODUCTION

New Jersey is a beautiful state of glorious contrasts: small but diverse, urban but agricultural, inland and coastal, industrial yet forested.

At 8,723 square miles, it's one of the smallest states, ranked 47th in size. Only Connecticut, Rhode Island, and Delaware are smaller. But New Jersey ranks first in population density, with 1,195.5 people per square mile, and is eleventh in total population. New Jersey is the only state in the union in which every county is considered "urban." The U.S. Census Bureau classifies an urban area as a territory that encompass at least 2,500 people, at least 1,500 of which reside outside institutional group quarters. Yet fully 29 percent of New Jersey's total land area has been permanently preserved by all levels of government. (The average number for the entire United States is 27 percent.) New Jersey exceeds national standards when it comes to protecting land by regulatory legislation.

Despite dense population and urbanization, the state has a strong tradition of agriculture. New Jersey is one of the top ten producers of blueberries, cranberries, peaches, tomatoes, bell peppers, eggplants, cucumbers, apples, spinach, squashes, and asparagus in the United States. Farms cover about one-sixth of the state's land area, and farm income per acre is among the highest in the country. Abraham Browning of Camden was remarkably prescient in 1876 at the Centennial Exhibition in Philadelphia (on New Jersey Day) when he nicknamed New Jersey the "Garden State."

Though people may not think of it as such, New Jersey is a peninsula. The Atlantic Ocean hugs the eastern coastline from Sandy Hook to Cape May. Delaware Bay, where the Delaware River meets the Atlantic, cradles the southern and western coastlines from Cape May to Fort Mott and separates New Jersey from Delaware. To the north, the Hudson River forms a boundary between New Jersey and New York. Tributaries of the Delaware and Hudson rivers crisscross the state. Altogether, New Jersey boasts 1,792 total miles of coast.

New Jersey has been an important center of manufacturing since the industrial revolution, but today forests cover 45 percent of the state, or 2.1 million acres, and provide abundant habitats for wildlife. In fact, the National Audubon Society has designated the Delaware Bayshore area one of Earth's most important stopovers for migratory birds.

Overlaid on this beauty is New Jersey's varied terrain: the rugged Kittatinny Ridge and Valley, Delaware Water Gap, and the Highlands in the north; the forested Ramapo and Watchung mountains in the middle of the state; and the flat expanse of the coast and the Pine Barrens in the south. Within these regions, New Jersey boasts 33 state parks, eleven state forests, one state wildlife management area, five national wildlife refuges, a national park, a national historic site, a national historical park, a national recreation area, and dozens of municipal parks.

Is there any doubt that New Jersey is an urban hiker's paradise?

With such a vast array of riches to choose from, selecting the hikes for this guide was a challenge. I did it in eight "easy" steps. First, I scoured many books and online guides to find the "best of" and "most popular" hikes in New Jersey. Second, I approached area hiking clubs and asked for their favorites: AMC chapters (especially my chapter, Delaware Valley), Outdoor Club of South Jersey, and TriState Ramblers were key sources. Third, I followed hiking blogs, most notably *Gone Hikin'* and *South Jersey Trails*, and other hiking websites, including those of the New York–New Jersey Trail Conference, NJ Hiking, and the New Jersey Trails Association. Fourth, I conferred with experts in New Jersey's recreational and environmental fields. Fifth, I decided to explore all 21 counties, resolving to cover some popular gems but also to showcase hikes that are underrated or have not been written about.

Sixth, I hiked! With hiking clubs; with friends; with my husband, Paul; and with my camera, notepad, and Garmin. Thanks to all who tolerated my slower pace and frequent stops to take photos and write down the moments that made each trip special.

Seventh, I wrote, drawing on my own experience as a hike leader and AMC member since 1996. I hope this "best of" guide will be useful for all who love the outdoors, and especially for beginning and intermediate hikers. Keep in mind that the word *best* is fluid and somewhat subjective. Age and physical ability influence perspective, as do experience and mindset. A 10-year-old child hiking the rustic boardwalk of an Atlantic cedar swamp for the first time will have a different sense of wonder about the smells, sounds, animals, and flowers than will a 65-year-old adult who hikes frequently.

Eighth, I wondered what to do with all the hikes that didn't make the cut, either because they are extensively covered in other publications or because there simply wasn't room in this book. Eureka! How about a reference section listing other hike-worthy trails in New Jersey? Please explore the hikes listed in the appendix of this book, and if you discover more hikes on your own, email amcbooks@outdoors.org. To get the most out of any hike, please download the latest maps listed for each hike, since trails do change.

When I was finished writing, I realized that hiking is more than exercise or fresh air or a social activity or a solitary pursuit; it's a way to connect with self, life, Earth, and the cosmos. I embraced (with a grain of salt) this opinion from John Muir:

*[Hiking!] I don't like either the word or the thing. People ought to saunter in the mountains—not hike! Do you know the origin of that word saunter? It's a beautiful word. Away back in the Middle Ages people used to go on pilgrimages to the Holy Land, and when people in the villages through which they passed asked where they were going, they would reply, "A la sainte terre," "To the Holy Land." And so they became known as* sainte-terre-ers, *or saunterers. Now these mountains are our Holy Land, and we ought to saunter through them reverently, not "hike" through them.*

Whether you saunter or hike, I hope this book helps you enjoy the journey. Thank you and AMC for making my own journey possible.

# HOW TO USE THIS BOOK

With 50 hikes to choose from, you may wonder how to decide where to go. The locator map at the front of this book will help you narrow down the trips by location, and the at-a-glance trip planner that follows the table of contents will provide more information to guide you toward a decision.

Once you settle on a destination and turn to a trip in this guide, you will find a series of icons that indicate whether fees are charged, the hike is good for kids, whether dogs are permitted, and whether cross-country skiing and snowshoeing are allowed.

Information on the basics follows: location, rating, distance, elevation gain, estimated time, and maps. The ratings are based on the author's perception and are estimates of what the average hiker will experience. You may find hikes to be easier or more difficult than stated. The estimated time is also based on the author's perception. Consider your own pace when planning a trip.

The elevation gain is calculated from measurements and information obtained from U.S. Geological Survey (USGS) topographic maps, landowner maps, and Google Earth. Each hike identifies the relevant USGS maps, if any, as well as where you can find additional trail maps. Most USGS topographic maps can be downloaded for free from store.usgs.gov. The boldface summary provides a basic overview of what you will see on your hike.

The directions explain how to reach the trailhead by car and, for some trips, by public transportation. GPS coordinates for parking lots are also included. Enter these coordinates into your own device for driving directions. Whether or not you own a GPS device, it is wise to consult an atlas before you leave home.

In the trail description, you will find instructions regarding where to hike, the trails on which to hike, and turn-by-turn directions. You will also learn about natural and human history along your hike, as well as information about flora, fauna, and any landmarks and objects you will encounter.

The trail maps that accompany each trip will guide you along your hike, but it would be wise to take an official trail map with you. They are often—but not always—available online, at the trailhead, or at the visitor center.

Each trip ends with a section titled "More Information" that provides details about restroom locations, access times and fees, the property's rules and regulations, and contact information for the place where you will be hiking. The "Nearby" section provides useful information on other sights, hikes, and points of interests in the area.

# TRIP PLANNING AND SAFETY

While elevations in and around New Jersey can be relatively low, and the hikes detailed in this guide aren't particularly dangerous, you'll still want to be prepared. Some of the walks traverse moderately rugged terrain along rocky hills, while others lead to ponds and fields where you'll have extended periods of sun exposure and slow walking. Many places in the region have complex trail networks, some of which are unmarked. Allow extra time in case you get lost.

You will be more likely to have an enjoyable, safe hike if you plan ahead and take proper precautions. Before heading out for your hike, consider the following:

- Select a hike that everyone in your group is comfortable taking. Match the hike to the abilities of the least experienced person in the group. If anyone is uncomfortable with the weather or is tired, turn around and complete the hike another day.
- Plan to be back at the trailhead before dark. Before beginning your hike, determine a turnaround time. Don't diverge from it, even if you have not reached your intended destination.
- Check the weather. Spring and fall bring unstable air masses to the area; summer features late-afternoon thunderstorms. If you are planning a ridge or summit hike, start early so you will be off the exposed area before the afternoon hours, when thunderstorms most often strike. Temperatures at higher elevations are often significantly lower than they are in the cities and suburbs and tend to fall quickly after sunset. Storms are a potential hazard throughout the area. If rain is in the forecast, bring waterproof gear.
- Bring a pack with the following items:
  - ✓ Water: Two quarts per person is usually adequate, depending on the weather and the length of the trip.
  - ✓ Food: Even if you are planning a one-hour hike, bring some high-energy snacks, such as nuts, dried fruit, or snack bars. Pack a lunch for longer trips.
  - ✓ Map and compass: Be sure you know how to use them. A handheld GPS device may also be helpful but is not always reliable.
  - ✓ Headlamp or flashlight, with spare batteries
  - ✓ Extra clothing: rain gear, wool sweater or fleece, hat, and mittens
  - ✓ Sunscreen
  - ✓ First-aid kit, including adhesive bandages, gauze, nonprescription painkillers, and moleskin

- ✓ Pocketknife or multitool
- ✓ Waterproof matches and a lighter
- ✓ Trash bag
- ✓ Toilet paper
- ✓ Whistle
- ✓ Insect repellent
- ✓ Sunglasses
- ✓ Cell phone: Be aware that cell phone service is unreliable in rural areas. If you are receiving a signal, use the phone only for emergencies to avoid disturbing the backcountry experience for other hikers.
- ✓ Binoculars (optional)
- ✓ Camera (optional)

- Wear appropriate footwear and clothing. Wool or synthetic hiking socks will keep your feet dry and help prevent blisters. Comfortable, waterproof hiking boots will provide ankle support and good traction. Avoid wearing cotton clothing, which absorbs sweat and rain, contributing to an unpleasant hiking experience. Polypropylene, fleece, silk, and wool all wick moisture away from your body and keep you warm in wet or cold conditions. To help avoid bug bites, you may want to wear pants and a long-sleeved shirt.

- When you are ahead of the rest of your hiking group, wait at all trail junctions until the others catch up. This avoids confusion and keeps people from getting separated or lost.

- If you see downed wood that appears to be purposely covering a trail, it probably means the trail is closed due to overuse or hazardous conditions.

- If a trail is muddy, walk through the mud or on rocks, never on tree roots or plants. Waterproof boots will keep your feet comfortable. Staying in the center of the trail will keep it from eroding into a wide hiking highway.

- Leave your itinerary and the time you expect to return with someone you trust. If you see a logbook at a trailhead, be sure to sign in when you arrive and sign out when you finish your hike.

- Poison ivy is always a threat when hiking. To identify the plant, look for clusters of three leaves that shine in the sun but are dull in the shade. If you do come into contact with poison ivy, wash the affected area with soap as soon as possible.

- Snakes, common in many hiking areas, are cold-blooded. Their body temperature rises and falls with the ambient temperature, and they hibernate during cold months. In summer, snakes may bask on exposed rocks or on open trails, although you also may find them near stone walls, brush piles, or fallen logs. Snakes usually avoid confrontation and are not aggressive toward humans; when surprised or provoked, however, they may bite. Most snakes in New Jersey are harmless, but northern copperheads and timber rattle-snakes have venomous bites that can be painful or, in rare cases, fatal. To reduce the chance of an unpleasant encounter for both parties, use proper snake etiquette, especially when hiking around rocky areas in the warm seasons: Look before taking a step or reaching in between rocks; if you see a snake, leave it alone. If you are bitten by a snake, seek medical attention as quickly as possible.

- Wear blaze-orange items in hunting season. Hunting seasons vary. Check nj.gov/dep/fgw/hunting.htm.

- Ticks, which can carry diseases, are common in many wooded and grassy areas in suburbs and exurbs, though uncommon on mountain ridges, and are active year-round in New Jersey. To reduce the chance of a tick bite, you may want to wear pants and a long-sleeved shirt. After you finish your hike, check for ticks on your clothes and body. The deer tick, which can carry Lyme disease, can be as small as a pinhead. Run a lint roller over your clothes. Take a shower when you get home and check for ticks again.

- Mosquitoes can be common in the woods in summer and fall. Although some carry diseases, their bite is mostly annoying. As with ticks, you can reduce the chance of bites by wearing long sleeves and pants. A variety of options are available for dealing with bugs, ranging from sprays that include the active ingredient N, N-diethyl-meta-toluamide (commonly known as DEET), which potentially can cause skin or eye irritation, to more skin-friendly products. Head nets, often cheaper than a can of repellent, are useful in especially buggy conditions.

# LEAVE NO TRACE

The Appalachian Mountain Club (AMC) is a national educational partner of Leave No Trace, a nonprofit organization
dedicated to promoting and inspiring responsible outdoor
recreation through education, research, and partnerships.

The Leave No Trace program seeks to develop wildland ethics, or ways in
which people think and act in the outdoors to minimize their impact on the
areas they visit and to protect our natural resources for future enjoyment. Leave
No Trace unites four federal land management agencies—the U.S. Forest Service, National Park Service, Bureau of Land Management, and U.S. Fish and
Wildlife Service—with manufacturers, outdoor retailers, user groups, educa-
tors, organizations such as AMC, and individuals.

The Leave No Trace ethic is guided by these seven principles:

1. **Plan ahead and prepare.** Know the terrain and any regulations applicable
   to the area you're planning to visit, and be prepared for extreme weather
   or other emergencies. This will enhance your enjoyment and ensure that
   you've chosen an appropriate destination. Small groups have less impact
   on resources and the experiences of other backcountry visitors.

2. **Travel and camp on durable aurfaces.** Travel and camp on established
   trails and campsites, rock, gravel, dry grasses, or snow. Good campsites
   are found, not made. Camp at least 200 feet from lakes and streams, and
   focus activities on areas where vegetation is absent. In pristine areas,
   disperse use to prevent the creation of campsites and trails.

3. **Dispose of waste properly.** Pack it in, pack it out. Inspect your camp
   for trash or food scraps. Deposit solid human waste in cat holes dug 6
   to 8 inches deep, at least 200 feet from water, camps, and trails. Pack out
   toilet paper and hygiene products. To wash yourself or your dishes, carry
   water 200 feet from streams or lakes and use small amounts of biodegrad-
   able soap. Scatter strained dishwater.

4. **Leave what you find.** Cultural or historic artifacts, as well as natural
   objects such as plants and rocks, should be left as found.

5. **Minimize campfire impacts.** Cook on a stove. Use established fire rings,
   fire pans, or mound fires. If you build a campfire, keep it small and use
   dead sticks found on the ground.

6. **Respect wildlife.** Observe wildlife from a distance. Feeding animals alters their natural behavior. Protect wildlife from your food by storing rations and trash securely.

7. **Be considerate of other visitors.** Be courteous, respect the quality of other visitors' backcountry experiences, and let nature's sounds prevail.

AMC is a national provider of the Leave No Trace Master Educator course. AMC offers this five-day course, designed especially for outdoor professionals and land managers, as well as the shorter two-day Leave No Trace Trainer course at locations throughout the Northeast. For Leave No Trace information and materials, contact the Leave No Trace Center for Outdoor Ethics, P.O. Box 997, Boulder, CO 80306; 800-332-4100 or 302-442-8222; lnt.org. For information on AMC's Leave No Trace Master Educator training course, see outdoors.org/education/lnt.

# SKYLANDS

Variety is the key word for the Skylands region, a diverse corner of northwestern New Jersey that comprises five counties: Sussex, Warren, Morris, Hunterdon, and Somerset. Both serious and casual hikers will find journeys here that explore the slopes, floodplains, wetlands, ravines, valleys, fields, waterfalls, streams, rugged ridges, and rock outcroppings. The Skylands region hosts New Jersey's highest point, as well as some of its flattest terrain. At 1,803 feet, the challenging High Point, in High Point State Park, is the highest elevation in the state; most of New Jersey's section of the Appalachian Trail runs through this area. On the other hand, parts of  the mainly flat, 70-mile Delaware and Raritan State Park Trail in Hunterdon and Somerset counties are universally accessible.

Not only is the terrain varied, but so is this region's character. History buffs will enjoy charming industrial and homestead remains and American Revolution stories. Rock hounds will enjoy "ringing rocks," kettle holes, and erratics, as well as old iron, copper, and zinc mines. Fairy glens and secluded waterfalls offer solitude. Hikers can gaze upon valleys and rivers and see across three states (New Jersey, New York, and Pennsylvania) at once. Birders will enjoy the havens for migratory fowl, the riparian corridors, and the floodplain forests that provide wintering grounds for bald eagles. Vernal pools nourish amphibians; the rare Atlantic white cedar swamps house many of these pools, which also protect the threatened bog turtle.

Every area in this region boasts pretty wildflowers (Trip 2: Duke Farms, even has a greenhouse of cultivated orchids), and the uplands harbor the small-whorled pogonia, a wild orchid. Deciduous trees blaze in autumn. Rattlesnakes, bats, bears, turtles, and small mammals live in these woods. Timber rattlesnakes especially enjoy the shale cliffs and rock formations. Don't bother them, and they won't bother you.

Facing page: A group treks along the Appalachian Trail
near Mohican Outdoor Center, in the Delaware Water Gap
National Recreation Area. Photo by Ryan Smith.

The jewel of the Skylands is the rugged Delaware Water Gap National Recreation Area (Trip 10), hugging 37 miles of the Delaware River (parts of which are designated a Wild and Scenic River by Congress) and sprawling across New Jersey and Pennsylvania. The New Jersey side of the recreation area comprises 31,000 acres and runs along the eastern edge of the Kittatinny Ridge. This area is largely shaped by the Kittatinny Ridge and Valley.

The Kittatinny Ridge and Valley spans 346,838 acres and 35 miles, from High Point State Park in the north to Worthington State Forest in the south. This forested greenway provides refuge for black bears, bobcats, red-shouldered hawks, and bald eagles.

The rugged Highlands area of New Jersey is part of the Kittatinny section and occupies about 980 square miles in the state, with major portions in the Skylands. The area is the ancestral home of the Lenni-Lenape people, many of whom live here today. Local iron ore provided munitions during the American Revolution. The Highlands Trail, when complete, will stretch 150 miles, from north of Bear Mountain in New York to the Delaware River in Riegelsville, New Jersey. Volunteers from the hiking clubs and organizations that make up the New Jersey Regional Trails Council maintain the trails. The Highlands Conservation Act, heavily supported by AMC, protects this valuable land. To learn more, visit outdoors.org/hca.

The Sourland Mountain Preserve, 90 square miles of wetlands and forest, and a major source of drinking water, is a unique ecological island of unbroken habitat. Migratory birds, rare plant species, and vernal pools for reptiles and amphibians are found here. The New Jersey Conservation Foundation and its partners—including the dedicated Sourland Conservancy, which has provided some excellent mapping—maintains this section.

Along with the Delaware and Raritan Canal (see essay on page 40), another notable route is Patriots' Path, covering roughly 90 miles, including side trails, primarily in Morris County. Patriots' Path links several federal, state, county, and municipal parks, along with watersheds, green open spaces, and historic sites. Some of the trail is universally accessible.

The hikes in this section cover parts of all the above areas for a diverse taste of the Skylands region. There is no shortage of adventure in the fourteen state parks, one national park, three state forests, one natural wildlife refuge, one national historical park, and many natural areas—including 9-mile-long Lake Hopatcong, New Jersey's largest—that occupy more than 100,000 acres in this corner of paradise.

# SOURLAND MOUNTAIN PRESERVE

Be amazed by huge boulders, fantastic trees that grow from rocks, a hidden stream that roars, "ringing rocks," and spotted salamanders in vernal pools.

## DIRECTIONS

Take I-80 west to Exit 43 and proceed south on I-287. Take Exit 17 and continue south on US 206 about 7.2 miles. Turn right onto Amwell Road (County Road 514; do not turn right at New Amwell Road) and proceed 2.8 miles to East Mountain Road. Turn left onto East Mountain Road and follow it 1.9 miles to the entrance to Sourland Mountain Preserve, on the right, with at least 50 parking spots. *GPS coordinates:* 40° 28.428′ N, 74° 41.655′ W.

## TRAIL DESCRIPTION

The Sourland region of New Jersey covers 90 square miles. The 3,025-acre Sourland Mountain Preserve is a sweet hike, despite the name, with 10 miles of blazed trails to choose from, and most are easy to moderate. This trip explores the longer, more scenic, and challenging white-blazed Ridge Trail, a perimeter journey through a deciduous forest, with a section on the unique red-blazed Roaring Brook Trail. Numbered green markers denote trail intersections, and arrows indicate trail direction. Connecting trails, marked with a "C," can shorten your hike, if so desired. Deciduous trees make Sourland beautiful in the fall and shady in the summer. Critters in vernal pools and wildflowers charm in spring, and icy rocks provide a challenge in winter.

Head toward the forest and the well-marked trailhead. The preserve is dog-friendly and provides "mutt mitt"

**LOCATION**
Hillsborough

**RATING**
Moderate

**DISTANCE**
6.3 miles

**ELEVATION GAIN**
700 feet

**ESTIMATED TIME**
3 hours

**MAPS**
USGS Rocky Hill; somersetcountyparks .org/geninfo/maps/ sourlandsmap.pdf

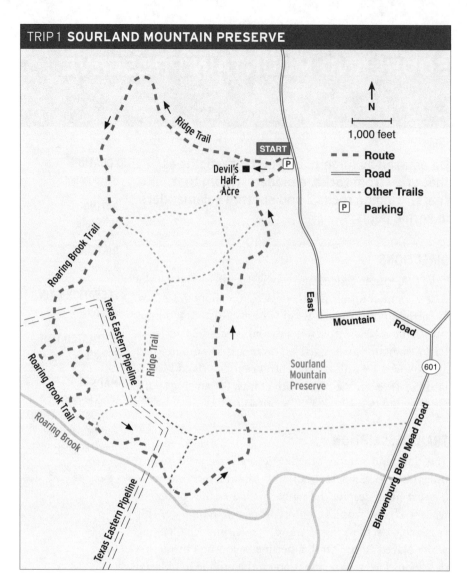

dispensers to clean up after your pet. Take advantage of the two chemical toilets in the parking lot, if needed, before heading out.

Start on the white-squared Ridge Trail, which follows the streambed on the left. Continue straight at 0.2 mile, passing green marker 1 on the left. At a bridge with railings, go straight (keeping the bridge on your left), and stay on the white-squared Ridge Trail that heads to the boulder field. Enjoy the flat, easy stepping-stones on the way. The trail becomes rockier as you near the boulder field. The drone of summer insects and loud *chuuree* of the yellow Kentucky warbler provide a comforting white noise. At 0.6 mile, pass one of many connecting trails to your left, marked with a "C." Keep straight and head up, still on the rocky Ridge Trail. Shadows of birds flit over the rocks, urging you higher in the bushy woods. Stop at the impressive boulder field. This amphitheater of diabase, or rock formed from molten magma that cooled far below the earth's surface, has presence. Tap on rock fragments to discover musical "ringing rocks." Ridge Trail leads to impressive car-sized boulders known as Devil's Half Acre, which you can go around on the right or slip through via a person-sized gap. Linger for a trail break.

There are lots of footpaths here, so be sure to stay on the white-squared Ridge Trail that cuts around the boulders on the right. If you slip through, be sure to pick up the trail. Maneuver past the tree growing in the path. Keep going straight. Soon a rhinoceros-shaped rock appears, wallpapered with lichens. Marvel at the tree growing in the rock, one of several such trees in Sourland. The boulder field ends, and the walk in the woods begins.

Enjoy the narrow, leafy trail, which is cool and refreshing most months of the year. There are fewer people now. You are walking on a ridge of hardened magma, or igneous rock, with views obscured by leaves. At about 1.9 miles, follow the fork to the right at marker 4, still on the white-squared trail; to your left is a round "C" sign. After about 100 yards, turn right at the round red sign for Roaring Brook Trail. (The trail is actually a floodplain and often flooded and wet in rainy months.) Look for vernal, or spring-only, breeding pools for amphibians, such as frogs and salamanders. The trees cohabit with the rocks, roots splaying and grasping. If trees could talk, there would be some amazing survival stories. Rock-hop for 50 yards, watching out for bounding deer. After a heavy rain on this sparsely traveled trail, you can hear the roaring of the stream, invisible beneath the boulders.

Go through a fallen-down metal fence. Note the many trees with interesting animal burrows. Walk through a gap in a picturesque rock wall into a grassy pipeline clearing, picking up the trail on the other side in the cooling woods. Enter another boulder field, not as dramatic as Devil's Half Acre, populated by "sleeping" rocks—large and lower to the ground, as if curled up in slumber. Lichens splash the rocks like black-and-white paint. At the fork, go right onto the red Roaring Brook Trail (ignoring the white connector trail marked by a "C" on the left). This well-maintained path gradually descends though a moderate boulder field. At the next fork, veer right onto the white-squared Ridge Trail. After 3.6 miles, at marker 7, you'll reach a rock cairn. Go downhill for a while, less than 10 minutes. A fence appears on the left; go through the gate toward marker 8, at 4.0 miles. Proceed straight (not left), going away from the fence, still on the white-squared trail.

A pleasant boardwalk meanders over a creek bordered by soft green grasses. Cross other boardwalks, still in the shade, and reach marker 9 at 4.4 miles. Go straight at the white-squared Ridge Trail and onto another boardwalk. Listen for bird songs and fussing squirrels; other wildlife includes pileated woodpeckers, bobcats, wood turtles, barred owls, Cooper's hawks, and bobolinks. At marker 10 (5.5 miles), the rock shapes once again become amazing—amateur

This fantastically twisted tree has grown over a rock in Sourland Mountain Preserve.

geologists should look for hornfels, or heat-altered rocks—and give way to roots on the path. Follow the white-square and white-triangle markers with a drawing of a tree on them; these eventually lead you toward the parking lot.

At 5.9 miles, pick some raspberries in the meadow at marker 11 and traverse a boardwalk into the woods. Look for ghostly Indian pipes, trout lilies, and wood anemones in season. Solitude gives way to dogs and people. At marker 12 (6.1 miles), go right at the white square/triangle markers to a beautiful pond nestled in a meadow, complete with a bench beneath a tree. At 6.3 miles, reach the parking lot and journey's end.

## DID YOU KNOW?

John Hart, a signer of the Declaration of Independence, hid in these hills during the American Revolution. The name Sourland comes from the Dutch *sauer landt*, probably because settlers found the rocky soils difficult to farm or perhaps because of the sorrel-colored dirt.

## OTHER ACTIVITIES

Turn right out of the Sourland parking lot, and in about 10 minutes (within 5 miles), you will see a lavender farm and food stop. Or drive 20 minutes to charming Princeton, about 10 miles away (south on East Mountain Road to US 206 S). Hike the 70-mile linear Delaware and Raritan Canal (see Trip 7). The entrance is 15 minutes away (about 8 miles), where Amwell (County Road 514) and Millstone roads meet. To reach canal parking, head east on East Mountain Road and turn right on County Road 514 to Millstone Road. Look for the new Stoutsburg Sourland African American Museum, at 189 Hollow Road, Skillman, NJ, 08558, to open around September 2019; ssaamuseum.org.

## MORE INFORMATION

No fee. Open dawn to dusk. Dogs allowed. Sourland is part of the nonprofit D&R Greenway Land Trust and Sourland Conservancy. Sourland Conservancy has detailed hiking maps of the entire region at sourland.org/sourland-trail-maps, as well as *Sourland Region Hiking Atlas*. For information on Sourland Conservancy, visit sourland.org. For information on D&R Greenway Land Trust, contact 609-924-4646; drgreenway.org. For information on Sourland Mountain Preserve, contact Somerset County Park Commission, 355 Milltown Road, Bridgewater, NJ 08807; 908-722-1200; somersetcountyparks.org.

# 2

# DUKE FARMS

Take an easy stroll on tobacco heiress Doris Duke's former estate, following mostly paved paths through woods and around lakes, fountains, an orchid greenhouse, a pet cemetery, and statuary.

## DIRECTIONS

From US 206 (Bayard Lane), turn left onto Dukes Parkway West. (If you reach County Route 583, you've gone too far.) After 0.7 mile, take the third left. In 0.1 mile, turn right. Take the first left, and the marked entrance is in about 100 feet. The parking lot has space for about 100 cars and offers car-charging stations. *GPS coordinates:* 40° 32.722′ N, 74° 37.397′ W.

## TRAIL DESCRIPTION

James Buchanan (J.B.) Duke, an American tobacco and electric power industrialist, originally transformed these 2,742 acres of farmland and woodlot into the estate known as Duke Farms. The landscape consists of an astonishing nine human-made lakes, 18 miles of trails, more than 45 buildings, and one of America's largest indoor botanical displays. After J.B.'s death in 1925, his fortune passed to his daughter, Doris Duke. She was an avid traveler, horticulturist, and philanthropist, doing much to protect and conserve Duke Farms, her primary residence. After her death in 1993, more than a decade passed while trustees of the Doris Duke Charitable Foundation decided how to fulfill her wish to promote conservation via Duke Farms. Eventually, in May 2012, Duke Farms opened to the public with a goal of teaching visitors to be good stewards of the environment. A variety of educational programs for children and adults, many held in the old Coach Barn building restored in 2015, help fulfill this goal.

**LOCATION**
Hillsborough

**RATING**
Easy

**DISTANCE**
4.9 miles

**ELEVATION GAIN**
496 feet

**ESTIMATED TIME**
2 hours

**MAPS**
USGS Bound Brook, USGS Raritan; dukefarms.org/visiting-duke-farms/property-map

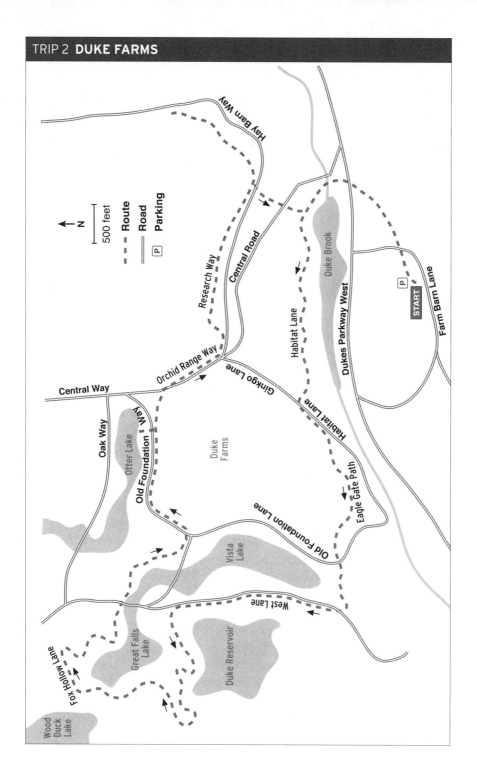

**Route**
**Road**
P **Parking**

N

500 feet

Hay Barn Way

Research Way

Central Road

Duke Brook

Habitat Lane

Dukes Parkway West

P
START

Farm Barn Lane

Orchid Range Way

Ginkgo Lane

Central Way

Oak Way

Old Foundation Way

Otter Lake

Duke Farms

Habitat Lane

Eagle Gate Path

Old Foundation Lane

Vista Lake

West Lane

Great Falls Lake

Duke Reservoir

Fox Hollow Lane

Wood Duck Lake

The hay barn on Duke's property burned down in 1915. It was later converted to a statuary garden by Doris Duke, with the original walls still standing. Photo by Siddharth Mallya, Wikimedia Commons.

Duke Farms offers 18 miles of well-marked trails on 2,742 acres of woodlands and meadows, passing lakes, lagoons, fountains, and sculptures—all clearly explained by signs. Beginning hikers, children, and those with limited mobility will like the tram stops and paved paths. Numbered markers indicate all intersections. The farm is most crowded and flower-filled from April through September but is open all year long. In winter snow, look for deer, rabbit, fox, coyote, bobcat, mink, skunk, and badger tracks. In fall, the blazing colors of the trees (maple, oak, beech, black cherry, and more) reflect in the lakes and other waters.

From the parking lot, make your way to the Orientation Center. Inside, grab a map, watch a short film, and visit the educational displays on conservation and preservation. The building itself is powered by a 2.6-acre solar array and geothermal wells. The Farm Barn Café offers locally sourced organic meals. With a driver's license for collateral, borrow an Eco-Kit: binoculars, compass, field guide, and nature journal for recording notes.

This hike goes through the middle of the park and Migration Woods, past five lakes, the site of an unfinished mansion at Old Foundation, the Orchid Range, and other sites, with scads of butterflies and dragonflies in season, plus bunnies and wood ducks. Look out for trams as you walk.

To start, take the pedestrian path from the right of the Orientation Center, turn right at the tram stop and sunflower field, go past the bluebird houses on the right, and head to marker 7. There, at South Gate Entrance, a guard will stop traffic so you can cross the road into the park.

Pause to admire Duke Brook, a minor tributary of the Raritan River, and the elegant falls. Watch for a great blue heron or a great egret. Continue on the paved and level Habitat Lane. Note the raspberries, black-eyed Susans, and cell phone "dial and listen" stops. Habitat Lane becomes gravel; stop to sit on one of the stone benches and admire the enormous trees.

Turn right onto Woods Lane, a dirt path, then left onto Eagle Gate, a path over a charming stone bridge. Left at the solar panel brings you back to gravelly Habitat Lane and the darling Blue Boy (1.2 miles), a statue of a lad who eternally examines his bare foot for an offending stone or thorn. Take a right onto West Lane toward Duke Reservoir on the left, which used to gravity-feed the farm's seven-lake system via a canal above the Raritan River. Today, new wells supply the water. (Lake elevations are listed on the hiking map.) Wheelchair-accessible bathrooms are on the left. Tables next to Mermaid Pool, a former swimming pool, make a perfect picnic spot where you can admire the stone balustrade that runs the length of the pool and lake (1.5 miles). Stone steps invite you down to a meadow to explore bird habitats, waterfalls, and flowers.

When you are ready, take a left onto Fox Hollow (1.6 miles), a dirt/gravel path through woods, to Great Falls Lake with a terraced, 30-foot, human-made waterfall that "turns on" at certain hours; check with staff. Stroll flat ground to Wood Duck Lake on the left, complete with Canada geese and wood ducks, and a solar panel on the right (2.1 miles).

Climb a gentle, tree-lined grade to a large ravine on the right, where an unannounced pet cemetery surprises atop a knoll. Here are the grave markers for about 60 birds, dogs, and cats—mostly Doris Duke's pets, including a camel named Baby, who died on September 13, 1994.

Continue downhill, passing through a stone tunnel with a resounding echo, until you reach marker 18 (2.7 miles). Take a left onto the paved Old Foundation Way, where another surprise awaits: a deep pit with the jutting footers of an unbuilt mansion. Take a minute to read the explanation.

Head down into the woods and toward the gazebo on the left. Follow the gravel path a few hundred yards left of the gazebo to view a giant clam shell, a statue of a little boy, and educational signs about orchids of the Northern Piedmont Range. At marker 21 (3.0 miles), you can take a side trip onto Great Meadow Path and explore the wildflowers and native grasses of the Great Meadow, once a high-maintenance lawn.

Make a detour at marker 22 onto Orchid Range Way (3.1 miles), a series of greenhouses with mind-boggling arrays of tropical and subtropical orchids. At the exit, there is a 9/11 memorial beneath a tree on the left.

Take paved Central Way toward the Hay Barn and segue left onto wood-chipped Railroad Path, where a narrow dirt path to the right of a bench leads to Research Way, through an ecotone field (a transitional area between two communities of plants and animals) and past the Farnese Bull statue (3.7 miles). Turn left onto paved Hay Barn Way to visit a statue garden ensconced in the shored-up stone ruins of the old hay barn (3.8 miles). Past the statue garden, a tiny dirt path on the left leads to Research Woods, a gated enclosure you can explore, if you'd like. Double back to Hay Barn Way and go left past the wheelchair-accessible Sugar Shack on the right then left onto paved Nursery Way, past restrooms on the left.

You can keep going straight and explore the upper part of the farm or, at the statue of Athena (4.2 miles), double back through the statue garden and take a left on Central Way toward the South Gate entrance, passing Duke Brook on the right. If it's after 6 P.M., the guard will be off duty, so push the button on the left of the gate to release it and walk past the sunflower patch back to your car.

## DID YOU KNOW?

A seasonal weekly farm-to-table market on the premises offers cheeses, wines, meat, vegetables, fruit, and more. Check dukefarms.org/classes--events/farm -to-table-market for featured vendors. The farm also has bike shares at selected locations.

## OTHER ACTIVITIES

Duke Island Park in nearby Bridgewater is part of the Raritan River Greenway and offers trails and summer concerts. See the Wallace House in Somerville, which served as George Washington's headquarters from 1778 to 1779. Visit the Sri Venkateswara Temple in Bridgewater (check venkateswara.org for hours), which has a cafeteria. US 206 also has many dining options.

## MORE INFORMATION

Hours of operation are 8:30 A.M. to 6 P.M. in spring and summer, and 8:30 A.M. to 4:30 P.M. in fall and winter. Closed on Wednesdays. A free Accessibility Shuttle from April 1 through October 31 is available between the Orientation Center and Orchid Range for those with limited moblility, but reservations are required; call 908-722-3700, extension 2. The parking lot closes when full, usually on weekends in nice weather, so check Twitter @DFParking or call 908-722-3700. Major events include the mid-March Sugar Maple Celebration, the early July Firefly Festival, and the late-October Creature Fest. Duke Farms, 1112 Dukes Parkway West, Hillsborough, NJ 08844; 908-722-3700; dukefarms.org.

# 3
# ROCKHOPPER AND DRY RUN CREEK TRAILS

Walk the woodsy road used by the Continental Army under General George Washington en route to battle at Monmouth and get a boulder-hopping cardio workout.

## DIRECTIONS

From I-95, take the Route 29 exit and follow Route 29 about 10 miles. At a light, take a left onto Route 179. In 0.2 mile, turn left at unused railroad tracks before a bridge to Pennsylvania. Drive through the Lambertville Station Restaurant and Inn parking lot to the Delaware and Raritan Canal (D&R Canal) lot behind the inn, with parking for about 25 cars. *GPS coordinates:* 40° 21.831′ N, 74° 56.786′ W.

## TRAIL DESCRIPTION

A ten-minute walk through historic Lambertville takes you to the solitude of Rockhopper Trail and onto an old road used by soldiers during the American Revolution. Keep going and in 3.2 miles, you'll cross Route 518 to pick up Dry Run Creek Trail on the other side. Both trails are blazed blue and are in the Sourland region, a 90-square-mile section of contiguous forest that is an important breeding ground for migratory songbirds and home to rare and endangered plant species. This hike includes a break at Howell Living History Farm. The trail markings are a little tricky to spot sometimes, but if you don't see a blaze for a while, simply backtrack. Rockhopper undulates, and Dry Run Creek is hilly. It's a good route for summer due to the heavy, almost continuous shade of oaks, beech trees, and sycamores; the length of the combined trails makes this a great cardio workout.

From the parking lot overlooking the Delaware River, walk past the Lambertville Station Restaurant and Inn,

**LOCATION**
Lambertville

**RATING**
Moderate to Strenuous

**DISTANCE**
9.3 miles

**ELEVATION GAIN**
1,000 feet

**ESTIMATED TIME**
4.5 hours

**MAPS**
USGS Bound Brook; sourland.org/sourland -trail-maps; njtrails.org/ trail; *Sourland Region Hiking Atlas*

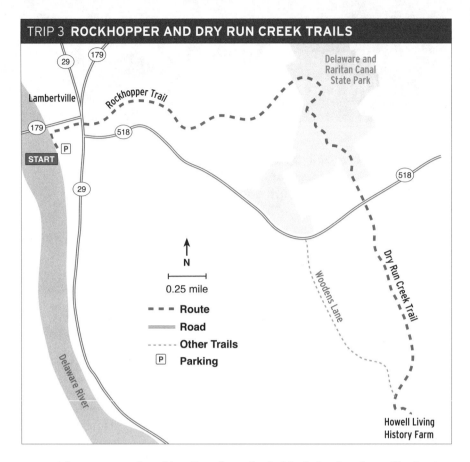

turn right to cross the old railroad tracks behind the Lambertville Station Restaurant (separate from Lambertville Station Restaurant and Inn), and take the small bridge over the D&R Canal to Ferry Street (0.2 mile), stopping to admire the adorable houses. Cross Route 29 and then Route 179 (large road, be careful), and take a left onto Quarry Street (0.4 mile). Here the picturesque houses on the right face a massive rock wall. Pass a stream, some apartment buildings, and woods on the right. Then turn right onto Stymiest Road–Rock Road (0.8 mile), cross a one-lane bridge, and veer left uphill onto a shaded gravel road. Climb up the gravel road, veering to the right. Look carefully for the next left—a house is at the intersection—and for the orange-blue trailhead markers at the edge of the woods. Take the orange-blazed trail, which will soon meet the blue-blazed Rockhopper Trail.

Pause a moment to consider that you will be walking a historic colonial road used by General George Washington's Continental Army during the American Revolution as they marched to Monmouth to do battle in 1778. The road was then called the Bungtown Road because alcoholic spirits, contained by a bung (or cork) in the barrel, were trudged to New York on this route. Toast the past with a drink of water.

Today the level dirt path leads into a welcoming mature hardwood forest and over several wooden footbridges. Briefly pop out into an open field with wildflowers on your left then pop into the woods again. The trail becomes rooty and rocky, living up to its name. This traprock, or blue-gray diabase, was used at one point for railroad ballast, concrete aggregate, and gravel roadbeds. Note the shallow pits scattered throughout where stone was quarried in the nineteenth century.

At the next clearing, the orange trail changes to blue (see marker) as you head back into the woods. Trees with interesting shapes enchant in this green oasis. You feel miles away from Lambertville and the twenty-first century. To the right are the Lambertville Lower and Middle reservoirs; you can't see them in summer when trees are in full leaf. Cross another wooden footbridge and pass an open field on the left. Go right at the fork and you'll see blue trail markers in a few yards. A lovely old stone bridge and stream are to the right (2.2 miles) before another footbridge. The rocks are in earnest now and will have you hopping! Be careful in wet weather. The path goes through a low, picturesque stone wall, dating back to 1792, staying in the cool woods. Cross a stream then a boulder field. At the fork, keep straight to remain on the blue-blazed trail (2.6 miles). Pass houses on the right as the path widens and becomes gravel. Note the picturesque old barn and group of buildings on the left. This is a nice spot for a photograph. The smell of crushed wild onions carries on the gentle breeze. Cross paved County Road 518 (Brunswick Pike) and enter the woods (3.2 miles).

You are now on blue-blazed Dry Run Creek Trail, a tributary of Moore's Creek, in the D&R (Delaware and Raritan) Greenway Land Trust Nature Preserve. Formed in 1989, the D&R trust has permanently preserved more than 1,500 square miles of watershed, farm, and canal lands.

AMC's Delaware Valley Chapter explores these historic woods.

The rocks magically disappear as you take the narrow dirt path into the dappled shade, crossing one (3.6 miles) of several wooden footbridges over dry streambeds, which can be very wet in spring. The path winds downhill, past a large, dry creek bed to the left. A bench at the beginning of some wooden steps leads down, and you soon walk through a low, well-constructed rock wall. The woods have a soft, hushed quality as you descend, smelling the sweet, hot green. Take a left onto the paved Valley Road (4.4 miles) at a large trail signage area that leads to Howell Living History Farm for a fantastic picnic-table lunch stop under giant trees. Flush toilets are available inside the visitor center, as well as honey, syrup, crafts, and more. Maintained by the Mercer County Park Commission, the farm is an educational facility that preserves and interprets farm life from about 1890 to 1910. Pigs, sheep, chickens, and oxen roam the grounds and are part of many educational programs for children. The farm also connects to the trails at Baldpate Mountain, for hikers who want to explore.

Throw your trash away and go back to the trail signage area, enter the woods (blue blaze), cross County Road 518 (6.2 miles), and stay on the blue trail. (*Note:* Be careful not to take the private drive to the left.) Retrace your steps: blue trail to stone bridge (7.2 miles) to Quarry Street (8.7 miles). Carefully cross Route 179 to Ferry Street. Traverse the bridge over the canal and the railroad tracks. Turn left to go behind Lambertville Station Restaurant, past the separate Lambertville Station Restaurant and Inn, and back to the D&R parking lot.

## DID YOU KNOW?

*The Road Along the Rocks 1758: "The Bungtown Road,"* by John P. and Barbara J. Hencheck, a book about the famous artery for the armies of the American Revolution (now part of Rockhopper Trail), is available for purchase from the Lambertville Historical Society (lambertvillehistoricalsociety.org).

## OTHER ACTIVITIES

Lambertville is rich in galleries, antiques, and restaurants. Walk a section of the approximately 70-mile-long D&R Canal that runs through town. The museum at nearby Monmouth Battlefield State Park, on the site of one of the largest battles of the American Revolution, is well worth visiting. If you'd care to bag another state, walk across the Delaware River via the car/pedestrian bridge to vibrant New Hope, Pennsylvania. Be sure to look for turtles sunning themselves on the river rocks below.

## MORE INFORMATION

Rockhopper Trail's canopy of white oaks might date to the 1700s. In spring, the forest floor dances with rue anemone, tiny orchids, and jack-in-the-pulpit. Dry Run Creek Trail is maintained by the D&R Greenway Land Trust, One Preservation Place, Princeton, NJ 08540; 609-924-4646; drgreenway.org.

## FOREST BATHING, OR *SHINRIN-YOKU*

Forest bathing is not an instructive nature walk, or a peak-bagging experience, or a bathtub filled with water in the woods. It is a contemplative walk in the woods, a meditative experience, a chance to be still and be changed by nature's healing magic. Along with being an enjoyable experience, forest bathing has well-proven benefits.

A 2015 study by Gregory Bratman of Stanford University showed that people who walked through the school's grassy Palo Alto campus instead of on a nearby busy road showed reduced neural activity in the area of the brain responsible for rumination, defined as "repetitive thought focused on negative aspects of the self." Similar studies of participants in natural versus urban settings indicate that walking in nature restores one's ability to pay attention and helps the brain replenish itself. Even the U.S. military is aware of the benefits of being in nature. In September 2016, the Institute for Integrative Health launched the nationwide Green Road Project, which puts wounded veterans in a natural setting to reduce anxiety.

In short, nature walks reduce the chatter in our heads.

With more than 50 percent of the world's population now living in urban areas, which are associated with increased levels of mental illness, forest bathing's time has come.

The Japanese Ministry of Agriculture, Forestry, and Fisheries coined the term *shinrin-yoku,* or "forest bathing," in 1982. Forest bathing simply means soaking up the smells, tastes, sounds, sights, and feel of nature in order to relax and heal. A 2010 study of forest bathers in 24 Japanese forests showed lower blood pressure, heart rate, and cortisol (or stress hormone) levels. Other studies show that forest bathing improves the immune function. Japan has even made forest bathing a part of its health care system, as has Korea, and they're expanding trails in an effort to reduce depression and chronic pain.

But you don't have to go to Japan or Korea to experience *shinrin-yoku.* The United States has quickly adopted this latest fitness practice, with California leading the way. The Santa Rosa–based Association of Nature and Forest Therapy was founded by wilderness guide Amos Clifford in 2012. Clifford, the author of *Your Guide to Forest Bathing: Experience the Healing Power of Nature* (Conari Press, 2018), teaches that the forest is your hiking companion. The association's trained forest therapy guides can lead you through a slow, quiet, sensual awakening to your surroundings. Tea from foraged foliage completes the 1-mile, three-hour experience.

And you don't even have to go as far as the West Coast to reset your brain with forest bathing. You can stay in the Garden State. The New Jersey Conservation Foundation sometimes offers "Forest Bathing in the Pines" (njconservation .org/2018ForestBathingFPP.htm) at Franklin Parker Preserve in Chatsworth (see Trip 49) and at Wickecheoke Creek Preserve in Stockton (see the introduction to the Skylands region). Glen Rock's Thielke Arboretum (460 Doremus Avenue) offers two-hour "baths" on weekends, as does Colonial Park Gardens in Somerset (156 Mettlers Road). September 8 is International Forest Bathing Day, so check local resources for bathing outings.

The power of forest bathing makes intuitive sense. After all, our brains developed in nature. Nature long has been a source of healing. Anyone who has spent much time in the woods knows that nature is a sentient being. The benefits of spending time with her linger for days.

Forest therapy guides are trained to connect you with sensory activities, but you don't need a guide to start. Find a tree and rest your hand on it. Feel the bark. Smell it. Notice the patterning and texture. Imprint your skin with its roughness or its smoothness. Listen to the birds through your window when you have your morning coffee. Note the texture of their song, the syllables, the pitch, the rhythm. Imagine each note as a dot of color suspended in the air. Lie in your yard or a local field. Feel the grass on your limbs, smell the earth, observe the color and form of the sky, reach your palm up to pat the clouds. Find a "sit spot," or a comfortable place to sit quietly, and be still for 20 minutes, without electronics, letting the surroundings slowly reveal themselves: flowers, bees, bunnies, caterpillars, butterflies, rays of sun, and drops of rain. Bathe your body in peace.

# 4

# MORRISTOWN NATIONAL HISTORICAL PARK: JOCKEY HOLLOW SECTION

Maximize the miles with an aerobic hike through the heart of Jockey Hollow over rolling terrain and experience American Revolution-era history as you visit reconstructed soldier huts.

## DIRECTIONS

From I-287, take Exit 30B (Bernardsville exit). Turn right at the top of the ramp. At the traffic light, turn right onto Route 202 North. At the next traffic light, turn left onto Tempe Wick Road (Route 646). Continue on Tempe Wick Road for about 1.5 miles. The entrance to Jockey Hollow will be on your right. The parking lot has many spots. *GPS coordinates:* 40° 45.691′ N, 74° 32.561′ W.

## TRAIL DESCRIPTION

The 27 miles of trails on what used to be the 1,400-acre Wick Farm are marked and easy to follow if you keep a sharp lookout (which may be difficult with the wonderfully distracting historical markers). The 10-mile meander on the yellow, white, green, blue, and red trails gets the most distance possible out of the park while covering the historical highlights. Some trails overlap with Patriots' Path, a unique cross-county trail system (morrisparks.net). In winter, enjoy clear, excellent views of New York City (Empire State Building and One World Trade Center). Spring and summer bring out the water plants, wildflowers, and vernal-pool amphibians.

Stop in at the Jockey Hollow Visitor Center and pick up a map for $1 (or download one beforehand). Be sure to view the exhibits and short film about the Continental Army's winter encampments in Jockey Hollow.

Head toward the fence on the paved path in front of the visitor center. Walk through another parking lot, past a red barn on the right, toward a beautiful fenced flower

**LOCATION**
Morristown

**RATING**
Strenuous

**DISTANCE**
10 miles

**ELEVATION GAIN**
1,250 feet

**ESTIMATED TIME**
5 to 6 hours

**MAPS**
USGS Mendham; nps.gov/morr/planyourvisit/maps.htm

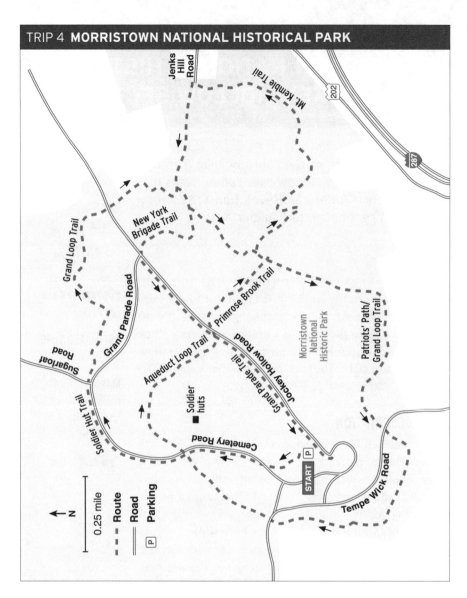

garden. At the one-way sign, veer right into the woods toward yellow-blazed Soldier Hut Trail. The pretty path with tall grasses slopes down crunchy gravel. Keep straight, staying on Soldier Hut Trail; enter a field and cross paved Grand Parade Road (1.0 mile). Pass a sign for the Pennsylvania Line Encampment site, where the First and Second Pennsylvania brigades were the backbone of Washington's army under General Anthony Wayne.

You soon reach the replicas of the soldiers' huts (1.1 miles). The original huts, built of timber from Wick Farm, were 14 by 16 feet and 6.5 feet high. They each housed up to twelve soldiers. Markers along the trail relay more information about the historical aspects of this hike.

Continuing on Soldier Hut Trail, veer right toward the white-blazed Grand Loop Trail and Grand Parade Road. At this junction, take a left toward Grand Loop Trail (1.3 miles). The trail heads down a dirt path and meanders through the woods. At marker 8, turn right onto Grand Loop Trail (1.5 miles), which descends and turns rocky before leveling off and widening into a lovely small green valley. After a slight ascent to a hilltop and a "Park Open" sign, cross the paved Jockey Hollow Road (1.9 miles), heading into the woods again at a metal gate.

Go right at the junction onto the blue-and-white-blazed trail (where Grand Loop Trail temporarily merges with New York Brigade Trail) (2.3 miles). (*Do not* go straight onto blue-blazed Mt. Kemble Loop Trail at marker 10.) Here the trail widens; watch for roots and rocks. Pass a beautiful, calm pond on the left, with a bench for rest and contemplation. Turn left at the next junction onto white-blazed Grand Loop Trail (2.4 miles), which follows a sweet meandering stream before widening and sloping down. Stay on Grand Loop Trail at marker 21 and cross a pretty footbridge over another stream. Cross two more footbridges and go uphill.

At the trail junction with Patriots' Path (2.8 miles), go straight. Watch your step on this downward, rooty path. Do not take the feeder trail to the left after the stepping-stones. Keep straight as the trail begins to ascend, passing the sign for the Connecticut Line Encampment Site on the right. Stay on the white-blazed trail at marker 55. (It overlaps with the Patriots' Path during some of this section.)

Descend a rocky hill and cross paved Mendham Road Trail (3.7 miles, not on map) to marker 56. Still on Grand Loop Trail, carefully cross Tempe Wicke Road (3.8 miles). Cross a footbridge over a trickling stream at marker 57. At the trail junction, go straight on Grand Loop Trail at marker 58. (*Do not* take New Jersey Brigade Trail/Patriots' Path, 4.0 miles.) The rocky trail leads up and narrows; bushes brush your thighs. At marker 59, the trail splits. Head toward a "Green Acres" sign and the picnic tables at the Boy Scout camp (4.7 miles), where you can pause for lunch or snacks. Return to the woods and go left to continue on lightly graveled Grand Loop Trail. Go downhill, past an iron gate, and cross Tempe Wick Road (5.0 miles).

Take the path on the left into the woods, past old-timey split rail fences. Continue straight up Grand Loop Trail (or go to the right and take the footpath back to the visitor center). The trail levels off for a delightful walk on a ridgeline and then slopes downhill into loose rocks and roots, so watch your step. At marker 3, take the fork to the right, onto the green-blazed Aqueduct Loop Trail (5.5 miles). Cross small paved Cemetery Road.

Go downhill on loose pebbles as the path widens into blowdown. Pretty rocks are scattered on the rise to the right. Pass an area enclosed by a 6-foot wire fence and keep winding through a beautiful forest. At the trail junction, turn right at marker 53 and continue on a soft, flat dirt path with lacy overhanging trees. Boulders in the streambed on the left look like bowling balls. Cattails wave in

Replicas show the cramped quarters in which Continental Army soldiers lived, twelve to a hut, during the Revolutionary War. By 1780, there were 1,200 huts in Jockey Hollow. Photo by Susan Bennett.

the marsh. Stay on the trail, which veers to the left before an iron gate. Cross a bridge over a brook and follow the "To Trail Center" sign at marker 34.

Come out at a paved parking lot with the Aqueduct Loop Trail sign on the left (6.2 miles). Take a moment to read a marker about Nathanael Greene, Washington's quartermaster. Then turn left (in the opposite direction of the one-way sign) onto paved Jockey Hollow Road at the Trail Center kiosk.

Turn right onto red-blazed Primrose Brook Trail, which parallels Patriots' Path, marker 28. The trail descends and becomes narrow, winding, and very rooty in the deep woods. Cross a meandering stream on a series of footbridges and stepping-stones. (*Note:* The water can get high in the rainy season.)

Take a left at marker 30 onto the wide, gravel Grand Loop Trail (6.6 miles). Turn right at marker 20 onto the blue-blazed Mt. Kemble Loop Trail (6.7 miles). At a junction atop the incline, go left at marker 19 into the woods. Stay right at marker 17, still on the well-worn Mt. Kemble Loop Trail.

Vista alert: Stop at the sign at Jockey Hollow View and admire the New York City skyline and the Watchung Mountains, a natural defense. Read the marker about Stark's Brigade Encampment. Back on the blue-blazed trail, pass another iron gate and a house to the right. At marker 14, go left (8.0 miles), still on

Mt. Kemble Loop Trail (blazed aqua here). Go right at a fork and head down a rocky dark-blue-blazed trail, then turn left—straight onto a slightly graveled path. At a culvert and marker 10, take the unnamed trail to the left (8.4 miles).

The trail is now blazed light-blue and white, where Grand Loop and New York Brigade trails merge. You'll revisit the pond and bench from earlier. At marker 22, take the light-blue New York Brigade Trail on the right (8.5 miles), going past a beautiful grassy meadow, to the restrooms (8.8 miles). At marker 23, read about the New York Brigade Encampment.

Head toward marker 24 and then 26, following signs to orange-blazed Grand Parade (not Grand Loop) Trail and Wick House. It's a straight shot and only 1.2 miles to the parking lot where you started.

## DID YOU KNOW?

Just minutes south of the park is Scherman Hoffman Wildlife Sanctuary, a New Jersey Audubon sanctuary, on 11 Hardscrabble Road in Bernardsville. Fort Nonsense in downtown Morristown provides great views of the Watchung Mountains without any of the effort. Bat lovers can travel 20 miles north to visit a hibernaculum for more than 26,000 of these furry mammals, at the Hibernia Mine in Wildcat Ridge Wildlife Management area in the Highlands region. Entrance to the hibernaculum is prohibited. (Take I-80 to Exit 37. Go north on County Road 513 toward Hibernia for 2.8 miles; turn right on Sunnyside Road. Parking area is 0.1 mile on left.)

## OTHER ACTIVITIES

See Cross Estate Gardens at the south end of the park. Visit Washington's Headquarters Museum and the Ford Mansion at the east end of the park (30 Washington Place). From here, walk part of the Washington-Rochambeau National Historic Trail, "only" 680 miles long from Massachusetts through Virginia. Morristown has a variety of shops and restaurants. Other attractions include Frelinghuysen Arboretum, New Jersey's largest horticultural park (353 E. Hanover Avenue), and Historic Speedwell, a National Historic Landmark, known as the "birthplace of the telegraph." The Factory Building museum has three floors of exhibits devoted to the development of Samuel F.B. Morse's telegraph, which was first successfully demonstrated here in 1838 (333 Speedwell Avenue).

## MORE INFORMATION

Park grounds are open from 8 A.M. to sunset. Building hours and days of operation vary seasonally. The 1.5-mile self-guided Aqueduct Loop Trail traces the history of New Jersey's first water company, built in 1799. Jockey Hollow Visitor Center, 580 Tempe Wick Road, Morristown, NJ 07960-6657; 973-543-4030; nps.gov/morr/index.htm.

# 5

# HIGH POINT STATE PARK: MONUMENT TRAIL TO APPALACHIAN TRAIL

This challenging hike offers panoramic views of three states from the highest point in New Jersey. Spot hawks and grouse in the unique Atlantic white cedar swamp.

## DIRECTIONS

Take I-80 West to Route 15 North, then take Route 15 North to Route 565 (Ross Corner Sussex Road). Take Route 565 to Route 23, just north of Colesville. Park in the Appalachian Trail parking lot, marked with a brown sign, on the left. There's room for about twenty cars. *GPS coordinates:* 41° 18.176′ N, 74° 40.051′ W.

## TRAIL DESCRIPTION

Get ready to summit New Jersey's 1,803-foot high point, appropriately named High Point; climb even higher on the 220-foot High Point Monument ($1 fee) for spectacular views of the Catskill Mountains to the north, the Pocono Mountains to the west, and the Wallkill River valley to the southeast. Thirteen marked trails cover more than 50 miles, over ridges, fields, and wetlands, through forests and an Atlantic white cedar swamp. Stop by the park office (just 1.2 miles north of the parking lot) and pick up a map. You'll hike part of the Shawangunk Ridge Trail (SRT), named after the rugged, rocky range—also called "the Gunks"—that extends north to New York and south to Virginia. The Appalachian Trail (AT) runs for 9 miles through the park, 884 miles from the AT's northern terminus at Katahdin in Maine and 1,330 miles from its southern terminus at Springer Mountain in Georgia. The park is spectacular in fall with blazing colors from oak, hickory, and birch trees; the cedar swamp is peaceful in winter. Enjoy blooming rhododendrons in spring and blueberries and huckleberries in summer.

**LOCATION**
Sussex

**RATING**
Strenuous

**DISTANCE**
7.9 miles

**ELEVATION GAIN**
1,250 feet

**ESTIMATED TIME**
5 hours

**MAPS**
USGS Port Jarvis South; state.nj.us/dep/ parksandforests/parks/ highpoint.html; *Kittatinny Trails Map, Trail Map 123,* Seventh Edition, New York-New Jersey Trail Conference

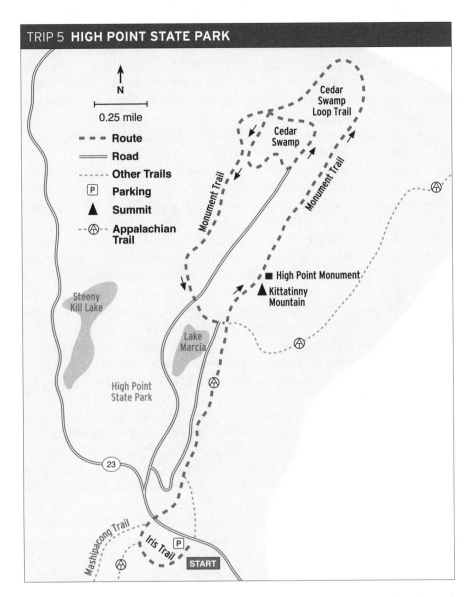

Directly from the parking lot, take the blue-blazed connector trail at the trail sign. The path becomes rooty and rocky as it progresses. After a turn to the right it becomes Iris Trail (red dot on white background, 0.2 mile) and slopes up gradually. This dirt path was originally built to be a bridle trail by the Civilian Conservation Corps between 1933 and 1941.

At the four-way intersection, turn right onto the white-blazed Appalachian Trail (AT, 0.4 mile). (Do not go straight onto the yellow-blazed Mashipacong Trail.) At the park office and kiosk, veer right into the woods, staying on the AT. Cross Route 23 (0.6 mile) and stay on the AT northbound—the sign is apparent across the road. Traverse a field and enter the woods at the AT sign.

Gradually ascend rocky terrain before entering a shady grove of tree tunnels. Big rocks give way to smaller rocks before you pop out on the ridgeline into open sky and welcome breezes. Enjoy the view and then descend about 1 mile to the raised observation platform (1.6 miles) with a 360-degree view of High Point Monument and the Delaware Water Gap to the south, the Catskills to the north, and Pennsylvania and Lake Marcia to the west.

Head through the woods toward the obvious monument by curving left onto the red-and-green-blazed Monument Trail, which overlaps just a bit with the blue-blazed SRT. Cross a boulder field and a park road (1.8 miles, watch for cars) and then head into the woods again, still on Monument Trail. Go right at a fork, climbing steeply uphill over large wooden water bars to reach the monument and the spacious parking lot with wheelchair ramp (1.9 miles).

Visit the small museum for information on the Kuser family, who donated the land, and on the formation of the Kittatinny Mountains. The museum offers coin-operated observation binoculars, a snack bar, and bathrooms.

Walk away from the monument to the end of the parking lot, where Monument Trail descends into the woods and goes up and down past beautiful oak trees, over challenging rocks, past a scenic overlook to the right, and then steadily descends. At a trail junction, go straight after the footbridge (3.1 miles), still on Monument Trail, which levels off briefly. Take a left at the next junction (3.6 miles) for a detour onto the magnificent but unmarked 1.2-mile Cedar Swamp Trail loop. (*Note*: Protect against chiggers—tiny red mites that bite and cause skin irritation—here in warm weather by wearing long pants, long-sleeved shirt, socks and boots, and insect repellent all over, including the entire foot.) Very soon, a sign reassures that you are on the Cedar Swamp Trail, which is unblazed. Take a right at a bench onto the unblazed Cedar Swamp Trail. At an elevation of 1,500 feet, the Atlantic white cedar bog here is believed to be the highest in the world.

High Point's website offers the *Cedar Swamp Trail Guide*, with eleven pages of more in-depth information on the Atlantic cedar bog. The trail also has nature signs to help you enjoy the flat dirt path and rich air, dense with green particles from hay-scented and bracken ferns, spongy sphagnum mosses, highbush blueberries, spruces, black gums, hemlocks, black birches, red oaks, carnivorous plants, and irises and callas (in spring). The rhododendrons are tall and dense. Take a left at the stone wall with an embedded metal plaque that reads "John Dryden Kuser Memorial Natural Area" to continue on the unmarked Cedar Swamp Trail (4.3 miles). Take a left at the next junction, still on the Cedar Swamp Trail (4.6 miles).

Back at the bench, turn right onto the SRT (4.8 miles) and walk for about 100 yards. Cross a magnificent boardwalk over a bog, then go left at a junction to return to red-and-green-blazed Monument Trail (5.7 miles). Ascend, passing a turnoff on the right for the SRT, traversing a gorgeous woods, before you pop out on a ridge for a good view of Port Jervis, New York, and Pennsylvania on

High Point Monument, as seen from the observation platform on the AT. Photo by Paul Wulfing.

the right. A gentle ascent takes you past a boulder field on the right and over a footbridge, where you can hear, but not see, the thundering falls to the left. Keep straight (do not take the blue-blazed trail to the right). Curving stone stairs lead to the top of the hill and a large "resting rock," shaped to the contours of a human back.

Turn left onto the paved road at the Stone House Nature Center (6.0 miles) toward Lake Marcia, a pretty spring-fed glacial pond at 1,570 feet. Head toward the brown building on the wide cinder path to the left of the lake. Continue on the path, keeping the lake to your right; turn left at the next intersection (6.2 miles) onto an unmarked trail, which becomes red-and-green-blazed Monument Trail in about 200 feet. Ascend over broken rocks, then cross the road and head straight into the woods. At a trail junction, turn right, going uphill onto the AT (6.3 miles).

Soon you'll see the observation platform; retrace your steps the 1.6 miles back to the parking lot, staying on the white-blazed AT. Cross Route 23, pass the kiosk on the left of the park office, and head into the woods. Turn left at the next two junctions to reach the parking lot.

## DID YOU KNOW?

The park was landscaped by the sons of Frederick Law Olmsted, who designed New York City's Central Park. Anthony R. and Susie Dryden Kuser donated the land. The High Point Monument is a 220-foot obelisk that honors all war veterans. Tri-States Monument, where New York, New Jersey, and Pennsylvania meet, is in the Laurel Grove Cemetery in Port Jervis, New York, beneath the I-84 underpass; for help in locating the monument, see roadsideamerica.com.

## OTHER ACTIVITIES

Stokes State Forest (33 miles of trails, including the AT) connects to High Point State Park via the light-green-blazed Parker Trail; hike Sunrise Mountain there, the second-highest point in New Jersey. Also nearby is Wallkill River National Wildlife Refuge in Sussex. Visit the Sterling Hill Mine Museum in Ogdensburg, the "fluorescent mineral capital of the world." Within 10 miles is Grey Towers National Historic Site in Milford, Pennsylvania, the former home of Gifford Pinchot, founder of the U.S. Forest Service.

## MORE INFORMATION

From Memorial Day weekend to Labor Day, parking at High Point Memorial parking lot carries a fee of $5, $7, $10, or $20 depending on time of week, type of vehicle, and whether or not you are a New Jersey resident. The free AT parking lot is at 1396 Route 23 in Sussex. The park office is 1.2 miles north on Route 23, but parking there is limited to two hours. Mailing address: High Point State Park, 1480 Route 23, Sussex, NJ 07461; 973-875-4800; state.nj.us/dep/parksandforests/parks/highpoint.html. Friends of High Point State Park, P.O. Box 817, Wantage, NJ 07461; friendsofhighpointstatepark.org.

# 6
# DEER PATH PARK: ROUND MOUNTAIN SECTION

This township park features paths that wind in and out of rustic woods and beautiful meadows, past historical farms and barns, a museum, and beehives.

**LOCATION**
Flemington

**RATING**
Easy to Moderate

**DISTANCE**
6.6 miles

**ELEVATION GAIN**
900 feet

**ESTIMATED TIME**
3.5 hours

**MAPS**
co.hunterdon.nj.us/
depts/parks/ParkAreas/
DeerPath/trailmap.pdf

## DIRECTIONS

Take Route 31 North and turn right onto West Woodschurch Road, following signs for Deer Path Park and the YMCA. Proceed about 0.7 mile on West Woodschurch Road to the park entrance on the right. Drive past the YMCA entrance to the parking lot on the left, with space for about 30 cars. *GPS coordinates:* 40° 33.208′ N, 74° 50.315′ W.

## TRAIL DESCRIPTION

This hike visits the Round Mountain section of Deer Path Park. Deer Path Park is one of 28 parks in Hunterdon County. Round Mountain is 600 feet above sea level, and the Lenni-Lenape used to camp here; the area has one of the nicest mature forests in Hunterdon County, with oaks, ashes, maples, and beeches.

Rolling terrain, sometimes rocky, slips repeatedly from meadows to woods, creating variety and interest. You'll visit a working farm and a historical farmstead on the Bouman-Stickney Loop (orange diamond), Woodschurch Farm Loop (yellow diamond), and Round Mountain Loop (white diamond). Following the blazes in and out of the woods can be a bit tricky; just keep a sharp lookout. In spring and summer, flowers bloom and birds are active. In fall, the meadows are bright with goldenrods and rimmed with a brilliantly colored forest. In winter, frozen grasses catch the sun, and bare trees lace the sky.

Grab a Round Mountain Trail System map from the kiosk in the parking lot. Then head toward the bathrooms

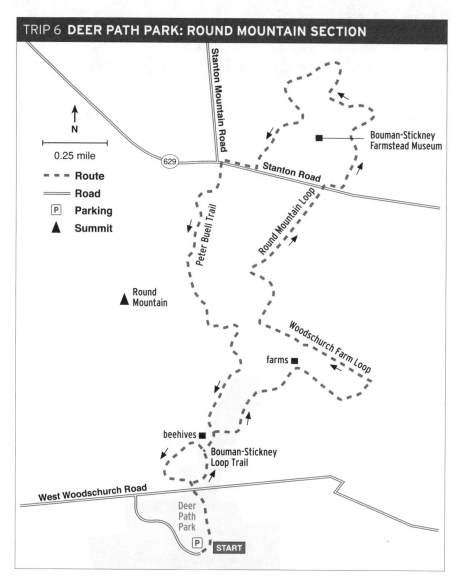

N

0.25 mile

- - - Route
═══ Road
P  Parking
▲  Summit

Stanton Mountain Road

629

Stanton Road

Bouman-Stickney
Farmstead Museum

Peter Buell Trail

Round Mountain Loop

Round
▲ Mountain

Woodschurch Farm Loop

farms ■

beehives ■

Bouman-Stickney
Loop Trail

West Woodschurch Road

Deer
Path
Park

P START

and take the paved path behind them. The path goes past brown buildings, through the soccer fields and across open fields before veering left to parallel the road on your right (West Woodschurch). Turn right to cross the road (0.4 mile), and enter the Round Mountain section of Deer Path Park.

Veer to the right, walking alongside a beautiful blooming meadow. As you stroll the many meadows and fields on this hike, be sure to stop and look up for hawks. You may even spot an eagle. When you are almost at the top of the meadow, turn right into the woods on the first path you see, which is the orange-blazed Bouman-Stickney Loop (0.6 mile). Go over a bridge that parallels a field. (*Note:* Be sure to wear a hat or have sun protection in this exposed area.) Take an uphill, uneven path into lush green woods—watch your footing. Still on the orange-blazed trail, veer left into another lovely meadow with soft, colorful grasses and seasonal flowers. Toward the end of the meadow, take the first path on the right into the cool woods. The rocky dirt path slopes down, soft grasses lining the way. At the public-lands-sign intersection (0.9 miles), veer right. Then veer left at a junction marked by posts. Follow the yellow-blazed Woodschurch Farm Loop (maintained by the Readington Trail Association) across another bridge.

You'll reach the Dobozynski Farm Park/Woodschurch Farmstead (1.4 miles) on the yellow-blazed trail. Take time to admire the house and historical barns. In the animal pens, chickens and usually a large tom turkey are fun to observe. The trail becomes a gravel road through the farm, then makes a left at the "Dobozynski Farm" sign and goes uphill.

Take a left onto the first road, a gravel path, and follow it to a gate and fence. Go through the gate and walk slightly uphill around another beautiful meadow. Enter the woods, then walk along a field, turning right into woods again on a dirt path (1.9 miles); note houses for orientation to your right. You are now on white-blazed Round Mountain Loop. Stay on this trail (eroded and rocky in spots) as it goes gradually up and in and out of fields and meadows. At 2.6 miles, Round Mountain Loop crosses Route 629. Turn right on the road, walk on the shoulder for 100 yards, and then cross the road and turn left to continue on Round Mountain Loop.

The Bouman-Stickney Farmstead Museum is in a stone building on the right. Take some time to visit the museum and learn about Howard Lindsay and Dorothy Stickney. This thespian couple entertained many luminaries at their retreat, including Julie Andrews, Shelley Winters, and Oscar Hammerstein, before Dorothy's death in 1998 at age 101. The reconstructed New World Dutch Barn is worth exploring. Walk the light-orange-blazed Stickney Interpretive Trail that circles the property. Go right and pass two footbridges to get back on white-blazed Round Mountain Loop. (*Note:* If you go left, you'll be backtracking.) As you enter a field, you'll see Route 629; head toward it and turn right on Route 629 and walk on the shoulder for 0.2 mile until you see Stanton General Store, a restaurant on the opposite side of the road. Stop for a drink or a meal. (*Note:* Restaurant closed in summer 2018 but is rumored to reopen in 2019.)

Leave the restaurant, walk across Route 629, and turn left to walk on the shoulder, keeping the wire fence on your right. When the fence ends, turn right, and then almost immediately left into the woods, still on the white-blazed trail. Here the trail is a very rutted dirt path, rooty and rocky. Take a left at the junction onto a white-and-red-blazed connector trail (5.0 miles), which widens and slopes downhill. Turn right onto the orange-blazed Bouman-Stickney Trail; a wooden sign labels this stretch Peter Buell Trail, in honor of a park employee. Hike down through the woods (5.3 miles).

Emerge in an open field, under power lines, and continue on the Peter Buell Trail. Cross a path and go straight downhill into the woods. Do not take the trail

In fall, goldenrod lines the path through beautiful meadows.

on left. Step over water bars and cross the creek bed (the creek is sometimes dry, sometimes wet, but still easy to cross). Turn right at the field and walk the perimeter, visiting the active beehives and honey trays on the left. Take a right at the fork to go toward the gate and cross West Woodschurch Road (6.3 miles). Stay straight. There will be a soccer field on the right and buildings and bathrooms on the left as you make your way back to the parking lot.

## DID YOU KNOW?

Some say Oscar Hammerstein wrote the score for *The Sound of Music* at what is now the Bouman-Stickney Farmstead. Round Mountain is a rest stop for migratory birds; look for eastern bluebird and American kestrel nesting boxes. Wild turkeys are a common sight, and watch for white-tailed deer and red foxes.

## OTHER ACTIVITIES

Myriad shops and restaurants crowd the area, especially Route 31. Visit the Hunterdon County Arboretum, less than 3 miles (5 minutes) away at 1020 Route 31. About 22 miles west (25 minutes), park at 182 Dennis Road in the town of Bloomsbury to explore 524-acre Musconetcong Gorge Preserve, especially the moderate-to-difficult Ridge and Highlands trails. Cushetunk Mountain Preserve (106 Old Mountain Road, Lebanon) has nesting bald eagles.

## MORE INFORMATION

Deer Path Park, a former summer camp, was acquired by Hunterdon County in 1977. The park features a fifteen-station fitness circuit and running trails. Round Mountain was formed by volcanic activity and reaches 600 feet above sea level. The Bouman-Stickney Farmstead (Stanton section) has programs for children (908-236-2327). The Round Mountain Trail System map is a combined effort of employees and volunteers of Readington Township and the Hunterdon County parks department. Township of Readington, 509 Route 523, Whitehouse Station, NJ 08889; 908-534-4051; readingtontwpnj.gov. Hunterdon County Division of Parks and Recreation, 1020 Route 31, Lebanon, NJ 08833; 908-782-1158; co.hunterdon.nj.us/depts/parks/parks.htm.

## NEW JERSEY HIGHLANDS

The Highlands region of New Jersey is large, both in physical dimensions and in ecological importance. Physically, the Highlands stretches for about 60 miles, from Milford in the southwest to Mahwah in the northeast, and encompasses more than 850,000 acres in New Jersey. The region lies within the boundaries of seven counties: Sussex, Warren, Morris, Hunterdon, and Somerset in the Skylands region; and Bergen and Passaic in the Gateway region (see hikes in the Skylands and Gateway regions).

In terms of ecological importance, the Highlands is a giant. This belt of green protects the drinking water resources on which 70 percent of the state's population depends. The Highlands supplies potable water to 5.4 million people, only 821,000 of whom live in the region itself. More than 200 threatened, endangered, or rare plants and animals live here. Wetlands, forests, lakes, and streams protect the blue-spotted salamander, the osprey, the silver-bordered fritillary butterfly, and the bog turtle, among others. The tiny bog turtle achieved rare status in June 2018, when Governor Phil Murphy designated it the official state reptile.

Given the Highlands' importance, it's no wonder serious attention was finally given to this geologic region in the 1980s. Many conservation organizations, state and local governments, and local businesses are now involved. The Appalachian Mountain Club (AMC) leads the four-state Highlands Coalition, an alliance of nearly 200 nonprofit, municipal, state, and federal organizations that advocate for federal funding to protect the region. Today the entire Highlands encompasses 3.5 million acres, from Pennsylvania through New Jersey, New York, and into Connecticut.

AMC has long been a key advocate for the Highlands. In 2004, AMC led the Highlands Coalition's advocacy efforts to secure passage of the Highlands Conservation Act, a tremendous milestone for the long-term protection of the Highlands, allowing Congress to allocate $10 million a year on open-space projects in the region. When the program expired in 2014, AMC led the charge to reauthorize the Highlands Conservation Act. Success came in 2018, after four busy years, and now the Highlands Conservation Act is effective through 2021. AMC continues to advocate for yearly funding through the Land and Water Conservation Fund, a visionary and bipartisan federal funding program designed to protect special places. AMC also oversees the Pennsylvania Highlands Coalition.

Work on the Highlands Trail (HT) began in 1995, via an inventive co-alignment of both established and new trails. When complete, the HT will stretch 150 miles, from Pennsylvania to Connecticut. In New Jersey, the HT is a rugged, sometimes challenging footpath that follows the spine of northwest New Jersey, crosses rolling hills and mountains, cuts through deep forests, and passes waterfalls, small rural communities, and land remnants of historical features, such as iron works, transport canals, and mansions. Some sections where it aligns with other trails can be confusing. But if you pay attention to the trail's distinctive teal, diamond-shaped blazes, especially at intersections, you will be amply rewarded.

One of the best ways to help protect the Highlands is to get out and hike it! Each footstep honors those who fight for it and brings awareness to this vibrant area.

According to the New Jersey Highlands Coalition, every $1 invested in state preservation programs returns $10 in economic value to the state. So while you're hiking, invite a buddy, take pictures, and share on social media with #NJHighlands and #LWCF (Land and Water Conservation Fund). You'll impress your friends, and Mr. Bog Turtle, the state reptile of New Jersey, will thank you.

For maps, see the *Jersey Highlands Trails* and the *North Jersey Trails* from the New York–New Jersey Trail Conference, as well as the online Highlands Trail Guide (nynjtc.org/region/highlands-trail-region). For more information on AMC's role in the Highlands, visit outdoors.org/conservation/where-we-work/mid-atlantic-highlands.

# 7

# DELAWARE AND RARITAN CANAL AND HORSESHOE BEND PARK

A flat walk along the Delaware River becomes a woodsy ramble through lush forests, over streams, and through rolling meadows.

## DIRECTIONS

Take NJ 29 toward Frenchtown. Turn onto Bridge Street (NJ 12) toward the Delaware River. Go 0.11 mile and turn left before you cross the bridge (just past Front Street). A free parking lot on River Road holds 20 to 30 cars. *GPS coordinates:* 40° 31.493′ N, 75° 03.785′ W.

## TRAIL DESCRIPTION

This fun adventure combines two trails in two parks: the Delaware and Raritan Canal State Park and Horseshoe Bend Park. Enter the southern end of Horseshoe Bend Park through a little-used access point off the Delaware and Raritan (D&R) Canal towpath. You'll hike only 2.5 miles along the D&R Canal; the entire route extends for 70 (mostly flat) miles. (For more information on the canal's history, see page 40.) The section in Frenchtown is known as a "feeder," supplying water to the main canal. Today the canal is lined with homes, woods, and whimsical garden creations. The 736-acre Horseshoe Bend Park has three trails spanning 11.5 miles, with the Cooley Preserve in the northwest corner and a 7-acre dog park in the northeast corner. Ravines, streams, and forests provide homes for pileated woodpeckers, hawks, and amphibians. Butterfly spotting is best from May to October when swallowtails, hairstreaks, fritillaries, skippers, and more float through the air. Foliage makes this a great fall hike; the flat trails are good in snow. Spring brings the running of the shad, the largest fish in the herring family, when they migrate from salt water to the Delaware River to reproduce. Don't miss the two-day shad festival in Lambertville, usually in late April.

**LOCATION**
Frenchtown

**RATING**
Moderate to Strenuous

**DISTANCE**
10.6 miles

**ELEVATION GAIN**
900 feet

**ESTIMATED TIME**
5.5 hours

**MAPS**
USGS Frenchtown; Horseshoe Bend Park: kingwoodtownship.com/ KT_ParksRec/ParkMaps/ HBPOverviewMap9.02.2014 .pdf; njtrails.org/trail/ horseshoe-bend-park

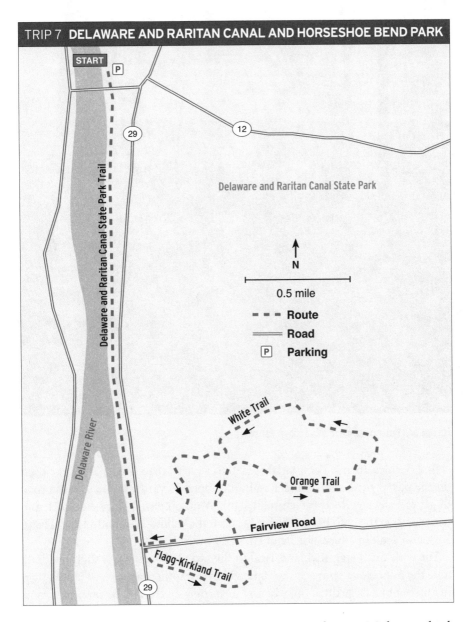

Start in the parking lot next to the bridge in Frenchtown. With your back to the parking lot and the beautiful Delaware River, walk to the D&R towpath and turn right (south) on the loose-gravel trail. As you begin the walk, note the family of gnomes on the left and a cemetery from the 1800s. On your right is the mighty Delaware River; just across the water is Pennsylvania. Soon you will traverse a field and walk through a green tunnel of trees, with an inviting bench on the left. As you continue along the towpath, be sure to pause and admire the river. Scan the banks for a bald eagle, red-tailed hawk, or northern goshawk. (*Note:* Be careful of speeding bicycles on this popular route.)

Foliage and butterflies make this an ideal fall hike.

At 2.5 miles, turn left at a gated area onto a paved road (Route 29). Take a left on the paved road and shoulder walk for about 30 yards, then cross the road to get to Fairview Road (green road sign). Walk on paved Fairview Road, and turn right on the path before the bridge onto the yellow-diamond-blazed Flagg-Kirkland Trail in Horseshoe Bend Park (2.9 miles).

The wide dirt Flagg-Kirkland Trail in this wooded area winds slightly uphill; note the impressive ravine to the right. Go over another ravine, still uphill, then in and out of a large ditch (may be wet in spring). In the fall, be careful of roots and rocks hiding under fallen leaves.

Stroll on a wooden boardwalk for a hundred yards or so. Then meander downhill through oak, beech, and hemlock trees, which offer brilliant foliage in the fall. In wet seasons, you'll cross a few small, clear streams.

At 4.2 miles, cross Fairview Road. (If you want to go back, turn left and walk down the paved road, which intersects Route 29. Continue to your car or wander farther south on the flat canal towpath.) Turn right to return to yellow-blazed Flagg-Kirkland Trail. Go uphill into a clearing where you'll see awe-inspiring massive overturned tree trunks. (The trail skirts private land, so be careful not to trespass.)

Take a right onto the appropriately orange-blazed Orange Trail (5.0 miles). Go over two wooden bridges. Ignore the trail to the left after the second bridge; keep straight on Orange Trail. A wire fence runs along the right, as well as a picturesque stone wall. Turn left onto a paved road in the park and head to a covered pavilion for lunch or a rest stop (5.8 miles).

Refreshed, go back down the paved road and past the trail sign on the right that you saw earlier. After 100 yards, turn left at the kiosk onto the white-blazed White Trail. Veer right into the woods on White Trail, being careful of rocks underfoot. At the fork, turn right to continue on White Trail. The trail then loops off to the right, but keep left (straight). White Trail follows Burke's Run for a while, making for a pretty and lush path. At the intersection with Orange Trail (6.3 miles), turn right onto Orange Trail. The narrow route goes uphill and is exposed to the elements, then plunges down a steep, rooty hill. Use caution on this hill. At 6.9 miles, turn right onto the yellow-blazed Flagg-Kirkland Trail. At the intersection with Fairview Road (7.5 miles), turn right onto Fairview. Fairview Road soon intersects Route 29. Turn left on Route 29 and walk on the shoulder for a few dozen yards. Cross the road carefully as you head back to the canal. Take a right on the canal and go 2.5 miles back to the parking lot, enjoying the Delaware River on your left. Take a good look at the 2-mile-long Marshall Island in the middle of the river; perhaps you'll glimpse an otter.

## DID YOU KNOW?

Many of the Irish workers who helped build the D&R Canal died during an Asiatic cholera pandemic in 1832 and are buried in unmarked graves along the canal. Visit a memorial, made from a 2-ton granite stone taken from a lock in the New Brunswick section in front of Bull's Island Recreation Area's office (2185 Daniel Bray Highway, Stockton, NJ).

## OTHER ACTIVITIES

Small, charming Frenchtown has a bookstore, antique stores, and upscale as well as more affordable shops. Rent skates (inline or quads) at an old-fashioned roller-skating rink just south of town on Route 29. In summer, companies set up in the parking lot to offer trips down the river on tubes or in canoes. Walk across the bridge, with seriously impressive river views sweeping north and south, and visit Pennsylvania on the other side.

## MORE INFORMATION

Delaware and Raritan Canal State Park, 145 Mapleton Road, Princeton, NJ 08540; 609-924-5705; state.nj.us/dep/parksandforests/parks/drcanal.html. Horseshoe Bend Park, 178 Horseshoe Bend Road, Frenchtown, NJ 08825; 908-996-4276; kingwoodtownship.com/parks.

## DELAWARE AND RARITAN CANAL STATE PARK

As you hike some of the 70 miles of trails in New Jersey's Delaware and Raritan Canal State Park, which runs from Milford to New Brunswick, consider its more than 400-year-old history.

In the early 1600s, during British colonization, canals and other transportation systems between colonies were discouraged because Britain wanted access to all of the colonies' raw materials, rather than having colonies trade with one another. Even though officials in New Jersey knew that a canal connecting the Delaware and Raritan rivers would circumvent the poor roads and shallow rivers that inhibited (forbidden) intercolonial trade, it took winning the American Revolution (1775–1783) and the opening of the Erie Canal in 1825 to bring "canal fever" to New Jersey. The Delaware and Raritan Canal (D&R Canal) was built from 1830 to 1834 and was the final link in the intercoastal waterway that runs from Massachusetts to Georgia.

Often referred to as "the Big Ditch," the original canal was 66 miles long, had fourteen locks to raise and lower boat traffic, cost almost $3 million (roughly $73 million today), and was hand-dug by workers, including 3,000 Irish laborers. The workers, mostly recruited from Ireland during a U.S. labor shortage, were paid $1 a day (roughly $25 today) and could earn an additional 25 cents for each tree stump they removed. Passage from Ireland was expensive, $27 for food and transportation, so many laborers borrowed the money from their employers, paying them back by working for "free" for a period of time, usually six months. With shovels, pickaxes, and wheelbarrows, they worked from sunrise to sunset, six days a week, living in tents, with no medical facilities or sanitation. Many died due to these conditions, and in 1832, an outbreak of Asiatic cholera killed hundreds more. Most are buried in marked and unmarked graves at Bull's Island and the Griggstown Cemetery, and along Ten Mile Run (a tributary) and the canal banks. Paul Muldoon's Pulitzer Prize–winning collection of poetry, *Moy Sand and Gravel*, honors these "navvies." A 2-ton carved granite stone, taken from a lock in the New Brunswick section of the canal, stands in front of the Bulls Island Recreation Area's office (2185 Daniel Bray Highway, Stockton, NJ) and pays tribute to the workers.

Mules towed boats on the newly built canal and were kept moving by "mule tenders." The tenders, mostly children, some younger than 9 years old, were tied to the barge so they could be hauled up if they fell in the water. The Mule Tenders Barracks Museum in Griggstown provides an excellent history of this era. Today you can take a one-hour mule-drawn canal ride starting in New Hope, Pennsylvania, to enhance your experience. Just walk over the Delaware River on the bridge that connects Lambertville, New Jersey, to New Hope.

By the end of the nineteenth century, railroads put the canals virtually out of business. The D&R Canal closed in 1932, and the State of New Jersey repurposed it to serve as a water supply system. By 1973, after some portions of the canal had been filled in and turned into highways, activists sought to save the canal from total destruction, and it was placed on the National Register of Historic Places. From 1974 on, the canal and corridors of land on both sides were made into a state park. In 1992, the park's trail system was designated a National Recreation Trail.

Museums, historical buildings, and picnic tables and grills are located along this magnificent trail that's perfect for hiking and biking. Several towns on the New Jersey side are worth a special trip. In Stockton, Prallsville Mills contains a sawmill, a gristmill, and a linseed-oil mill. Kingston has Lock 8 and the lockkeeper's house and station. View bridgetenders' homes in Griggstown and Blackwells Mills. Visit old homesteads at Six Mile Run Reservoir in Somerset County (see Trip 12).

Wherever you go on this 70-mile trail, history nudges you, slows your step, and brings a thoughtful and grateful dimension to your hike.

For more on the D&R Canal, see two books by Linda J. Barth: *The Delaware and Raritan Canal* and *The Delaware and Raritan Canal at Work* (Arcadia Publishing). Also contact Delaware and Raritan Canal State Park, 145 Mapleton Road, Princeton, NJ 08540; 609-924-5705; state.nj.us/dep/parksandforests/parks/drcanal.html.

# 8

# JENNY JUMP STATE FOREST

Enjoy open views of the Kittatinny Ridge and Valley, plus dramatic rock outcroppings and boulders in rolling terrain.

## DIRECTIONS

Take Route 80 to Exit 12 to the Village of Hope. Turn onto Route 519 north at the blinking light. At the third right, turn onto Shiloh Road. Drive approximately 1 mile and turn right onto State Park Road. There is limited parking at the park office, so go a few hundred yards uphill past the office and park in the lot there, which has space for about twenty cars. *GPS coordinates:* 40° 54.708′ N, 74° 55.507′ W.

## TRAIL DESCRIPTION

Jenny Jump State Forest is in the New Jersey Highlands region and has 14 miles of trails. For rock lovers, the light-blue-blazed Jenny Jump Trail is a fun hike over moraines (rocky mounds made by glacial deposits) and past unusually shaped glacial rock outcroppings and boulders. Be sure to wear sturdy boots. You'll enjoy views to the west of the Highlands and the Kittatinny Mountain Ridge and Valley. If you climb to the top of Jenny Jump Mountain, you can see Great Meadows to the east. The forest is mainly hardwoods and white pines. A winter hike showcases excellent views of the Delaware Water Gap and is mercifully bug-free.

Head to the park office and pick up a map. (Geology enthusiasts should grab the brochure for a self-guided tour of the forest's moraines, kettle holes, and large rocks called "erratics" that were transported by glaciers. The geology tour is not covered in this hike, but you can see two large erratics outside the park office.) From the office parking lot, get on the light-blue-blazed Jenny Jump Trail, a beautiful boulder-lined path, and head south. (*Note:* The

### LOCATION
Hope

### RATING
Moderate

### DISTANCE
4.9 miles

### ELEVATION GAIN
900 feet

### ESTIMATED TIME
3 hours

### MAPS
USGS Blairstown; state.nj.us/dep/parksandforests/parks/maps/jennyjumpareamap_reduced.pdf

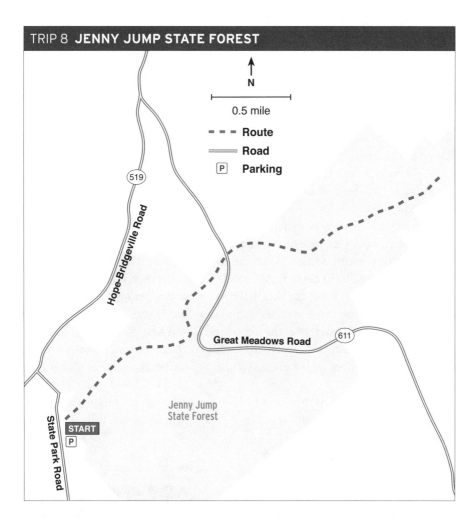

trail can be icy in winter, so be prepared with poles or traction cleats.) Keep straight on Jenny Jump Trail. Don't turn left on the yellow-blazed trail.

Enjoy the undulating hills and a lovely ridge to the left. In winter, bare trees allow a good view of the Village of Hope, named in an optimistic moment by early Moravian settlers from Germany in 1769, who believed in the Bible rather than the infallibility of the Catholic pope and also in education for both boys and girls (unusual for the late 1700s). After almost 40 years, the Moravian planned community "experiment" in Hope ended. The main culprits were smallpox and financial troubles. The entire village was sold for $48,000 to Nicholas Kramer and Abraham Horn. (The Moravian community moved to Bethlehem, Pennsylvania, and is still there today.)

Turn right at a large glacial boulder, still on Jenny Jump Trail. Cross over a path that appears after 20 yards and stretch your muscles by going straight up a hill, but watch your footing on the rocks. Cross white-blazed Orchard Trail (0.3 mile), but stay on the light-blue-blazed trail. Enjoy views of the Village of

Hope and the Delaware Water Gap, as well as Mount Tammany (New Jersey) and Mount Minsi (Pennsylvania). Routes 611, 521, and 519 crisscross below.

Keep walking past impressive rocks along a ridge exposed to the elements, admiring the views. At a fork, there's a faded blaze on your right indicating a side trail toward an excellent vista of the Delaware Water Gap (1.7 miles). Legend has it that this vista marks the spot where Jenny jumped, hence the name Jenny Jump State Forest. Hundreds of years ago, according to legend, 9-year-old Jenny was gathering berries with her father near this ridge. When her father saw Lenni-Lenape people approaching, he became frightened and yelled at her to jump. Some say she died and her small ghost wanders the cliffs forever; others say she survived.

Backtrack to the light-blue-blazed trail, which meanders through the woods to another hilltop. Get ready for a rugged trek over boulders; be sure you are wearing sturdy boots. At the top of the hill, pause to catch your breath, then follow steep switchbacks down into the valley. In winter, wet, icy leaves and rocks make tricky footing; however, this is the sunny side of Jenny Jump Mountain. The beauty of the brown leaves and white snow are worth it. Cross a boulder-strewn stream and turn right at the light-blue blaze at a fork (2.2 miles) to stay on Jenny Jump Trail. Keep a sharp eye out for the blazes as the trail here is winding. There is a lovely valley with a gorge to the right. You may see some tom turkey tracks here.

Go down over boulders; green moss lines the path. You are on the ridge road, and the valley is to the right. It's tricky walking, so tread carefully. Go down

Rambling stone walls along this hike offer a welcome resting place or lunch stop.

rock steps to NJ 611 (2.7 miles); Jenny Jump Trail cuts right across the road and is prominently blazed (light-blue) on the guardrail. Cautiously cross the road, stepping over the guardrail, for a short, steep, rocky descent (poles come in handy). A very narrow fern-lined trail winds across the gently rolling contours of the hill, beneath the roar of CR 611 traffic. A valley stretches imperially to the right, with an open field at the bottom that glows like a heavenly footprint. Remains of a massive stone wall are to the left.

Carefully cross a stream, usually partially frozen in winter (3.1 miles). A stone wall near the stream provides a good lunch spot. You can continue on the light-blue-blazed trail for 2.6 more miles one-way to reach Lake Just-It, a small lake with a dam, if you'd like more exercise. Otherwise, save your energy for the return trip, and begin retracing your steps. At the fork, take the light-blue-blazed trail uphill away from the field, cross NJ 611, go uphill, and keep following the light-blue blazes. At the top of the hill, follow the light-blue blazes to the right; cross two trail intersections, staying on light-blue. At the third intersection, veer to the right on light-blue. A gigantic glacial boulder makes for a good photo op. Stay straight at the fork on the light-blue trail. The walk down the stone-lined path is reminiscent of a stroll through ancient Incan ruins. You will arrive back at the parking lot shortly.

## DID YOU KNOW?

The ghoulishly named Shades of Death Road skirts the eastern section of the forest. A former peat mining company there supplies pitcher's mound material for all major league and most minor league ballparks.

## OTHER ACTIVITIES

The Village of Hope is on Route 512, 1.0 mile south of Exit 12 on I-80. The Greenwood Observatory off of Fairview Road (open April to October) is 0.4 mile south of the park entrance, via State Park Road. Pequest Trout Hatchery and Natural Resource Education Center is 13 miles south in Oxford. The Delaware Water Gap National Recreation Area (100 miles of trails, including 27 on the Appalachian Trail) is 12 miles northwest; great hikes include Mount Tammany and Sunfish Pond. About 10 miles east is 9,000-acre Allamuchy Mountain State Park.

## MORE INFORMATION

The park office has information on the surrounding area and local attractions, including the Greenwood Observatory, and offers a nice selection of taxidermy and plaster animal tracks. There are no bathrooms, but turn left out of the office parking lot, and a bathhouse with flush toilets and showers is on your left. Jenny Jump State Forest, 330 State Park Road, Hope, NJ 07844; 908-459-4366; state.nj.us/dep/parksandforests/parks/jennyjump.html.

# 9

# WHITE OAK TRAIL TO LOCKATONG CREEK

Take a woodsy loop past old stone walls and ruins, over wetlands and wooden bridges, and along a creek.

## DIRECTIONS

Take I-287 or Route 22 to the intersection with Route 202 in Somerville. Follow Route 202 south for 26 miles to the exit for Route 29 North. Go north for about 6 miles. The entrance is on the left. The parking lot at the Bull's Island Recreation Area visitor center has room for at least 40 cars. *GPS coordinates:* 40° 24.571′ N, 75° 02.148′ W.

## TRAIL DESCRIPTION

Start at the visitor center at the Bull's Island Recreation Area and pick up a map. This out-and-back hike connects White Oak Trail and Wescott-Zega Lockatong Trail in Delaware Township. The Wescott-Zega Lockatong Trail consists of three trails: red-blazed Hunterdon Land Trust Alliance Trail (previously known as Mimi's Trail), Ralph Peters' Trail, and Wescott Trail. (You will not hike Wescott Trail on this journey.) Spring, when the trees are bare, is a good time to see the stone ruins that dot the trails, particularly the former Mimi's Trail. However, spring flooding and March mud may make access tricky—wear boots and maybe gaiters just in case. Summer and fall ensure drier paths, but the foliage covers the ruins. Winter may be the most rewarding season to hike these trails.

From the visitor center, walk away from the Delaware River and over a pedestrian bridge then cross Route 29 (0.1 mile). Turn right and walk about 100 feet, then turn left onto blue-blazed White Oak Trail. The narrow dirt path rises slightly, aided by switchbacks, to a field on the

**LOCATION**
Stockton

**RATING**
Moderate

**DISTANCE**
5.8 miles

**ELEVATION GAIN**
725 feet

**ESTIMATED TIME**
3 to 4 hours

**MAPS**
USGS Lumberville; White Oak Trail: dandrcanal.com; Wescott Preserve: co.hunterdon.nj.us

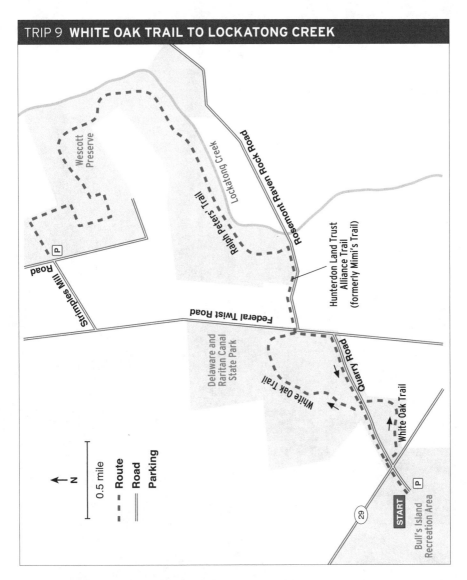

right, and another gentle incline. Keep a lookout for interesting blowdowns and trees. Worth noting, in order, are a large sycamore, a large white oak, a black locust stand, a large tulip poplar tree, and a dogwood and cedar stand. The blue-blazed trail levels off. Reach a dirt-and-gravel road (Quarry Road, 0.4 mile), turn left, and walk for a few hundred yards, then turn right at the state park boundary sign (after the bridge), onto the blue-arrowed White Oak Trail.

The trail climbs gradually and then widens onto a wooden bridge. Note the oak-hickory regeneration area. Soon cross some planks over a ravine, go down another ravine onto another bridge, and pass through a picturesque rock wall (0.7 mile). This section can be muddy and wet in spring, so use caution when crossing the planks.

Entering the ruins along the trail, stone walls are evidence of previous homesteading in this area.

As you walk this section, White Oak Trail, see if you can spot the springhouse in the woods on the right (difficult to see when leaves are on the trees). Pass a stand of beech trees and another stone wall. Soon after a remarkably tall American holly, you'll reach paved Federal Twist Road (1.1 miles).

Cross Federal Twist Road onto paved Rosemont Raven Rock Road. Cross over a pretty stream, lined with daffodils and other spring flowers in season, and then cross another stream. An attractive one-lane iron truss bridge (the Raven Rock Road Bridge, built in 1878) lies just ahead; red sheds and a red barn sit to the right. Turn left onto the path before the bridge, entering the woods (1.4 miles). Do not cross the bridge unless you simply want the experience of crossing a historical truss bridge. You are now in the Zega-Lockatong Preserve of the Hunterdon Land Trust (you will see a sign), about to embark on the Wescott-Zega Lockatong Trail system, which often parallels the cascading Lockatong Creek.

Veer right, going uphill. You may smell pungent crushed green onions as you walk. Cross an open meadow, home to kestrels, bluebirds, and other grassland fowl, and then head downhill and pass through a picturesque stone wall.

You are now on red-blazed Hunterdon Land Trust Alliance Trail, previously known as Mimi's Trail. (Mimi Upmeyer was a dedicated conservationist and founding Land Trust member.) Cross a stream flowing from Lockatong Creek on wooden planks. Another stone wall is to your left; make another stream crossing. Early spring wildflowers, including yellow marsh marigolds, dot the red-blazed trail. Walk on the gravel path alongside Lockatong Creek, a native trout stream that can overflow its banks in early spring. A bench near the stone wall that lines the creek provides an opportunity to rest; look for crayfish, and perhaps find tracks from deer, raccoons, and other animals. Peer into the creek for crayfish (2.0 miles).

From here, red-blazed Hunterdon Land Trust Alliance Trail changes to orange-blazed Ralph Peters' Trail (2.1 miles). The rock wall is now on your left, and when the trees are bare you can see foundations where Ralph Peters, the previous owner of this land, had his homestead.

The orange-blazed trail curves to the left, through a narrow gap between two trees. Look to your left to see the remains of an old barn with a dilapidated ramp. Cultured daffodils that bloom in spring are evidence of previous homesteading.

In less than half a mile, you are back at Lockatong Creek with the stone wall to your right and dramatic stone cliffs to your left—only visible when trees are bare. You are walking through part of Wescott Nature Preserve (named after Lloyd Wescott, an agriculturalist and philanthropist). If the creek is low, just follow Ralph Peters' Trail through a stand of mature hemlocks. (If a flooded creek cuts off the trail, scramble to the left up a steep but short hill.) The orange-blazed trail meets a stone wall at the top of the hill and veers left. An attractive open field is to your right. The trail intersects the field at a downed tree.

Turn around (3.0 miles) and retrace your steps. Look for water cascades and falls along Lockatong Creek. When you reach Federal Twist Road (5.0 miles), take a left and walk 0.1 mile to Quarry Road; turn right onto it (5.1 miles). (For reference, the blue-blazed White Oak Trail you came in on is to the right, near a hitching post. But you are looping back on Quarry Road.) Cross the stream, with a rock cliff to the left. Cross Route 29 and head back to the parking lot over the bridge and stream, with a lovely picnic area below. End at the Bull's Island Recreation Area visitor center parking lot (with flush toilets) where you began.

## DID YOU KNOW?

Spanning Lockatong Creek, the restored iron truss bridge on Rosemont Raven Rock Road may be the oldest bridge in the world still standing with Phoenix columns (patented pin-connected truss structures that protect against cracking and ensure stability). The bridge is included in the National Register of Historic Places and is 127 feet long and only 15.7 feet wide.

## OTHER ACTIVITIES

In Stockton, visit the Prallsville Mills complex, listed in the National Register of Historic Places. Frenchtown is a short drive north on Route 29 and is home to many fine restaurants and shops. Lambertville is equally charming and just a short drive south on Route 29. Drive or walk the Delaware and Raritan Canal path to Stockton (3.3 miles) or Lambertville (7.2 miles).

## MORE INFORMATION

Wescott-Zega Lockatong Trail, Hunterdon County Division of Parks and Recreation, 1020 State Route 31, Lebanon, NJ; 908-782-1158; co.hunterdon .nj.us/depts/parks/ParkAreas/Wescott/trailmap.pdf. Lockatong Creek, Hunterdon Land Trust, 111 Mine Street, Flemington, NJ 08822; 908-237-4582; hunterdonlandtrust.org. Bull's Island Recreation Area, 2185 Daniel Bray Highway, Stockton, NJ 08559; 609-397-2949; state.nj.us/dep/parksandforests/ parks/bull.html.

# 10

# DELAWARE WATER GAP NATIONAL RECREATION AREA: MILLBROOK VILLAGE TO VAN CAMPENS GLEN LOOP

Delight in river views, old foundations, waterfalls in a wooded glen, wildflowers, and historical buildings in the middle of the Delaware Water Gap National Recreation Area.

**LOCATION**
Hardwick

**RATING**
Strenuous

**DISTANCE**
7.1 miles

**ELEVATION GAIN**
850 feet

**ESTIMATED TIME**
4 hours

**MAPS**
USGS Flatbrookville; nps
.gov/dewa/planyourvisit/
maps.htm; *Kittatinny Trails
Map, Trail Map 121*, Sixth
Edition, New York–New
Jersey Trail Conference

## DIRECTIONS

To the Millbrook Village parking lot (capacity at least 40 cars): Take I-80 West to Exit 12, turn right onto County Road 521 North (Hope Blairstown Road/Hope Road), and go about 5 miles to NJ 94. Turn left and go 0.25 mile to the first traffic light, making a 60-degree turn onto Bridge Street (do not turn onto County Road 521). From here go 0.25 mile on Bridge Street uphill to the end of the road, turn right, go 50 yards on High Street, and then turn left onto Millbrook Road (County Road 602) toward Millbrook. Continue 7.5 miles to Millbrook Village, parking in the lot on the right (near the intersection of Old Mine Road and Millbrook Road in Hardwick). GPS may say "Columbia" or "Blairstown." *GPS coordinates:* 41° 04.442′ N, 74° 57.785′ W.

## TRAIL DESCRIPTION

This hike is in the middle part of the Delaware Water Gap National Recreation Area (DWGNRA) and goes from historic Millbrook Village via the orange-blazed Pioneer Trail and the blue-blazed Hamilton Ridge Trail to the yellow-blazed Van Campens Glen Trail in rugged Van Campens Glen. It connects with Watergate Recreation Area on a brief road walk and enters the rear of Millbrook Village past historical buildings. Along the way, hikers pass an old lime kiln, the Delaware River, an

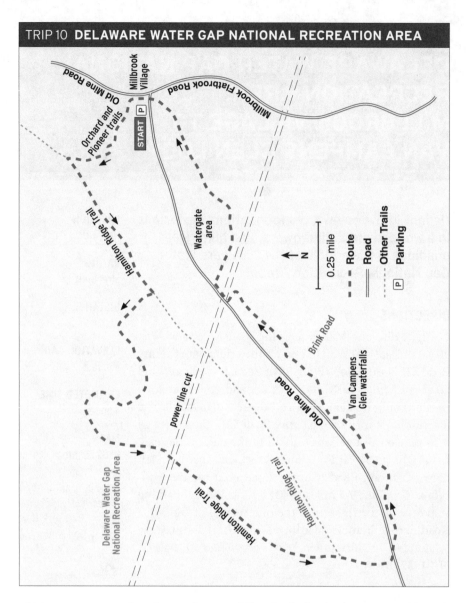

1800s cemetery, and a glen with waterfalls, rhododendron, mountain laurel, and hemlock. Spring brings high water and a profusion of yellow-blooming spicebush and wildflowers. Pastel bluets, white rue anemone, trout lilies, blue violets, white daffodils, and many others gild the paths. Summer brings crowds and bugs but also kaleidoscopic shades of green: emerald moss, vivid barberry bushes, asparagus ferns, and more. In the fall, colorful foliage and red spicebush berries delight. Winter creates a frozen solitude with open views.

Begin in the parking lot at Millbrook Village, which boasted a gristmill in 1832 and grew to a community of 75 inhabitants and several noteworthy buildings by 1875. On summer weekends some buildings are open, and Millbrook

Village Society volunteers give living history demonstrations. With the parking lot and buildings to your back, walk to the right out of the lot, cross Old Mine Road, and enter orange-blazed Orchard Trail in the woods. (*Note:* Old Mine Road is sometimes closed to cars in winter.) The walk is uphill, rocky and rooty, with many wildflowers in spring as a reward for your efforts. The trail soon turns grassy and mossy as you follow a picturesque rock wall on your left. Enjoy fresh woods smells as you carefully walk downhill on the mossy path. When you come to paved Ridge Road (0.6 mile), turn left and continue walking on the trail (this is not the road walk), admiring the mayapples and dogwoods, the white rue anemone, and the bluets. (*Note:* The trail is flat and slippery when wet.)

Soon, turn right onto Pioneer Trail, also blazed orange (1.3 miles), and enter a pine glen where the terrain is alternately flat and soft, then rooty and rocky. Veer right to stay on Pioneer Trail for a gradual downhill adventure. Begin looking for the old lime kiln on the right at 1.4 miles, about 50 feet off the path. Notice the beautiful small valley to your right and enjoy slipping through gaps in old stone walls. Burgeoning young ferns unfurl in spring. Switchbacks lead you down. The ravine to the left is home to a gorgeous stream and yellow violets. The path rolls up and down to follow views of the majestic Delaware River on your right through the trees. Notice the former homesteads—old foundations and clearings left when residents relocated to accommodate Tocks Island Dam (see essay on page 57), which was never built; instead, the DWGNRA sprang from the seized lands. The trail flattens out and showcases spring violets. Go through a clearing under power lines at 2.8 miles and back into the woods, where a forest of invasive Japanese barberry bushes cluster. At the junction, go straight, following the orange-blazed trees. Enjoy a flat stone-and-gravel road lined in greenery. It's interesting to look around and pick out foundations and clearings where the houses used to be.

At the intersection of Hamilton Ridge Trail and Pioneer Trail, go straight onto blue-blazed Hamilton Ridge Trail (3.7 miles). In about 0.15 mile, there is a faint, unmarked side path to the right that leads to a nearby 1800s cemetery for the Depue family that is worth the short detour.

If you are lucky, you'll see some orange witches'-butter fungus (also known as yellow brain fungus) growing on dead wood. At the intersection with two-lane Old Mine Road (County Road 606, 4.0 miles), turn left onto the road, and walk about 100 feet before turning right at the sign for Van Campens Glen. Chemical toilets are in the small parking lot. (*Note:* This place is very popular and crowded in summer.)

Start climbing up the yellow-blazed Van Campens Glen Trail at the end of the parking lot along Van Campens Brook. Because of the brook, the trail can be rocky and wet, with slippery footing, so be careful. The brook cascades powerfully over the rocks, creating churning pools and mighty falls. The path widens and flattens, level with the stream. Enjoy the large rhododendrons and hemlocks lining the route; the rhodies may be in glorious bloom from mid-May through

A waterfall in Van Campens Glen is just one of the highlights of this 7-mile hike through the DWGNRA.

June. Cross a bridge to a beautiful lunch spot across from a waterfall, with flat boulders for seats. Then climb the steps, still on the yellow-blazed trail, out of the ravine. (*Caution*: The trail is narrow, slippery, and rocky.) In April and May, weeds have not yet overtaken the path, and the water flows strongly. Follow the yellow-blazed trail as it again becomes level with the brook. Turn left at the junction with an unnamed trail. At the next bridge, make a right just *before* the bridge to follow the path out (5.27 miles). You are now on unmarked trails, so stay alert. The stream slows to a gentle flow to your left along a soft, straight path.

Cross Brink Road (5.4 miles) and then take a left over a bridge onto a paved path. At an iron gate, the path intersects Old Mine Road (5.9 miles). Turn right onto the road, watching for traffic. After a brief (0.15 mile) road walk, turn right at a gorgeous stone gate etched with the words *Water* on one column and *Gate* on the other (6.1 miles). Go around the gate and over a bridge. Admire the pretty lake to the left, where wild strawberries bloom in spring. A stream and a clearing with a picnic area are on the right (6.3 miles). Past the picnic tables, to the left, lies the grave of George Busch's beloved pup Bozo, who died in 1956. Busch was a jeweler, and Watergate was his estate back in the 1950s.

Continue to a swamp on the left. You are on a gravelly path that used to be a road, with a stream on the right. A pond emerges on your left; keep a lookout for snapping turtles. At the junction with an unnamed path, go straight. The gravel path changes to grass. Stroll past the historical buildings of Millbrook Village, including the old schoolhouse on the left, and peek in the windows. (Look for the old cemetery rumored to be at the top of the hill behind the schoolhouse.) The trail becomes eroded. Check out the garden to the right, behind the wooden fence, and then cross Old Mine Road. Turn left to go back to the parking lot where you began.

## DID YOU KNOW?

The Van Campen in Van Campens Glen refers to Colonel Abraham Van Campen, a settler who built a home in 1725 along the waterway now known as Van Campens Brook and later built a mill nearby. In 1756, his home was used as a frontier fort during the French and Indian War.

## OTHER ACTIVITIES

The DWGNRA has dozens of trails: Some highlights are Buttermilk Falls, Beulahland, the Appalachian Trail, Sunfish Pond, Dunnfield Creek, and Mount Tammany. AMC's southernmost facility—Mohican Outdoor Center—is here on a beautiful glacial lake. Mohican provides meals, cabins, camping, swimming, kayaking, snowshoeing, and hiking, as well as guided activities. Mohican Outdoor Center, 50 Camp Mohican Road, Blairstown, NJ 07825; 908-362-5670; reservations 603-466-2727; outdoors.org/mohican. In Layton, visit Peters Valley School of Craft and Walpack Center. Cross the river to Pennsylvania to hike two waterfalls on the popular and accessible Dingman's Falls Trail (this trail was closed as of August 2018 due to damage from March 2018 storms; check with the National Park Service for trail opening information; nps.gov/dewa/planyourvisit/conditions.htm). While in Pennsylvania, visit the Pocono Environment Education Center, one of the largest and longest running residential environmental education centers in the northeastern United States (peec.org/programs/school-programs).

## MORE INFORMATION

Millbrook Village is open seasonally, and the trails are always open. Call 908-841-9531 for information. Millbrook Village and Van Campens Glen are operated by Delaware Water Gap National Recreation Area, with headquarters at 1978 River Road, Bushkill, PA 18324; 570-426-2452; nps.gov/dewa.

## DELAWARE WATER GAP NATIONAL RECREATION AREA: DIVIDED IT STANDS

There are two sides to the Delaware Water Gap National Recreation Area (DWGNRA)—literally! This 70,000-acre parcel, part of the National Park Service, is split down the middle by the mighty Delaware River, which flows 330 miles from New York through Pennsylvania, New Jersey, and Delaware on its way to the Atlantic Ocean. The DWGNRA nestles along either side of the Middle Delaware River, a section that is generally more peaceful, smooth, and secluded than the upper and lower parts.

To the west of the river lies the Pennsylvania side of the DWGNRA and to the east, the New Jersey side. The Jersey side is split lengthwise by the two-lane Old Mine Road, which runs north to south, becoming part of US 209 at Port Jervis, New York. New Jersey farmers relied on the Old Mine Road, constructed in the mid-1600s, to bring crops to market. Today the road is a popular driving and biking route, leading to historical buildings, areas of natural beauty, and hiking trailheads.

A variety of hiking guidebooks further split the DWGNRA into northern, middle, and southern trails. The National Park Service provides a good basic grouping of which trails fall in these three divisions (nps.gov/dewa/planyourvisit/trails.htm).

The Water Gap itself is another divide, created by the river. The Middle Delaware River powers through the low forested mountains and rocky cliffs of the Kittatinny ridgeline, thus forming a gap of water, or a "water gap."

The Appalachian Trail (AT) crosses the river at the Water Gap and follows the eastern perimeter of the DWGNRA. The AT continues northward through Worthington State Forest, a 6,660-acre park adjacent to the DWGNRA. When visitors hike the popular Dunnfield Creek and Sunfish Pond natural areas, they are actually in Worthington State Forest, which is part of the Water Gap but not part of the DWGNRA. If this is confusing, visit the Kittatinny Point Visitor Center on the Jersey side for a map that shows the geography more clearly. North of the Kittatinny Visitor Center lies the Millbrook Visitor Center, near Walpack Bend, where the Delaware River makes a long, lazy S.

The recreation area was also formed by a split—of the political kind. In 1955, Hurricane Diane wreaked havoc along the Delaware. Seeking to control flooding, the U.S. Army Corps of Engineers asked Congress to authorize the building of a dam at Tocks Island, a small island on the Jersey side of the Delaware River, just north of what is now the DWGNRA. Congress complied, and soon about 600 families and property owners were displaced to make way for the dam. Then came the 1960s, a politically and socially charged era that galvanized several causes: Vietnam War protests, the civil rights movement, and a newly energized environmental push. Finally, in 1975, after many years in which squatters and hippies staked their claims on abandoned houses, the Delaware River

Basin Commission voted to shelve the Tocks Island Dam project. No one saw any wisdom in turning a beautiful river into a lifeless body of water. The result was Delaware Water Gap National Recreation Area, with 40 miles of protected, free-flowing river.

Today, whether you visit the Kittatinny Ridge, the AT, or the area's waterfalls, ponds, lakes, and ravines, the DWGNRA is a playground paradise for hikers, cyclists, and paddlers.

Kittatinny Point Visitor Center, Columbia, NJ 07832; 908-496-4458 (closed late fall through spring). Millbrook Village, Millbrook, NJ 08817 (near Hardwick); 908-841-9531 (open in summer only). DWGNRA park headquarters and visitor center, 1 River Road, Bushkill, PA 18324; 570-426-2452 (open daily May 25 through September 3, open Monday through Friday starting September 4); nps.gov/dewa; outdoors.org/DEriver.

# 11

# MARBLE HILL
# NATURAL RESOURCE AREA

Enjoy a lightly traveled area with mature rhododendrons, an abandoned iron mine, and a historical water pump; bonus: excellent views of Phillipsburg and the Delaware River.

**LOCATION**
Phillipsburg

**RATING**
Easy

**DISTANCE**
4 miles

**ELEVATION GAIN**
900 feet

**ESTIMATED TIME**
2 hours

**MAPS**
USGS Easton;
warrenparks.com/park/
marble-hill-natural
-resource-area

## DIRECTIONS

Take I-78 West to Exit 3 for West Phillipsburg Alpha; travel 2.8 miles. The road bears to the left to become US 22/Memorial Parkway. Continue on US 22 west for 1.4 miles, then take a slight right off the highway, following signs for South Main Street/Phillipsburg. Go 0.3 mile and turn right onto North Main Street (County Road 621, also known as River Road). In 1.9 miles, County Road 621 (now signed River Road) intersects Marble Hill Road; go right on Marble Hill Road. After about 0.2 mile, turn right into the gravel parking lot at the trailhead, with space for fifteen to twenty cars. *GPS coordinates:* 40° 43.436′ N, 75° 10.852′ W.

## TRAIL DESCRIPTION

This hike will take you past impressively mature and dense rhododendrons, the old Fulmer Mine, a historical pump house, a scenic view of the Delaware River, and intriguing rock structures left over from iron ore mining in the late 1800s. Marble Hill is also a gateway to the blue-blazed Warren-Highlands Trail (part of the Highlands Trail, which is teal-blazed in most sections), a cooperative effort among state and local governments, the New York–New Jersey Trail Conference, Metrotrails, the Highlands Project, and others. When complete (no projected completion date at the time of this writing), the Highlands Trail will cover 150 miles, with 32 miles in Warren County. The more than 270-acre Marble Hill Natural Resource Area has been officially designated a

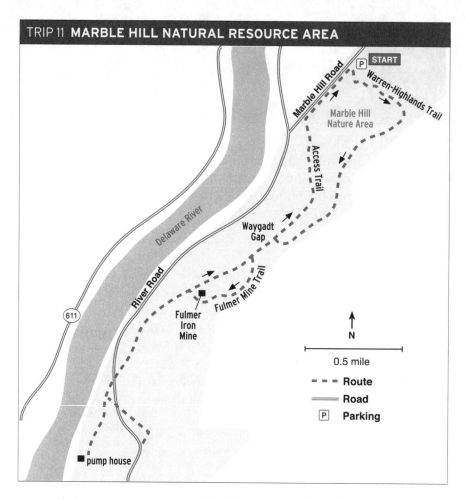

National Geographic Geotourism Destination. Marble Hill is a watershed protection to the Delaware River, and its deciduous forest provides coverage for many migratory songbirds. When trees are leafless, you can enjoy excellent river views of the "Little Water Gap"—the narrows north of Phillipsburg (New Jersey) and Easton (Pennsylvania). Spring brings a plethora of rhododendron blooms and wildflowers; summer ferns are magical. Generally, foot traffic is light on this somewhat secluded trail.

Looking at the Marble Hill kiosk, facing the woods, take the short yellow-blazed Marble Hill Road Access Trail uphill to the right. (*Note*: There are no toilets at this facility.) Turn right at the yellow blaze on a tree and climb a rocky hill. The steep ascent continues when you take a left at the next yellow blaze. In summer, trees provide shade and melodious bird songs. The ferns lend a prehistoric air of mystery to this pretty section. Turn left, away from power lines, to continue on the Marble Hill Road Access Trail. Turn right through the greenery at the next yellow blaze to go uphill. Look carefully in summer; thick undergrowth may obscure blazes. The Marble Hill Access Trail ends at a T intersection (0.3 mile).

Turn right to begin on the blue-blazed Warren-Highlands Trail, crossing a clearing under power lines. Take a moment to let your gaze follow the power lines for a dramatic view of Phillipsburg. Continue across the clearing to where the trail enters the woods. Blue blazes become visible after entering. Turn right onto a flat trail with pretty flowers. The trail gradually slopes down for a few minutes and crosses a picturesque old stone wall left over from mining days. Large old trees keep you company and provide some scenic blowdowns among the rocks. The path veers left over a series of rolling hills. Turn left at the next blue blaze.

Carefully cross a deep ditch with an unnamed stream at the bottom and get ready for more steep ups and downs in the deep woods. Go left at the next blue blaze and traverse a small ditch, probably created during mining activity. A red trail blaze appears on the left (0.7 mile). This red-blazed path leads to the 80-acre Lopatcong Municipal Park, which has a swimming pool, large pavilion, recreation fields, a playground, and a concession stand in season. This hike does not follow that route, but the option is there if you'd like to explore it. Instead, keep right on Warren-Highlands Trail, which goes downhill. Soon the trail widens and clears; hop over three tiny ditches and take a right, staying on the blue-blazed trail. At the next intersection, bear right again. You can hear the sounds of Route 22 in distance, but you are well hidden in the thick woods. At 0.9 mile, the yellow-blazed trail will be on the right. Continue to a scenic marker (1.0 mile) for an excellent view of the Delaware River narrows ("Little Water Gap"), which is actually Waygadt Gap, north of Phillipsburg (New Jersey) and Easton, Pennsylvania. You can count the cars on Highway 611 on the Pennsylvania side. If the day is clear and trees are leafless, you can see the rock outcrop known as St. Anthony's Nose in Gollub Park (Pennsylvania).

Keep straight on the blue-blazed trail as it winds uphill through big rhododendrons; watch your step on this steep, rocky incline. A valley opens to the right. At a T intersection, turn left on the orange-blazed Fulmer Mine Trail (1.1 miles). As might be expected from the name, the trail gets rockier. Clamber up a bank and admire some of the pretty stones. A rugged ravine spreads out to your right. Keep climbing past a deep fissure in the rock on your right.

Stay straight on the orange-blazed trail, heading down through rocks and rhodies. The sign for Fulmer Mine pops up on the left at 1.3 miles. (The mine is known locally as the "Ice Cave" because of the ice formations that form inside during winter.) Take some time to investigate this hematite (iron) mine that dates back to 1860, but do not enter the mine. Head downhill on the rocky path, noting the stone walls to the left and right, which were possibly former mines or shelters. At the junction, go left on the blue-blazed Warren-Highlands Trail (1.4 miles), admiring the pretty ravine and rock slide to the right, spilling through the ferns and rhodies.

The path continues downhill on the old "tote" (mining) road. The Delaware River and River Road are close by. Keep going straight, ignoring the spur to

Hikers can explore around the entrance to Fulmer Mine (a.k.a "Ice Cave") but may not enter it.

the right. Reach paved River Road/County Road 621 (1.8 miles); cross it at the blue blaze on a metal post. To begin a 0.4-mile round-trip detour, enter the gates (if open) to view a historical pump house, colloquially called "Big Allis." (The area is posted "Do Not Enter" by the New Jersey Department of Transportation, so please view only and do not enter the pump house.) Big Allis is a 51-foot-tall triple expansion steam-powered water pump engine, manufactured by the Allis-Chalmers Company of Milwaukee in 1913; the machine stands 30 feet below the floor of the pump house. Drawing from the Delaware River, this 300-horsepower pump used to deliver 4,200 gallons per minute to the Phillipsburg area. For information about the pump (which is being restored) and possible viewing, call the Friends of the New Jersey Transportation Heritage Center, 908-217-3553. (Warren County owns the land and building.)

Retrace your steps and cross River Road to return to the blue-blazed Warren-Highlands Trail and go right (2.2 miles). Continuing on the blue trail, cross an overgrown field under power lines, and turn right onto a gravel path at a blue-blazed metal post. Here is a small parking lot for the River Road trailhead, across from a commercial water company (2.4 miles). This is an optional turnaround point to road walk back to your car, heading toward green mile marker 1.

Return to the blue-blazed trail, and head back the way you came. When you reach the intersection of the orange-blazed Fulmer Mine Trail and blue-blazed Warren-Highlands Trail, take a left to stay on the blue-blazed trail (3.0 miles). Soon you'll see a nature sign for rhododendrons on the right. Pass the river view of the narrows. Warren-Highlands Trail again intersects Fulmer Mine Trail at

3.2 miles; go left, following the blue-blazed trail, which descends steeply and is rocky. At the next intersection, go left onto the yellow-blazed trail (3.3 miles), in and out of small ravines. The trail meanders in a crazy fashion, and rogue paths crisscross, but try to have fun with it (you can always road walk on River Road if you get frustrated). Veer right to go uphill on the yellow-blazed trail, then make a quick left at the Y intersection. Tromp up and down over a ravine and stream. At a yellow-blazed iron post, turn right (not left, no matter what the blaze indicates) into an overgrown and pretty uphill path crowded with ferns. Turn left at the next two yellow blazes onto the faintest of trails. You'll feel like an explorer—watch for brambles. At the T intersection, go left to follow yellow blazes; there's a clearing with power lines, and River Road is to the left. Go straight across the clearing into the woods—the path is hard to see in the clearing, but it's blazed yellow once you enter the woods (3.8 miles). Walk over a collapsed rock wall and back to the parking lot.

## DID YOU KNOW?

In the 1700s, serpentine was quarried near Phillipsburg; the United Methodist Church in Washington (Warren County) was built from local serpentine. Warren-Highlands Trail runs from the Delaware River in the west to the Musconetcong River in the east, a distance of 52.4 miles.

## OTHER ACTIVITIES

Train enthusiasts will enjoy the Phillipsburg Railroad Historians train museum and Delaware River Railroad Excursions, both in Phillipsburg. Washington Township offers Roaring Rock Park, with trails along Brass Castle Creek, and Merrill Creek Reservoir, a tranquil 650-acre body of water and preserve. Cross the river to Pennsylvania and climb to Saint Anthony's Nose in Gollub Park for excellent views of New Jersey and Pennsylvania. Young children will enjoy the Crayola Experience across the river in Easton, Pennsylvania.

## MORE INFORMATION

Open from dawn to dusk. Warren County Department of Land Preservation, 500 Mount Pisgah Avenue, Oxford, NJ 07863; 908-453-2650; warrenparks.com.

# 12

# SIX MILE RUN RESERVOIR

Zigzag between pastoral fields and welcoming woods, along a creek, over streams (with a stop at a lunch-worthy bridge), and across rolling terrain for a soul-lifting experience.

## DIRECTIONS

Take US 1 to Ridge Road. In 1.0 mile, Ridge Road becomes Heathcote Road. In 0.3 mile, Heathcote Road becomes County Highway 603. In 1.8 miles, County Highway 603 becomes Canal Road. After 5.4 miles, turn left to stay on Canal Road. In 1.0 mile, turn into the parking lot on the left, with room for 30 cars. *GPS coordinates:* 40° 28.404′ N, 74° 33.929′ W.

## TRAIL DESCRIPTION

The blue-blazed trail in Six Mile Run Reservoir is part of the 70-mile Delaware and Raritan Canal system (see page 40), and so has two names: D&R Canal Trail and Blackwells Trail. It intersects red-blazed Creek Trail, a rugged, fun route with great views of Six Mile Run Creek. You'll take these three trails (and one unmarked trail), and pause on a shaded, picturesque bridge spanning Six Mile Run Creek. Rolling terrain and small bridges over streams keep the journey interesting. The area is the largest agricultural district in New Jersey and is listed in the National Register of Historic Places. The 3,037 acres were intended to be a reservoir site, but alternative water supplies were located, much to hikers' delight. Many deciduous trees make this a glorious fall trip. Green shade and sparkling water are cooling in summer. Spring brings a profusion of woodland wildflowers. Snow-covered open fields in winter are stunning. (*Note:* To preserve the easily eroded soil, do not hike here during mud season, usually April and May in New Jersey.)

**LOCATION**
Somerset

**RATING**
Easy

**DISTANCE**
6 miles

**ELEVATION GAIN**
400 feet

**ESTIMATED TIME**
2.5 hours

**MAPS**
USGS Monmouth; dandrcanal.com/pdf/ SixMileRun_Trails_ 3-2010.pdf

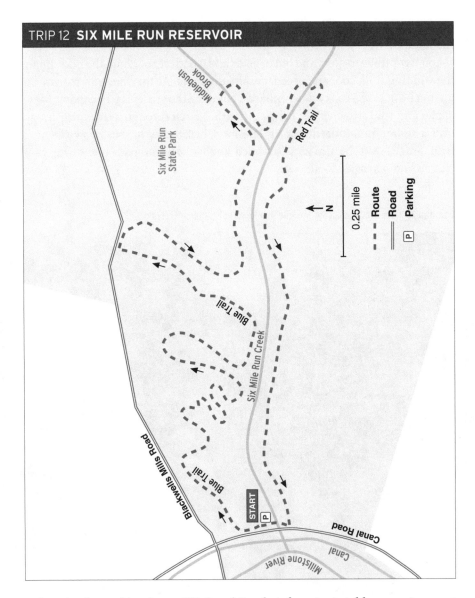

Start in the parking lot at 625 Canal Road. A few picnic tables promise a rest at hike's end. Be aware that this area is quite popular on the weekends, so those tables may be occupied. Facing Canal Road turn right and cross the paved access road to enter the woods on the blue-blazed Blackwells Trail. The pleasant path winds for a while through woods and open fields with birdhouses. In summer, daisies are prolific; goldenrod and milkweed attract butterflies and birds in season. Note the shagbark hickory trees and spicebush. You may smell honeysuckle that blooms near the trail's edge. The path becomes rooty and a bit muddy with gentle ups and downs. Be sure to walk in the middle of the path; do not skirt the edges and expand the trail. Go through a field briefly and then tread a boardwalk in a woodsy wetland. Enter an open field briefly again before heading back into the woods.

You'll continue to go in and out of fields and woods throughout the hike. Enjoy the winding trail, cool and green, despite the roots. At the blue trail marker on an iron post, take a rocky downhill trek, enjoying the graceful tree canopy. Mayapples and wild strawberries fringe the path. March through a tree tunnel; skip over a stream on a boardwalk. In late June, blackberry bushes show ripening fruit. Small, steep hummocks (rounded knolls) keep the path interesting as it narrows onto a lovely footbridge.

Boardwalks aid in the trek across Six Mile Run Reservoir's marshy terrain.

Go around an open field, with a housing development on the left, following the trail sign. The blue sky frames a golden-grained wheat field to the left, the stalks close enough to brush your cheeks.

Now the path goes gradually uphill and reenters the woods at the trail sign. Watch your footing on the following rocky downhill section. The trail heads toward the road, still following blue-blazed Blackwells Trail. Take the footbridge over a clear stream (2.6 miles) and the path becomes wider as you walk the woods' edge with the wheat field again to the left. Go straight, ignoring the path on the right, but then turn right at the blue Blackwells Trail sign. The trail forks again; go left into the woods. Enjoy the lovely temperature contrasts between shaded woods and open fields.

Soon you briefly leave the woods and enter an open field. At the Blackwells Trail sign, turn right and go back into woods, over yet another footbridge. Watch out for blackberry bush thorns as you move from woods to field onto a wooden boardwalk over a heavily eroded area. Eventually you reach a sunny clearing, where a long, dramatic boardwalk slices through the tall green grasses. Cross another bridge (3.7 miles) over a stream and go gradually downhill to a rather lengthy bridge, high above Six Mile Run Creek. The bridge is a good opportunity for lunch or a rest.

Say goodbye to the bridge and go onto the well-marked but rugged red-blazed Creek Trail (4.4 miles) and over a hill. (*Caution:* You may encounter speeding mountain bikers on weekends.) Take a sharp right on the red-blazed trail at the sign for Creek Trail (it's really a U-turn). Go uphill through a lovely tunnel of cedar trees and down a steep bank. The creek is nearly eye level on your right. At the Y intersection, go right to stay on Creek Trail (white-blazed Cedar Trail is to the left, 4.6 miles). Traverse a hiking bridge over a stream, parallel to a high, curved mountain bike bridge. Go straight (or right) at the next Y. You are now on a wide, grassy path with naturalist signage for eastern red cedar and black walnut trees. Read about forest succession, whereby a disturbed natural area rebuilds.

Go right onto an unmarked trail (5.2 miles). Cross a watery ditch and follow the sign for the red-blazed Creek Trail. The path here is narrow, shaded, and rooty. Enjoy an elevated walk between a field on your left and Six Mile Run Creek to your right. The contrast is one of the loveliest parts of this hike.

Some fencing begins on the left, then you plunge into a steep downhill, where the ground can be rutty. Look for spots where you can walk down and visit Six Mile Run Creek. The route takes more ups and downs, in and out of the woods, even going through a cut-out log. At a T intersection with a paved road (5.9 miles), turn right for a brief 175-yard road walk. (*Caution:* There's no shoulder.) A stone bridge passes over the river and then you turn right into the parking lot.

## DID YOU KNOW?

Nearby are eighteenth-century farmhouses, Dutch-framed granaries, and barns that tell the story of the first settlers to this region in the 1700s. The local eastern red cedars produce cedar oil, obtained from the wood and leaves, which can repel insects and provide antiseptic properties.

## OTHER ACTIVITIES

Browse farmers markets and visit Davidson's Mill Pond Park in South Brunswick for the E.A.R.T.H. Center, a horticultural education facility operated by Rutgers Cooperative Extension of Middlesex County. Walk along the Raritan River for 2.5 miles at Johnson Park in Piscataway. The 20-acre Elmer B. Boyd Park in New Brunswick has views of the city skyline and a historical swing bridge. Colonial Park in Somerset features outstanding horticultural displays.

## MORE INFORMATION

Open dawn to dusk, year-round. Administered by the Delaware and Raritan Canal State Park, 625 Canal Road, Somerset, NJ 08873, 609-924-5705; and by the State of New Jersey Department of Environmental Protection, Division of Parks and Forestry, 401 East State Street, Trenton, NJ 08625-0402, 609-777-3373; njparksandforests.org/parks/listserv.html.

# 13

# MOHICAN OUTDOOR CENTER: COPPERMINES–KAISER– APPALACHIAN TRAILS LOOP

Enjoy delightful woods, secluded waterfalls, and remarkable ferns on this ridgeline walk–with some fun rock-hopping–for views of Paulinskill Valley and the Delaware Water Gap.

## DIRECTIONS

Take Route 31 North to Route 46 in Buttzville. Left on Route 46 West for 1.0 mile to Route 519. Route 519 North to Route 521 North in Hope. Then take Route 521 North to Route 94; turn left to head south. Take Route 94 South for 1.1 miles through Blairstown to Mohican Road; turn right on Mohican Road, and follow Mohican Road 3.5 miles to Gaisler Road (bear right at forks on the winding road). Turn left and take Gaisler Road for 0.5 mile, then turn right onto Camp Road, which turns to dirt. Drive across the Appalachian Trail, passing Mohican Outdoor Center on your left as you pull into the large dirt parking lot on your left, which has room for about 30 cars. *GPS coordinates:* 41° 02.144' N, 74° 59.990' W.

## TRAIL DESCRIPTION

Take a clockwise loop that follows the iconic white rectangular blazes of the Appalachian Trail (AT) to Kaiser Trail (blazed with white squares), which leads to red-blazed Coppermines Trail. Waterfalls, wildflowers, and birds make this a great spring hike. Fall brings foliage and hawks gliding the thermals. In winter, the reservoir, valley views, and the Delaware Water Gap shine through the leafless trees. Summer provides seclusive greenery. Be sure to wear gaiters and waterproof boots right after the spring thaw when the streams are full.

**LOCATION**
Blairstown

**RATING**
Moderate

**DISTANCE**
5.7 miles

**ELEVATION GAIN**
900 feet

**ESTIMATED TIME**
3 hours

**MAPS**
USGS Bushkill, USGS Flatbrookville; *Kittatinny Trails Map, Trail Map 120* and *Trail Map 121,* Sixth Edition, New York–New Jersey Trail Conference; amcdv.org/assets/ mohican-area-hikes.pdf

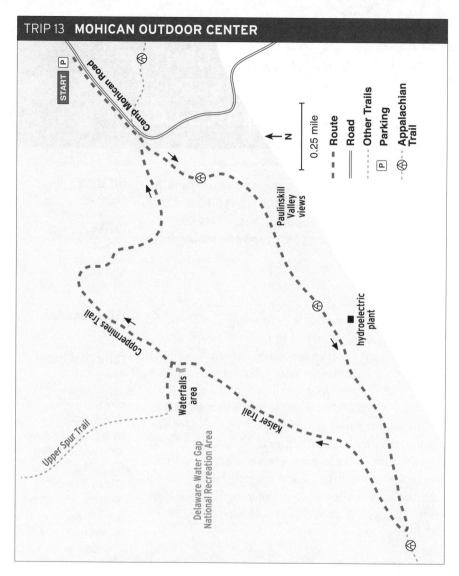

Turn right out of the parking lot at Mohican Outdoor Center (MOC) onto Camp Road. Stop at the lodge to get a map, then walk past the lodge and onto a gravel road. Pass the MOC sign on the left. Take a right at the AT sign (0.4 mile), cross a white-blazed wooden bridge over a pretty stream, and navigate around some impressive rocks. Approximately 100 yards from the bridge, veer left to stay on the AT (red-blazed Coppermines Trail is to the right). Unique, long, flat rocks make a "pavement" uphill, leading to more rocks and boulders. The path narrows and becomes slightly less rocky and is shaded all the way. Keeping on the white-blazed AT, get ready for a big ascent on this path lined with blueberry bushes and enjoy an exposed ridge walk with nice views of the Paulinskill Valley before heading back into the woods.

The AT narrows and is still rocky and uphill. (*Caution*: You may see rattle-snakes and bears in this area. To avoid snake encounters, don't reach under rocks. Make noise if you see a bear; they are gentle, easily frightened mammals. Keep your distance from both.) Take time to admire the Paulinskill Valley on the left (1.0 mile). (Below you is the Paulinskill Valley Rail Trail—check it out on your next trip.) Soon the AT levels out, relatively speaking, and rocks diminish as you walk through an oasis of ferns and trees. At 1.5 miles, reach an east-facing clearing with excellent panoramic views of Lower Yards Creek Reservoir, a hydroelectric plant in the Paulinskill Valley. Look to your far right (south) and you can see the beginning of the Delaware Water Gap, notably Mount Tammany.

After appreciating the views, walk through a lovely fairyland of grass and trees. Peeks of the Delaware River appear through the trees to the left. Enjoy this glorious walk on the ridge in and out of shade, alternatively warming and cooling. The elevated green plateau is relatively rock-free.

At the Y intersection (2.4 miles), turn sharply right (a U-turn) at the sign for Kaiser Trail (a white square marker, not the white-painted rectangle of the AT). Kaiser Trail (an old mining road) used to be blue-blazed, and there may still be some remnants of blue paint; don't get confused. (If you want to hike into the Water Gap, go straight on the AT for about 2.5 miles on Raccoon Ridge—with excellent vistas—to reach Sunfish Pond, a popular destination.) The grassy downhill walk is pleasant. The terrain slopes up to the right and down to the left for a wonderful sensation of walking between worlds as the path loses rocks and gains borders of moss. Note the impressive boulder field to the right. Sun patches glow on the ferns.

The path descends slightly for a few minutes, with an impressive gorge on your right. Just before the next trail junction, a fern forest blooms in summer. Take a right on the 0.2-mile spur to red-blazed Coppermines Trail. (*Note:* For more mileage, you could continue straight on Kaiser Trail for about 0.5 mile before veering right at the junction toward Old Mine Road and the remnants of the old Pahaquarry Copper Mine, a 2.2-mile round-trip diversion. The mine itself is barricaded and protected for bat roosting; see more under "Did You Know?")

Cross a stream on conveniently placed rocks. Look for toads. Make a left at the T intersection to descend slightly on rocky Coppermines Trail (3.4 miles). Another gorge is to the left. At 0.2 mile, turn left toward the falls, which roar in spring. If the water is flowing, admire the upper falls; otherwise, sit and appreciate the rugged rock formations before pushing through the brush to the lower falls. This gorgeous glen resonates with bird songs and water music.

When you are ready, go uphill back the way you came. At the T intersection, go left to stay on Coppermines Trail. Traverse a picturesque log bridge and continue uphill through a peaceful, shaded grove. A rock fence is to your left as the path rolls gently up and down under the canopy. Follow Coppermines Trail to the left as it goes uphill over interesting rocks and a plethora of scrub oaks with intricate acorn clusters. Have fun walking the flat-rock "pavement." Rocks line

Lower Yards Creek Reservoir as seen from the AT, in the Delaware Water Gap.

the red-blazed trail on either side, framed by ferns. At 5.2 miles, go left at the Y intersection onto the white-blazed AT; cross the wooden bridge you came in on and go back to the road, taking a left to the parking lot.

## DID YOU KNOW?

Mohican Outdoor Center is the Appalachian Mountain Club's southernmost property. The Dutch discovered copper in the Kittatinny Mountains in the seventeenth century and built a 100-mile-long road to transport the ore to Kingston, New York. The mine was not profitable, but Old Mine Road continues to be used and maintained by the Delaware Water Gap National Recreation Area. Pahaquarry Copper Mine (a side trip off the Kaiser Trail) is a bat hibernaculum, one of at least 20 known bat hibernation refuges in New Jersey. A gate across the entrance protects bats from people and from contact with the fungus that causes white-nose syndrome, a disease discovered in 2006 that killed 90 percent of little brown bats. For more bat-finding, visit Hibernia Mine (see "Did You Know?" Trip 4).

## OTHER ACTIVITIES

Canoe and swim in MOC's crystal-clear Catfish Pond. Hike Rattlesnake Swamp Trail for minimal effort, maximum view: Walk left out of the parking lot; in about 0.25 mile, turn right at a cabin onto the Rattlesnake Swamp Trail, marked with a wooden sign and orange blaze, and then go right at the fork to climb a short, steep, rocky hill for an excellent ridge view, where the AT intersects the orange trail. Turn left or right to extend the hike along the AT and ridgeline (For all MOC hiking maps, see amcdv.org/assets/mohican-area-hikes.pdf). Tour Lakota Wolf Preserve in Columbia. Stroll the 665-acre White Lake Natural Resource Area in Hardwick. Stroll Blairstown's shops and restaurants. Visit the Blairstown Museum to learn about regional history. The Blairstown Theatre (Roy's Hall), a former silent movie theater built in 1913, features films and live performances.

## MORE INFORMATION

Mohican Outdoor Center, 50 Camp Mohican Road, Blairstown, NJ 07825; 908-362-5670; reservations 603-466-2727; outdoors.org/mohican; Delaware Water Gap National Recreation Area, 1978 River Road, Bushkill, PA 18324; 570-426-2452; nps.gov/dewa/index.htm.

## BLACK BEARS IN NEW JERSEY

New Jersey has a lot of black bears. The northwestern part of the state has one of the densest and most productive black bear populations in the nation, with large litters and high survival rates. New Jersey also has a lot of humans; it's the most densely populated state in the nation. A 2013 study put New Jersey's human population at 8,791,894 and its black bear population at 3,400. The black bear's natural life span is about 33 years or more, while the average life span in unprotected black bear populations is only 3 to 5 years. Given that New Jersey is the most densely populated state for both humans and black bears, it is likely that hikers and bears will overlap.

Statistically, a hiker is most likely to encounter a bear in northwestern New Jersey, such as in the Kittatinny and Appalachian mountains or the Delaware Water Gap National Recreation Area. The latest estimates (as of 2017) say that 2,500 black bears live in the northwestern part of the state, but you won't necessarily see them just because they're there. Black bears are shy, timid creatures, and often wary of people. But they can be oblivious when on the trail of a tasty smell (they can detect scents more than 2 miles away) and can cross paths unintentionally with hikers. If the bear is curious, it may stand on its hind legs to see and smell better, which many hikers falsely take as a sign of aggression.

If you do see a black bear, it's smart to have a healthy fear, but don't panic and run. Instead, make noises to scare it and slowly back away. Don't approach it for that once-in-a-lifetime photo and *never* feed it.

New Jersey's bears aren't only in the northwestern part of the state. As the overall bear population increases, the southern and eastern regions have seen bear populations increase. Humans and bears are often drawn to the same habitat, such as wooded suburbs, forested parks, and developments in former agricultural areas that have retained some degree of wildness. Black bears really like forested slopes and riparian corridors where urban areas meet wildlands, and they thrive there. Female bears who live in close proximity to human development actually have more cubs than those living in the wild, although the suburban cub survival rate is lower. As the black bear population increases, suburban encounters between bears and humans are more likely to occur.

Human suburbanites who live in areas where there is known bear activity must properly manage outdoor food and garbage. Even though bears are shy, they are dedicated foodies. A bird feeder, improperly managed compost pile, pet food left outside, or smelly garbage container (even if empty) might attract investigation by a curious bear. And, this bears repetition: *Never* intentionally feed a bear. Trouble arises when bears associate humans with food.

Please don't report a bear as a problem if it is simply passing through your neighborhood, doing no harm. Bears that wander into residential areas, usually attracted by food smells, often end up in trees because they are confused and scared, as are the homeowners. If you do need to alert law enforcement, an officer will usually tranquilize and relocate the bear, typically to state-owned land, such as a wildlife management area. Bears are aversely conditioned with rubber buckshot or killed on the rare occasions when they pose a public safety threat.

Keep in mind that predatory attacks by black bears are extremely rare. There has been only one documented bear fatality in New Jersey's history, the 2014 death of a hiker in northwestern New Jersey for reasons that remain unclear.

Unfortunately, bear populations cannot be effectively controlled by bear relocation or bear birth control. Bear harvesting (i.e., bear hunting), although controversial, has been shown to control bear populations and to reduce human-bear conflicts by creating a "landscape of fear," or looked at another way, by creating a healthy respect for humans. We should return the favor and develop a healthy fear of and respect for bears.

Don't contribute to poor human-bear relations by being ignorant and over-reactive. Black bears are large land mammals, native to New Jersey, who are gracious enough to share their home with day hikers, even as we share our suburbs with them. Whether you are in their forested homes or they are in your suburban ones, be a good neighbor. In the woods, announce yourself by singing, talking, clapping, and making other noises. Bears, being shy and ever so polite, will simply try to stay hidden, leaving you to enjoy your hike. When bears are in your territory, don't tempt them with food and never tease or approach them.

With the ever-increasing human population, it's important to remember we share this planet with animals. Being a good neighbor is more important than ever.

For bear safety tips at home and in the outdoors, see "Know the Bear Facts: Black Bears in New Jersey" at state.nj.us/dep/fgw/bearfacts.htm and "Black Bear Safety Tips" at outdoors.org/bears.

# GATEWAY

The Gateway region of New Jersey is home to part of Ellis Island, the "gateway" through which many immigrants entered the United States. (The other part of the island belongs to New York State, according to a 1998 Supreme Court ruling.) Of the six geographic regions in New Jersey, Gateway best exemplifies the contrasts between this state's urban and rural bounties. With a population of more than 4 million, Gateway is the most urban part of the state and yet is home to some of its most beautiful and even secluded trails. The largest shopping mall in New Jersey is in Bergen County, but the same county also boasts the 4,269-acre Ramapo State Forest and Palisades Interstate Park. Ramapo State Forest is a stream-crossed and hilly sanctuary for wildlife, with views of the New York City skyline, and 2,500-acre Palisades Interstate Park offers 30 miles of hiking on the uplands and cliffs of the Hudson River shorefront, tucked incongruously just off the Palisades Interstate Parkway. You could easily have dinner in Manhattan after hiking in the Palisades.

Gateway encompasses New Jersey's six largest municipalities (Newark, Jersey City, Paterson, Elizabeth, Woodbridge Township, and Edison) and four major rivers (Hudson, Hackensack, Passaic, and Raritan). The urban/rural sprawl includes the Meadowlands and the Palisades in the northeast, the valleys and hills of the Watchung Mountains in the west, the Ramapo Mountains in the north, and the tidal plains of the Raritan River to the south. The Watchung Mountains are a group of three long, low ridges, the product of volcanic activity 200 million years ago, that range from 400 to 500 feet in height. The Watchungs are known for scenic vistas of New York City and parts of New Jersey, traprock areas, and isolated ecosystems that contain rare plants, endangered wildlife, and rich minerals. The Ramapo Mountains, a forested chain of the Appalachians, range in height from 900 to 1,200 feet. The Ramapos are known for their

Facing page: Autumn colors the steep basalt cliffs of the New Jersey Palisades. Photo by Liz D. Imperio, AMC Photo Contest.

preserves and their concentrations of gneiss, granite, and marble. New York's Harriman State Park is located in these beautiful mountains and is home to the Appalachian Mountain Club's Stephen & Betsy Corman AMC Harriman Outdoor Center.

Long ago, the Lenni-Lenape people resided in what is now called the Gateway. In 1609, Henry Hudson sailed into what is now Sandy Hook and Weehawken Cove; by 1660, the first chartered village was established at Bergen Square on the North River. Many of the hiking areas bear Lenape names today, such as Ramapo, Watchung, and Cheesequake State Park. The latter is anglicized from the Lenape word *chichequaas*, meaning "upland," or *chiskhakink*, meaning "at the land that has been cleared." Cheesequake is a transitional zone between two ecosystems: coastal salt marshes and upland forest.

Industry came in earnest to this region in 1755 with the first steam engine, and Alexander Hamilton helped found the Society for the Establishment of Useful Manufactures, which used water from the Great Falls of the Passaic River, near one of the hikes in this section (see Trip 14). Thomas Edison also left his impression here: Visit his laboratories in Edison and his home in West Orange to learn more about the Wizard of Menlo Park.

The Central Railroad of New Jersey Terminal, a symbol of immigration and industry, is featured in the Liberty State Park hike (Trip 24). You can visit historical displays here. The railroad was chartered in 1838 and accommodated 30,000 passengers a day at its peak in 1900. It ceased passenger operations in 1967.

The Gateway boasts 26 parks, including three state forests and five state parks; eleven are covered in hikes featured in this section.

# 14

# GARRET MOUNTAIN RESERVATION

Expect excellent New York City views in all seasons, especially from 75-foot-tall Lambert Tower, and a beautiful urban walk in the fall.

## DIRECTIONS

Take I-80 west to Exit 56. Turn left at the bottom of the ramp onto Squirrelwood Road. (If you are coming from the west, take Exit 56A and proceed south on Squirrelwood Road.) Continue along Squirrelwood Road for 0.7 mile, then turn left onto Weasel Drift Road. Go approximately 0.5 mile to the entrance to the park, on the left. Turn left into the park and proceed north on Benson Drive/Park Drive (pass the equestrian center on your right). In about 0.3 mile, parking is on your left, across from the observation tower (Lambert Tower). There are about twelve parking spots here, but bigger lots dot the park; see online map at right. *GPS coordinates:* 40° 53.999′ N, 74°10.178′ W.

**Public Transportation:** From New York City's Port Authority Bus Terminal to Lambert Castle at Garret Mountain Reservation, take NJ Transit bus 192 (Clifton–New York). Get off the bus at the intersection of Valley Road, Mountain Park Road, and Fenner Avenue (ask bus driver if you're unsure). Walk one block east (toward Paterson Avenue); the entrance to the castle's driveway is on the left. Walk up the driveway. From Lambert Castle parking lot, take the Morris Canal Greenway (MCG) Trail (yellow octagon) to the top of mountain (0.15 mile). At the top, with the observation tower on the left, turn right on MCG. For more information, please contact NJ Transit at 800-772-2222 or njtransit.com. Travel time from New York City to Lambert Castle is 48 minutes. You can access trails from Lambert Castle.

**LOCATION**
Woodland Park

**RATING**
Easy

**DISTANCE**
2.8 miles

**ELEVATION GAIN**
400 feet

**ESTIMATED TIME**
2 hours

**MAPS**
USGS Paterson; nynjtc.org/sites/default/files/GarretMtnRes_Map_v1-1.pdf

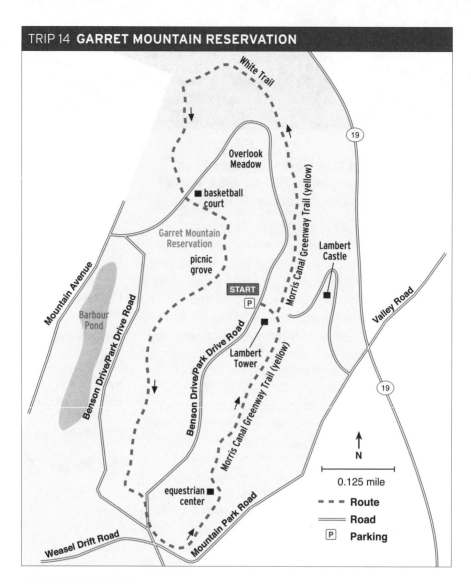

## TRAIL DESCRIPTION

Hikes in 560-acre Garret Mountain Reservation combine history, city views, rocky cliffs, and paved and dirt paths. The area is especially beautiful in the fall. December brings festivities at Lambert Castle, which serves as headquarters for the Passaic County Historical Society and is also a library and art museum (check posted hours and admission fees). Spring brings the return of a wide array of warblers, vireos, thrushes, sparrows, flycatchers, swallows, and wrens. Summer can be crowded, with lots of activity at the picnic groves and basketball courts.

From Lambert Tower, take the Morris Canal Greenway Trail (MCG), blazed with yellow octagons, to the White Trail to the Yellow Trail (blazed with white and yellow rectangles, respectively). This route along the eastern edge of the reservation and down through the middle is easy to follow, even though unblazed and minor trails branch off.

Walk across Mountain Park Road to the marker for Watchung Ridge; you are on the third-highest peak (about 500 feet) of the Watchung Mountains. Enter the gray stone Lambert Tower, marked by a green sign and named for Catholina Lambert, who emigrated from England in 1834 and founded a silk dynasty in Paterson (the Silk City of the New World). Lambert lived in Lambert Castle and used the tower as an observatory and summer house. He died in 1923, and his son Walter sold the castle and land to the city of Paterson. (Lambert had eight children. Seven predeceased him, leaving Walter as the only heir.)

Climb the 75 steps of the 75-foot tower (with interior historical signage), which is 502 feet above sea level, for excellent views of the George Washington Bridge and, in New York, Bear Mountain State Park and the Verrazano-Narrows Bridge, as well as New York City. Leave the tower, perhaps walking to the protected edge of the 150-foot sheer cliff to look down on the now-blocked "Devil's Staircase," a dangerous fissure once used by adventurous young visitors.

Facing the view, with your back to the tower, turn left (north) onto the cinder path rimmed by a massive stone wall, with views of Lambert Castle below. You are on the yellow-octagon-blazed MCG. This 1-mile path was reclaimed from the 102-mile-long Morris Canal, completed in 1831 and retired in 1923 when overshadowed by the railroad. The MCG, once all municipal trails are connected to the canal route, will stretch across six counties, creating a continuous 111-mile greenway; the 2018 MCG Corridor Study identifies 38 miles of existing trails. (For maps and more, see morriscanalgreenway.org.)

Follow the wall that runs between you and the cliffs, and go down stone steps onto a fairly flat dirt path with a few rocks. Many side trails lead to the right for fine views of Paterson and the same areas that are visible from Lambert Tower. Keep on the MCG, skirting the huge parking lot to the left, suitable for buses and around 100 cars. Reach an open field and veer right to follow the MCG. To the right is I-80 far below, and to the left is pretty Overlook Meadow. The MCG goes downhill and merges with the paved White Trail (rectangular white marker) at another parking lot.

Turn right (0.5 mile) to follow the White Trail around the far edge of the parking lot for some more fine views. See if the 25-cent observation binoculars work. Go down the steps to the right, following the stone wall, to stay on the White Trail. The paved path ends, and picnic tables and benches are conveniently located on your left. Head downhill into the woods, where white birches buffer the car noises. Keep going down on a well-maintained path through a section that is beautiful in fall. A ravine is to the right.

The White Trail goes up past huge boulders, perhaps remnants of the rock quarries (primarily brownstone and traprock, including amethyst and prehnite) that thrived in this area for more than 150 years. At the trail junction with the

Yellow Trail (1.0 mile), go left to stay on the White Trail (also known as the Bridle Path). Keep left on the White Trail to a gravel parking lot and basketball court. Cross the parking lot and road to stay on the White Trail, heading toward Rocky Hollow Picnic Grove (green sign). The dirt-and-gravel path widens in this nice patch of woods. (*Caution:* Unmarked trails dot this section, so be alert.)

Veer left to stay on the White Trail. Pass more big rocks on the right. Turn right at the first junction to follow the White Trail (1.2 miles); a concrete picnic table is on the right. The path widens at the second junction; go right there and at the third junction to stay on the White Trail. At the fourth junction, veer left, and take a few minutes to notice the fantastic tree shapes, the woods' smells, and the curious rock formations.

The White Trail ends at a gravel path, and the Yellow Trail (metal yellow rectangle) picks up; take a left on the Yellow Trail (1.9 miles)—*do not go straight.* As you head down toward the equestrian center, you may see deer and other critters.

Exit the woods, cross paved Benson Drive, and turn right in front of the attractive stone gates to stay on the Yellow Trail. The road will be to your right, a startling reminder of this reservation's accessibility. Weave through three small

This urban hike features stunning views of the New York City skyline.

boulders. Enter a beautiful, delicate woods and head uphill to a house on the right. Brush through tall, wheat-colored, whispery grasses and autumn wild-flowers. You are now on a very pretty hill, with the equestrian center on the left (2.2 miles). Turn left at a bend at the far end of the equestrian center. Follow the Yellow Trail between some rocks before it veers right into open grasses. Walk over some unusual black rocks, the color highlighted by bright yellow blazes, and head uphill for an excellent view of New York City to the right (2.6 miles), more secluded than the earlier views. Sounds of gunfire may drift up from the private police shooting range below. Lambert Tower ahead marks the end of the hike. Go downhill and cross the road to your car. If taking public transportation, access MCG from Lambert Tower, descend 0.15 mile to Lambert Castle, go down the castle's driveway, and walk one block west (away from Paterson Avenue) toward the bus stop at the intersection of Valley Road, Mountain Park Road, and Fenner Avenue.

## DID YOU KNOW?

Three ridges (called First, Second, and Third Watchung Mountain) make up the Watchung Mountains. Garret Reservation covers the northernmost part of First Watchung Mountain, sometimes called Orange Mountain. Second Watchung is also called Preakness, and Third Watchung is called Hook. Volcanic magma formed the ridges nearly 200 million years ago.

## OTHER ACTIVITIES

This area is especially rich in labor and industrial history. Plan to spend a few days and visit Thomas Edison National Historical Park (his home and lab) in West Orange; go to Paterson Great Falls National Historical Park and hike around the dramatic 77-foot-high falls, a source of water power; stop by the Paterson Museum in the Thomas Rogers Building; check out the American Labor Museum/Botto House in Haledon; and explore downtown Paterson.

## MORE INFORMATION

Open dawn to dusk, year-round. Eight Mountain Avenue, Woodland Park, NJ 07424; 973-881-4833; passaiccountynj.org/passaic_county_park_system/parks/garret_mountain_reservation.php.

# 15

# PALISADES INTERSTATE PARK: STATE LINE LOOKOUT TO PEANUT LEAP CASCADE

Enjoy Hudson River vistas, rocky cliffs, steep hills, the ruins of an Italian garden, and a rocky beach with waterfall nearby.

## DIRECTIONS

Head north on the Palisades Interstate Parkway. After Exit 2, go 1.8 miles and you will see a well-marked blue sign for the State Line Lookout exit. Follow signs to State Line Lookout parking (room for around 50 cars). *GPS coordinates:* 40° 59.327′ N, 73° 54.428′ W.

**Public Transportation:** Take Rockland Coach's Number 9 bus, which departs from Port Authority's George Washington Bridge Terminal in New York City (175th Street station on the A express subway line) or from the Port Authority Bus Terminal (42nd Street), with stops at Bridge Plaza in Fort Lee. The Number 9 then travels north up U.S. Route 9W, to the state line by the entrance to Lamont-Doherty Earth Observatory. Follow the concrete roadway of Old Route 9W (closed to traffic) to State Line Lookout. Total distance is about 1.5 miles. The old roadway follows an uphill grade going to State Line Lookout. Allow about 45 minutes for each direction, up and back down.

For additional bus schedule information for the Number 9 bus, visit Rockland Coaches (Red and Tan Lines, web.coachusa.com/rockland/ss.tickets.asp) or call 201-384-2400 or 212-279-6526. For connecting bus information, also check NJ Transit, njtransit.com.

## TRAIL DESCRIPTION

Prepare for a short but dramatic hike from atop the 520-foot-high Palisades Cliffs overlooking the Hudson River to the rocky beach at river's edge. The high cliffs

**LOCATION**
Alpine

**RATING**
Moderate

**DISTANCE**
3 miles

**ELEVATION GAIN**
600 feet

**ESTIMATED TIME**
1.5 to 2 hours

**MAPS**
USGS Yonkers;
njpalisades.org/pdfs/
hikeStateline.pdf

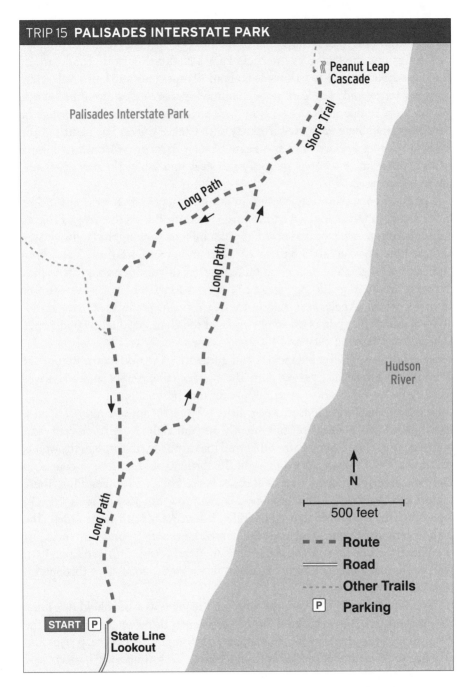

provide a superb vantage point for observing birds and butterflies. In autumn, look for sharp-shinned hawks, ospreys, broad-winged hawks, peregrine falcons, and monarch butterflies. Bald eagles and ducks spend winter on the cliffs, and more than 5 miles of cross-country skiing trails crisscross the park. Spring brings great blue herons and swallows. In summer, watch double-crested cormorants dry their wings, red-tailed hawks soar, and tiger swallowtail butterflies float. It's no wonder the U.S. Department of the Interior and the National Park Service designated the Palisades Interstate Park a National Historic Landmark in 1965. The 2,500-acre New Jersey side is about 12 miles long and half a mile wide. The New Jersey and New York sides combined span 42 miles, from the George Washington Bridge in Fort Lee, New Jersey, to the Bear Mountain Bridge in Bear Mountain State Park, New York. This hike takes you on Long Path, which leads to the rocky Shore Trail and Peanut Leap Cascades. Wear sturdy hiking boots because many sections are rocky and steep and can be slippery when wet, icy, or leaf covered.

Start at the cozy, picturesque Franklin Roosevelt–era WPA State Line Café for food, drink, guidebooks, and bathrooms. (Franklin Roosevelt's Work Projects Administration made the café possible.) The cliffs overlooking the Hudson River at State Line Lookout are a birder's paradise and great for fall hawk-watching and leaf-peeping. Use the observation binoculars or your personal pair to pick out some landmarks. The Tappan Zee Bridge lies to the far left; the water tower from the defunct Anaconda Cable and Wire Company is almost straight ahead. To its right are the twin brick smokestacks of the abandoned Glenwood Power Station, built between 1904 and 1906 and known locally as "the Gates of Hell," because of its use in zombie movies and allegedly, gang initiations. Rumors of renovation plans surface periodically. The big blue cube you see in Yonkers was part of a factory and is now a sound stage for film production.

Facing the majestic Hudson River, turn left (north) toward marker 1 on a paved path. Picnic tables are conveniently on your right. Very soon, veer right onto the aqua-blazed Long Path, a dirt trail that heads north through the woods (0.2 mile). The Hudson is to your right. In spring, you may see the courtship flight of peregrine falcons, a series of dives, barrel rolls, and somersaults. These raptors can also briefly invert (fly upside down) to grasp prey on the wing. On a weekday, the woods are serene and quiet, but weekends can get crowded. The path widens and flattens and begins to descend, becoming rooty and rocky. At the Y intersection, go straight at the signs for Trail E (ski trail) and Long Path North. The aqua blazes lead to the right, down some stone steps through an opening in a wire fence.

Carefully descend, following the fence and using it as a handhold (0.7 mile) because you are exposed to the cliffs and the river far below on your right. In the distance is a stunning view of the Tappan Zee Bridge. The very steep steps end on a flat, rocky path that goes away from the river. Technically, you have crossed into New York; a 6-foot-tall state line boundary monument, erected in 1882, is somewhere nearby.

Descend across three wooden footbridges. Turn right on the white-blazed Shore Trail (1.1 miles), which flattens out briefly and in autumn has a golden carpet of oak, maple, sweet gum, and tulip leaves. Begin a steep descent with a deep ravine to the right.

Hikers ascend from the Hudson River and garden ruins at Peanut Leap Cascade.

Pick your way over some fascinatingly contoured boulders and walk under a large fallen tree. Keep following the white blazes to your left. Admire the Hudson below; you will soon be there. Descend some steep wooden steps, listening to the waves lapping on the rocky shores of this mighty river, 3 miles wide at one point. At the bottom of your descent (1.3 miles) awaits a fairy-tale warren of steps and hobbit-like habitats on the banks of the Hudson. Capricious stonework, downed columns, a maze of stone walls and ramps, brick archways, and plunging stone steps are the remains of an Italian garden designed by the artist Mary Lawrence-Tonetti around 1900. She and her family entertained lavishly in the garden. After her death, the family donated the land to the park commission.

Linger on a lopsided bench jutting from tree roots, or stand on the rocky beach and dip your toes into the Hudson River; it's a good spot for lunch or a rest. To the right, admire the Palisades sill (an outstanding example of igneous rock intruded between sediment layers), noting the scarred areas where quarries in the 1800s produced diabase traprock for paving stones and blocks. (Mining stopped in 1900 when the park commission took over.) Smell the brackish scent: The Hudson River is part salt water and part fresh water. Imagine immense quantities of shad ascending to the headwaters to spawn in late March and early April.

Go back the same way. Before you leave, stop to admire Peanut Leap Cascade, a waterfall to the left of the ruins. In some seasons, the cascade merely trickles.

To ease your return, skip the three wooden footbridges by going straight on the rooty and rocky aqua-blazed Long Path (2.0 miles). Keep the stream on your left.

At the Y intersection, take a left toward State Line Lookout (sign) on an unblazed trail. Head upward over roots and rocks. In summer, look for stalks of turtlehead and black-eyed Susans; fall brings white snakeroots, foxgloves, and asters. Go through the gate at the wire fence, then take a left on the paved road. A gentle ascent takes you straight to the café, where you might spot soaring ravens. If you have time, take a short walk to the interesting Women's Federation Monument (see "Other Activities").

## DID YOU KNOW?

Palisades Park has its own song, a tribute to its days as an amusement park: "Palisades Park" was written by Chuck Barris in 1962 and has been recorded by Freddy Cannon, Gary Lewis and the Playboys, the Beach Boys, and the Ramones.

## OTHER ACTIVITIES

For a challenging hike, turn right (south) at the Peanut Leap Cascade area to follow the talus-ridden shoreline of the Hudson and climb the difficult Giant Stairs. (The Giant Stairs are not suitable for dogs or young children, and involve a scramble over a mile-long boulder field before ascending a steep trail.) For an easier hike, face the river at State Line Café, and follow the clear signage for the unblazed Women's Federation Monument Trail, a charming 0.6-mile walk on the New Jersey Women's Heritage Trail, to a mini castle honoring the role of the New Jersey State Federation of Women's Clubs in shutting down the quarries and preserving the Palisades. Visit Kearney House, a home illuminating two centuries of family life on the Hudson River (open weekends May through October), and Fort Lee Historic Park, an American Revolution encampment atop a 33-acre cliff (visitor center open Wednesday through Sunday).

## MORE INFORMATION

Open during daylight hours, 30 minutes before sunrise and 30 minutes after sunset. Restaurant and gift shop on premises. Palisades Interstate Park Commission, P.O. Box 155, Alpine, NJ 07620; 201-768-1360; njpalisades.org.

# 16

# WATCHUNG RESERVATION: WHITE TRAIL TO FELTVILLE

Discover hidden history deep in the woods as you explore an abandoned village and an eighteenth-century graveyard.

## DIRECTIONS

Take I-95 North to NJ 18 North toward New Brunswick. After 4.33 miles, take the Metlars Lane ramp, and keep left at the fork. Then stay straight to follow County Highway 609. In 0.58 mile, turn left to stay on County Highway 609. In 1.02 miles, stay straight to go onto South Washington Avenue/County Highway 665. In 1.32 miles, turn left onto County Highway 529/Stelton Road. In 3.42 miles, turn right onto US 22 East. In 6.67 miles, turn right onto Glenside Avenue (County Highway 527). At a T intersection, turn left onto Sky Top Drive. In less than 0.5 mile, parking is on both sides of street. You'll see a picnic pavilion. *GPS coordinates: 40° 40.211' N, 74° 23.593' W.*

## TRAIL DESCRIPTION

This historical, charming loop path follows the White Trail through the "deserted village" of Feltville/Glenside Park to the purple-blazed History Trail, to the Blue Trail, and back to the White Trail.

About 47 miles of trails are located in the 2,142-acre Watchung Reservation, the largest of Union County's 36 parks. The Union County Parks system was designed by the Olmsted brothers. The site is on both the New Jersey and National Registers of Historic Places. Since 1600, the reservation has hosted a copper mine, printing business, recreational resort, sawmill, and Boy Scout camp. Situated between First and Second Watchung mountains, with Blue Brook Valley in between, the reservation includes wetlands, ponds, rivers, hardwood swamps, forests, and meadows and is an important link in the Union County greenway. Migratory birds rest and refuel here. Other

**LOCATION**
Scotch Plains

**RATING**
Easy

**DISTANCE**
3.9 miles

**ELEVATION GAIN**
550 feet

**ESTIMATED TIME**
2.5 hours

**MAPS**
USGS Chatham;
ucnj.org/parks-recreation/
paths-trails-greenways/
watchung-reservation/

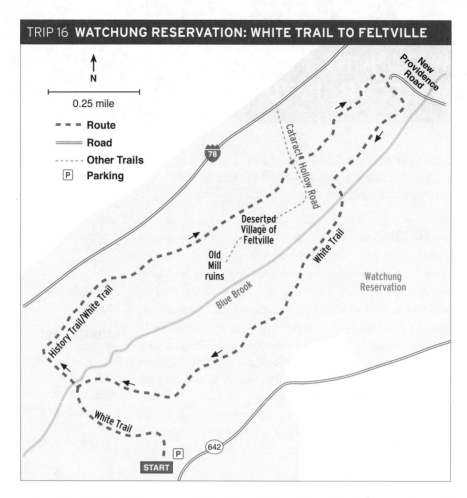

animals include red foxes, woodchucks, red-shouldered hawks, great horned owls, and bats. Trees include American beeches, oaks, dogwoods, and tulip poplars, making a beautiful fall and spring palette.

At the kiosk in the parking lot nearest the picnic pavilion, pick up a map and self-guided tour of the Deserted Village of Feltville and Glenside Park (cell phone QR codes are on maps). Chemical toilets are available seasonally. The route starts at the Sky Top Picnic Area (sign). Turn left at the picnic area onto the White Trail. Cross a stream and veer right at the fork, still on the White Trail. In winter, pine trees provide greenery. The broad, rooty, and rutted dirt trail soon heads down. Take a right at a wide road and then an immediate left to stay on the White Trail and head down the gravelly, rocky path.

Go up steps and cross a wooden bridge, noting the incredible shapes of downed trees. At the Drake Farm sign (0.6 mile), observe the stone foundations of a farmhouse and barn. The farm originally provided food for the residents of Feltville. The property was also used for grazing cattle and later converted to the summer resort of Glenside Park.

You are now on the purple-blazed History Trail, which merges with the White Trail. Turn right after the farmhouse, then right again, staying on History Trail. The trail narrows and becomes dirt before crossing a bridge over a stream. Descend and cross a streambed (dry in winter); the high, picturesque banks make the path cozy. Veer left at the Y intersection. Note deep erosion to the right caused by a microburst (intense thunderstorm with strong bursts of wind). The trail widens and becomes less rooty as it winds pleasantly through a clearing.

Enter a large, paved road (the purple-blazed History Trail and the White Trail) and enjoy Masker's Barn on the right—a restored and heated barn that holds 150 people and can be rented for parties (1.4 miles). Built in 1882, Masker's Barn held horses and carriages that transported businessmen to the train station at Murray Hill. Their families stayed behind at Glenside Park to enjoy golf, tennis, croquet, baseball, fishing, and horseback riding at the resort.

Take some time to explore the remaining buildings in the Deserted Village of Feltville and Glenside Park—although some are occupied today. In about 1736, Peter Willcocks built a sawmill along Blue Brook to produce lumber. The sawmill operation cleared hundreds of acres of forest. In 1845, David Felt bought 760 acres of Willcocks' land. Visit the house of David Felt, founder of Feltville, who lived here with his family from 1845 to 1860. Felt ran a stationery business in New York City. He built a paper mill here along Blue Brook and then built an entire town to support the operation. The self-guided tour booklet contains some interesting details about his life.

Go behind the Felt house (which has an indoor bathroom) and down a path with handrails. Turn left at the Y intersection and head uphill to a 1700s cemetery. Linger a while, paying homage to Phebe Badgley Willcocks and others buried here. It's believed that the cemetery holds about two dozen family members. The purple History Trail ends.

Continue straight on what is now just the White Trail, noting the steep ravine to the right. At the Y intersection, take a left and keep bearing left onto a narrow, smooth dirt path. At the T intersection, go right, still on the white-blazed trail, down a wider dirt path, with eerie, windblown trees. Take a right at the Y intersection, crossing over a drainage pipe, and go down a wide dirt path. Traverse a charming dirt bridge with brick railings and go right at the Y intersection.

Take a hard right onto a dirt boardwalk onto the Blue Trail (2.4 miles). Go over a bridge, up a narrow dirt path, and take a left at the Y intersection to stay on the Blue Trail. The terrain is a bit rugged with roots and rocks; a stream is to the right. Cross the stream. In winter, you'll hear the bare trees creak.

You are now back on the White Trail. Go left at the white blaze on a steep, rooty path. Stay left to keep on the White Trail, which merges with the Pink Trail temporarily (2.6 miles). Turn right at the junction to stay on the White Trail as it goes up and down a muddy path (wetlands). The White Trail turns left. Cross a ravine and climb a steep, rocky incline up to a ridge (about 2.9 miles). Take a right at the Y intersection to stay on the white-blazed trail. Private homes

The cemetery holds about two dozen people, though only one headstone is original.

are ahead on the left. Go straight at the next intersection and go downhill over a streambed, which can be wet in spring and bone-dry in winter, but is always rooty and rocky. At the road, stay to your left to remain on the White Trail. Go up some timber steps to your left, traipsing through a forest of toothpick-thin trees and up a muddy trail. Suddenly you are back at the picnic area, where you can stop for lunch or return to the parking lot.

## DID YOU KNOW?

Feltville was deserted—three times. The first time was by Feltville's creator, David ("King David") Felt, who built this quasi-utopian mill town from 1845 to 1847. For 15 years, it thrived under his benevolent leadership, fueled by his Unitarian ideals to provide a better lifestyle for urban industrial workers, and boasted 175 residents in 1850. In August of 1860, for reasons unknown, Felt sold the business and property to Amasa Foster, and supposedly said, "Well, King David is dead, and the Village will go to hell."

His prediction seemed to come true as ownership of the property changed hands six times over the next twenty years, and all businesses initiatives failed. For a while, the town may have been completely abandoned, earning its first reputation as a deserted village. In 1882, Warren Ackerman purchased Feltville at public auction, for the bargain price of $11,450, and built the summer resort of Glenside Park. In 1916, automobiles rendered proximity to the local train station less important and the village became almost deserted for the second time.

In the 1920s, the Union County Park Commission purchased the property, and incorporated it into the Watchung Reservation; the park commission rented the houses to full occupancy until the 1960s. Again, for reasons unknown, Feltville was virtually deserted by 1984, although a few people still live here today, with a long waiting list for residency. See the online magazine *Weird N.J.* for entertaining rumors of ghosts and satanic rituals (weirdnj.com).

## OTHER ACTIVITIES

Be sure to stop at the amazing Trailside Nature & Science Center. It has an ATM and a Wi-Fi lounge upstairs. One highlight is an enclosed exhibit called "Into the Night," where visitors mingle with owls, raccoons, and other nocturnal creatures. Diners galore dot the area around the reservation. Kids will enjoy Bowcraft Amusement Park and Ponderosa Park in Scotch Plains. The nearby charming, upscale town of Westfield is worth a visit.

## MORE INFORMATION

Open dawn to dusk, year-round. Department of Parks and Recreation, County of Union, 10 Elizabethtown Plaza, Elizabethtown, NJ 07207; 908-527-4000; ucnj.org/parks-recreation/.

## 17

# BRANCH BROOK PARK

Enjoy the largest urban collection of cherry trees in the United States and hike the Lenape Trail, which ends in Newark.

## DIRECTIONS

Take I-95 North to Garden State Parkway North. After 20.0 miles, take Exit 148 toward County Highway 506 (Bloomfield Avenue). In 0.4 mile, merge onto John F. Kennedy Drive North. In 0.3 mile, turn right onto Franklin Street (County Highway 509). In 1.25 miles, Franklin Street becomes Heller Parkway. Street parking is available on Heller Parkway just past Sixth Street, at the intersection of Heller and Franklin streets. (*Note:* The Cherry Blossom Welcome Center is a few blocks north on First Street, with parking for about 100 cars, but the lot fills up quickly during cherry blossom season.) *GPS coordinates:* 40° 46.691′ N, 74° 10.447′ W.

**Public Transportation:** Take Newark Light Rail to the Branch Brook Park Stop. Walk left, under the overpass and away from the tennis courts. For more information, see njtransit.com.

## TRAIL DESCRIPTION

This gorgeous, well-groomed park sprawls in the North Ward of Newark among the neighborhoods of Forest Hill, Roseville, and Belleville. It has the largest collection of cherry trees in the United States—more than 5,000 trees and more than 20 varieties (larger than even Washington, D.C.'s display). Nature is capricious, but it's best to get there mid-April to mid-May, though blooms have been known to pop as early as March. When you arrive, head straight to the Cherry Blossom Welcome Center for a free map (the online map is rather small) to traverse this 360-acre, 4-mile-long public park.

**LOCATION**
Newark

**RATING**
Easy

**DISTANCE**
4.5 miles

**ELEVATION GAIN**
160 feet

**ESTIMATED TIME**
2 hours

**MAPS**
USGS Orange;
essexcountyparks.org/
parks/branch-brook-park

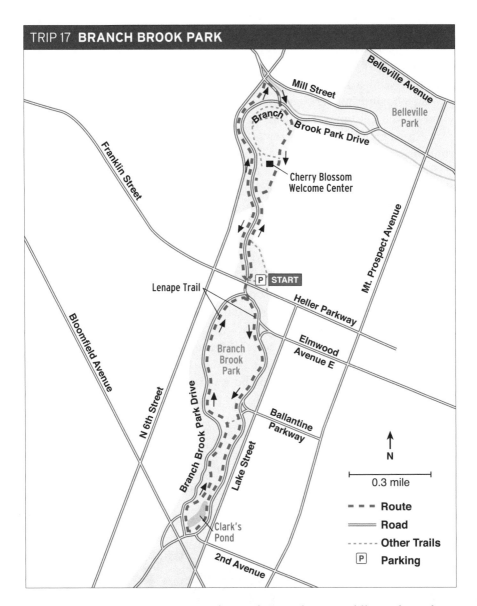

Technically, the area is separated into the Northern, Middle, and Southern divisions and the Northern Extension. You have to cross paved roads to stay on the park's footpaths, but it's simple to do. This guide suggests one possible route, but any path in the park will be easy to follow back. Ponds, streams, and lakes link the divisions, and nineteen art deco bridges cross the waters.

As in many sprawling urban parks, you can start your hike from anywhere in Branch Brook Park, but in spring, start in the Northern Extension, which has the heaviest concentration of cherry trees. Park along Heller Parkway, just past Sixth Street, by the Althea Gibson Tennis Center, away from the crowds at Cherry Blossom Welcome Center. You are near the sign for Forest Hill, a pre–World

War II neighborhood known for uniquely designed homes. Walk toward the tennis center and a large Branch Brook Park sign, cross the street to the Patricia Chambers Cherry Tree Grove sign, and take a right. The Branch Brook train station is on your left, and tennis courts are across the road. As you stroll down the paved path admiring the blooms, take advantage of the self-guided cell phone tours via the QR (quick response) bar codes posted periodically through the park. To access the QR tour, you will need to download a QR code reader from your smartphone's app store. Soon you'll walk under an art deco bridge.

Cross Branch Brook Park Drive to the parking lot, wander under the pink cloud of cherry blossoms to the unnamed paved path, and walk to the welcome center (0.5 mile). Get a map, enjoy the exhibits, and use the facilities, if necessary. Or plan your hike in the covered pavilion outside.

Walk past the baseball fields on your left. At the double yellow trail blaze, take the right fork. The path crosses a parkway (Branch Brook Park Drive, 0.7 mile). Turn left and follow the path up a steep hill, noting the many types and varieties of cherry trees. Pause to sit on a park bench and admire the blooms across the road and down the hill. Then continue going straight on this picturesque, tree-lined path.

When you reach another art deco bridge, cross Branch Brook Park Drive again and walk under the ancient blooming cherry trees through the parking lot. If you'd like, use your map and wander the northern, blossom-laden extension of the park some more. To get in some mileage, head south to the paved Lenape Trail.

Walk under the first art deco bridge again, following the path beneath it. Stay on the path toward the 2-mile loop of the Lenape Trail (from Heller Parkway to Bloomfield Avenue). Cross Grafton Avenue (1.9 miles). The train station is to the right, the tennis courts to the left. Walk over Heller Parkway, scoot across the

Boasting more cherry trees than Washington, D.C., this trip is best hiked mid-April to May for optimal bloom.

edge of the park, and cross Elmwood Road toward the paved walking path. The path is paved but springy because it's made from Porous Pave XL, a rubber chip, aggregate, and binder material. Turn left on the path (2.2 miles), admiring the beautiful green grass on your right. Time your walk with the concrete markers every 0.25 mile.

A pond and some stunning cattails appear on your right. Appreciate the stone bridge that spans the pond Attractive stone bridges dot the park, as do workout stations and benches. Tangled woods and another bridge pop up on the right.

Watch for two fountains that suddenly spout from the pond. Old city homes are to the left. Stay on the path as it circles to the right.

Enjoy the spectacular views of the pond and stone bridges as you circle around on the path. In April, across the road to your left, yellow trout lilies sprout, and white and pink wildflowers and clover coat the field like candy floss. Walk over a bridge and then another, noting the urban high-rise apartment buildings to the left. Stop at the Lenape Trail sign at the end of the 2-mile loop. Plan to explore the entire 34-mile Lenape Trail another day. Established in 1982, it links a dozen county and municipal parks and was a joint undertaking of the Sierra Club and the Essex County Department of Parks, Recreation and Cultural Affairs. The trail starts in Millburn and ends in Newark (see page 98).

Head to the right, back toward the tennis courts, and make your way to the Branch Brook Park sign and your car.

## DID YOU KNOW?

Conceived by Frederick Law Olmsted Sr. in 1867, Branch Brook Park was America's first public county park. It is on the New Jersey and National Registers of Historic Places. Branch Brook is a tributary of the Passaic River, and the original park encompassed the Branch Brook valley, hence the name.

## OTHER ACTIVITIES

Strap on roller skates or grab a tennis racket, basketball, or softball. A roller-skating rink, playing courts, and a ball field are in the park. Explore the Cathedral of the Sacred Heart, one of the largest Gothic-style churches in the country, in the park's Southern Division. Just minutes away, visit the Newark Museum and Newark Public Library or take in an event at the New Jersey Performing Arts Center or the Prudential Arena. There are many shops and restaurants in Bloomfield and Forest Hill.

## MORE INFORMATION

Essex County Department of Parks, Recreation and Cultural Affairs, 115 Clifton Avenue, Newark, NJ 07104; 973-268-3500; essexcountyparks.org/parks/branch-brook-park. Branch Brook Park Alliance, c/o 115 Clifton Avenue, Newark, NJ 07104; 973-268-2300; branchbrookpark.org/index.html.

## THE LENAPE TRAIL AND AL KENT

Almost 1 million people live within 5 miles of the Lenape Trail, but relatively few know it exists. This unique urban trail in densely populated Essex County was established in 1982 and runs from Millburn to Newark, linking a dozen county and municipal parks, including Branch Brook Park (Trip 17), Mills Reservation (Trip 20), Eagle Rock Reservation, and South Mountain Reservation. About 30 percent of the 34-mile trail is on-street, winding through municipalities such as West Orange, Montclair, and Belleville. Distinctive yellow markers on trees and telephone poles (first painted in 1979) and a variety of other signage mark the Lenape Trail.

The trail was a joint undertaking of the Sierra Club and the Essex County Department of Parks, Recreations and Cultural Affairs. But it was the brainchild of Albert "Al" Kent, who worked as a trail coordinator for the Morris County Park System after retiring from the fuel oil industry. Kent wanted to create a trail through urban and rural areas that everyone could enjoy. His passion for accessibility was so great that he went on to plan and help establish the 156-mile Liberty–Water Gap Trail, which runs across the entire state of New Jersey, from Liberty State Park in the east to the Delaware Water Gap National Recreation Area in the west (and includes the Lenape Trail). In 2010, at age 84, he walked the entire Liberty–Water Gap Trail to publicize it. His daughter, Susan Bennett (who took the photo for Trip 4), remembers hiking with him as a child and says that even in his 90s, her father still manages daily walks.

The Lenape Trail is full of places to explore as you wander. Visit the Nutley Museum, featuring fine art and items owned by the sharpshooter Annie Oakley, who moved to Nutley in 1892 and stayed for more than 10 years. In Montclair, the tiny (11.5 acres) Yantacaw Brook Park has a tranquil pond. Planned reroutes will include the nearby 19.68-acre Alonzo F. Bonsal Wildlife Preserve, Prospect Park in Livingston, Riverfront Park in Newark, the Presby Memorial Iris Gardens in Upper Montclair, and the 9/11 Memorial at Eagle Rock Reservation in West Orange. Presby, known as the "Rainbow on the Hill," has the largest public iris display in the United States: 14,000 plants with more than 100,000 blooms. Hike the Lenape Trail to the 9/11 Memorial at Eagle Rock Reservation. Here, on the Watchung Mountains' ridgline, a statue of a soaring bronze eagle faces midtown Manhattan. Other tributes include a wall of remembrance and World Trade Center artifacts that encourage visitors to linger in silence.

Hike the trail on your own or go in October with the FreeWalkers (freewalkers. org) on their annual 34-mile journey beginning at Millburn Station and ending at Penn Station in Newark, with seven bail-out train stations in between. Called the Origins Walk, it usually coordinates with the weekend before Columbus Day, also known as Indigenous Peoples' Day, and is meant to raise awareness of the Lenni-Lenape.

A Lenape Trail marker shows the signature yellow markers, first painted in 1979.

When European settlers arrived, the Lenni-Lenape were living in the areas that are now New Jersey, Delaware, southern New York, and eastern Pennsylvania. Among many Algonquian people along the East Coast, the Lenni-Lenape were considered "grandfathers" or "ancient ones" from whom other tribes originated. One of the first tribes to encounter European colonization, they were pushed north and west in the eighteenth century. Tribal communities now live in Oklahoma, Kansas, and Wisconsin in the United States, and in Ontario, Canada. The public can learn more about the group's 10,000-year-old heritage by attending the annual Nanticoke Lenni-Lenape Powwow in June at the Salem County Fairgrounds in Woodstown, New Jersey.

For a varied walk rich with history and natural delights, take the Lenape Trail for an urban and rural adventure through Essex County, one of the most densely populated counties in the United States, and thank Al Kent for his long-ago vision to bring the outdoors to the urban masses.

The Lenape Trail is maintained by the New York–New Jersey Trail Conference, in partnership with local park conservancies and the Essex County Park System. See a map of the trail at nynjtc.org/park/lenape-trail.

# 18

# NORVIN GREEN STATE FOREST (SOUTH)

Scramble up, down, and over boulders in this rigorous workout. Your reward? Excellent 360-degree views of New York City and Wanaque Reservoir.

## DIRECTIONS

Take I-287 North to Exit 55 toward Wanaque (Ringwood Avenue/County Road 511). Go 4.0 miles north on Ringwood (becomes Greenwood Lake Turnpike) and turn left onto Westbrook Road. In 2.0 miles, turn left onto Snake Den Road, and in 0.31 mile, take the first left to stay on Snake Den Road. In 0.45 mile, you arrive at 150 Snake Den Road (New Weis Center for Education, Arts & Recreation). There is a parking area with room for 50 to 60 cars. *GPS coordinates:* 47° 04.191′ N, 74° 19.297′ W.

## TRAIL DESCRIPTION

The 5,416-acre Norvin Green State Forest offers some of the most rugged hiking in New Jersey through an undisturbed forest and over old logging and mining roads. Hiking maps divide the park into two sections, one north of West Brook Road and one south of West Brook Road. This trip covers the south section, which has about 30 miles of crisscrossing trails. The north section has about 24 miles of trails, including the very difficult but worthwhile 9-to-10-mile Stonetown Circular Trail, with about 2,500 feet of elevation gain. The forest is mainly deciduous trees, including the American chestnut, with pitch pines and eastern red cedars at higher elevations. In the many wet areas, look for toads and red efts (a juvenile newt, or salamander). Black bears have been seen, as well as blueberry bushes. Fall, spring, and summer are good times to hike. Winter can

**LOCATION**
Ringwood

**RATING**
Strenuous

**DISTANCE**
5.4 miles

**ELEVATION GAIN**
1,800 feet

**ESTIMATED TIME**
4 to 5 hours

**MAPS**
USGS Wanaque; state.nj.us/dep/parksandforests; *Kittatinny Trails Map, Trail Map 115*, Sixth Edition, New York-New Jersey Trail Conference

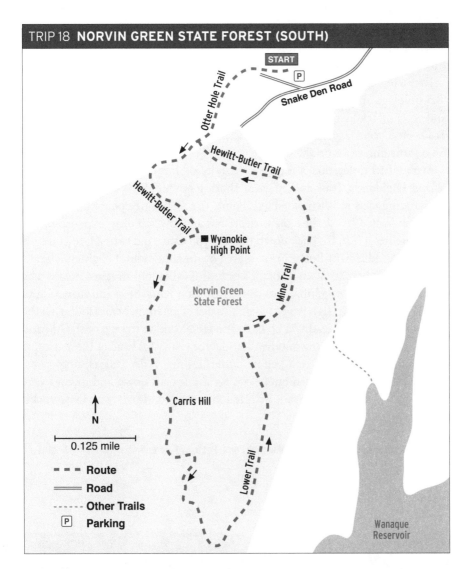

be tricky because of the rocks and water (ice). Enjoy excellent 360-degree views of New York City and the Wanaque Reservoir from Wyanokie High Point and Carris Hill. (*Note:* There are no bathroom facilities at this park.)

On this hike you take green-blazed Otter Hole Trail to blue-blazed Hewitt-Butler Trail to white-blazed Carris Hill Trail, then work your way back on Lower and Mine trails (blazed white-on-white dots and yellow-on-white dots, respectively) to Hewitt-Butler and Otter Hole trails for a rigorous workout with maximized views. Trail markers overlap, so stay focused on the primary markings.

Head toward the sign for the New Weis Center for Education, Arts & Recreation. Walk down a paved road, which soon turns into a packed-dirt path that leads to a sign saying "To All Trails." In spring, note the beautiful blooming forsythia on the right in the field with picnic tables.

Go straight at the trailhead and turn left at the Y intersection onto rooty, rocky, green-blazed Otter Hole Trail. A lovely waterfall and brook are on the left. The steep path includes some impressively large boulders.

Take a left onto a bridge. At the intersection and Richard Warner Trail kiosk (0.5 mile), go straight onto blue-blazed Hewitt-Butler Trail. Carefully hike up and across a boulder field. At the Y intersection, stay straight on Hewitt-Butler Trail. Find your favorite glacial erratic rock; there are many to choose from. Enjoy amazing views on the way up.

At about 1.1 miles, take a tiny detour to the left onto the turquoise-diamond-blazed Highlands Trail and make a short scramble up the boulders for an outstanding view at Wyanokie High Point. The 360-degree panorama includes the New York City skyline on a clear day and the winding expanse of the Wanaque Reservoir. Go back down the way you came and turn left to continue on blue-blazed Hewitt-Butler Trail, shared by the southbound Highlands Trail.

A rocky, rooty hike down through a beautiful valley and streams, followed by a climb up a steep, long hill, takes you to Yoo Hoo Point. Stop and turn around to gaze at Wyanokie High Point, where you just came from, before following the yellow markings that lead you up to Carris Hill. Walk to the top of the hill and spend some time admiring another 360-degree vista, this time of the Wanaque Reservoir. Hawks circle, and yellow butterflies flit. Wild azaleas, dogwoods, and mountain laurels spread out below. Scramble back down and follow steep, yellow-blazed Carris Hill Trail, with tough footing on leaves and loose rocks.

Wanaque Reservoir as seen from Wyanokie High Point. Photo by Paul Wulfing.

The path finally begins to gently slope, though it's still rooty and rocky. Cross a couple of streams, then turn left at the intersection onto white-blazed Lower Trail (2.8 miles), at the sign for the Weis Center.

The hike briefly gets flatter and easier. At the intersection, turn right to stay on Lower Trail. Violets and wildflowers abound in the beautiful valley to the right. A stream gurgles (probably Blue Mine Brook) as you go downhill over a rocky trail with slippery leaves. Watch for salamanders. Turn right where the teal Highlands Trail and Wyanokie Circular Trail (red on white circles) join (4.1 miles). Cross a stream.

At the Y intersection, go left (4.2 miles) onto Mine Trail (blazed with a yellow dot on a white circle) and head uphill. At the next intersection, keep straight on Mine Trail for one of those end-of-hike killer inclines. At the T intersection at the kiosk, turn right onto blue-blazed Hewitt-Butler Trail (4.9 miles). Cross a path to go straight onto green-blazed Otter Hole Trail, heading back to the parking lot. Turn right after crossing the bridge. You'll pass the Highland Natural Pool (see "Other Activities").

## DID YOU KNOW?

Take a self-guided geologic tour of the southern section of Norvin Green State Forest (see page 7 of state.nj.us/dep/njgs/enviroed/freedwn/NorvinGreenSF .pdf). Roomy Mine (named for surveyor Benjamin Roome) is closed, except to bats. The New Jersey Field Office of the U.S. Fish and Wildlife Service designates this cave a bat hibernaculum for hibernation and breeding. (See also "Did You Know?" Trips 4 and 13.) For more on bats, investigate the nonprofit New Jersey Bat Sanctuary in Milford, njbats.org. A few miles north in West Milford lies Long Pond Ironworks State Park; the ironworks was a source of iron during the American Revolution and the Civil War.

## OTHER ACTIVITIES

Visit the New Weis Center for Education, Arts & Recreation at 150 Snake Den Road on the grounds of the state forest. Call 973-835-2160 for hours and programs. The center is privately owned and operated by the Highlands Nature Friends Inc. (highlandsnaturefriends.org/home.html).

Get a day pass for the Highlands Natural Pool, a stream-fed freshwater swimming pool at the start of Otter Trail (973-835-4299). Visit Ringwood's 96-acre New Jersey Botanical Garden, and explore the historical estate and grounds at Ringwood Manor.

## MORE INFORMATION

Norvin Green State Forest is open 8 a.m. to 8 p.m., year-round. Mailing address: c/o Ringwood State Park, 1304 Sloatsburg Road, Ringwood, NJ 07456-1799; 973-962-7031.

# 19

# PLAINSBORO PRESERVE

Soothe your soul with a secluded woods hike to a peaceful, 50-acre lake; the nature center is a must for children.

## DIRECTIONS

Follow Route 1 North or South to the Scudders Mill Road exit in Plainsboro Township. Take the Scudders Mill exit, and follow the road to the traffic light that intersects Scudders Mill Road and Dey Road (County Route 614). Turn left onto Dey Road. At the first light, turn left onto Scotts Corner Road. The preserve's entrance is 1.0 mile up on the left. A gravel parking lot holds 50 to 60 cars. Two parking spots are wheelchair-accessible to the Rush Holt Environmental Education Center. *GPS coordinates:* 40° 20.972′ N, 74° 33.584′ W.

## TRAIL DESCRIPTION

If you seek peaceful, easy walks, head to the 630-acre natural area of the Plainsboro Preserve. Quiet waters, warblers, deer, flowers, soothing greens, and quiet fields will revive your spirits. More than 5 miles of marked trails wander through wet meadows and mature beech woods and around the 50-acre human-made McCormack Lake.

A cooperative project among Middlesex County, Plainsboro Township, and the New Jersey Audubon Society, the preserve boasts the excellent Rush Holt Environmental Education Center, with a reference library, gift shop, and bathrooms. (*Note:* When the center is closed, there are no bathroom facilities available at the preserve.) Inside are exhibits on turtles, snakes, and frogs.

In spring, the preserve teems with wildflowers and mating birds. Monarch butterflies flit in summer, as well as mosquitoes (wear repellent). Fall brings a canopy of

**LOCATION**
Cranbury

**RATING**
Easy

**DISTANCE**
4.9 miles

**ELEVATION GAIN**
200 feet

**ESTIMATED TIME**
2.5 hours

**MAPS**
USGS Highstown;
njaudubon.org/places-to
-visit/plainsboro-preserve

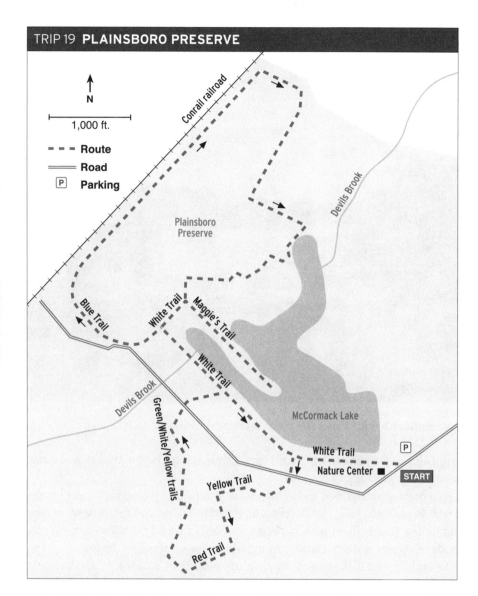

color. Flat trails make winter walks accessible, and the wide water grows blossoms of ice.

Start on the White Trail, and stroll trails blazed from yellow to red to green to blue before returning on the White Trail. You'll pass through an upland forest, across a stream and a wet area, through scrublands, and along a lake. The markings can be a little confusing, but with only 5 miles of trails and a lake to anchor you, don't worry about getting lost.

From the parking lot, head left to the trailhead sign (the environmental center is on your right) and take the White Trail, a wide gravel path that gives way to dirt with fields on either side, to head toward the Yellow Trail. Ignore the Orange

A memorial bench on McCormack Lake peninsula offers quiet contemplation.

Trail almost immediately to your right. This leads to a nature trail that you can visit on the way back to your car.

Keep going straight on the White Trail, glimpsing McCormack Lake on the right through the trees. Walk past adorable birdhouses and informative nature signs. The lake is lined with bayberry shrubs. Sit on a bench and admire this body of water, created by sand mining, which shaped much of the preserve. The lake is alive with fish, reptiles, amphibians, waterfowl, and plants. Look closely in the shrubbery to your right for a concrete structure, once part of a sand mining operation.

Continue on the White Trail past many numbered birdhouses. At birdhouse 48, the trail splits; turn left toward the Yellow Trail (0.3 mile). Walk past a grassy field (still farmed). Enter the woods at the trail sign and go straight onto the Yellow Trail. The wide, flat dirt path is shady and cool, courtesy of the American beech forest microclimate. You may observe some of the salamanders that live here near logs and rocks.

At the Y intersection, turn left onto the Red Trail (0.5 mile). Walk a gorgeous, sand-dappled dirt path lined by logs. Bird songs abound in spring. It's a little rooty—wear sturdy hiking boots. Ferns, downed trees, and pretty moss complete this quiet, peaceful sanctuary. At the T intersection, go left on the Yellow

Trail (0.9 mile) for about 50 yards before veering to the right toward the Green Trail. (*Note:* If you go straight instead of right, you will reach a "No Trespassing" sign.) The trail is essentially narrow and flat, rooty, and a bit wet—mosquitoes may be a nuisance here in summer. At the next Y intersection, near the bench, take a left toward the green, white, and yellow trail markers (1.3 miles). The shaded, grassy path narrows to dirt and roots. Go past two rings of wooden log "seats" to your right. The Yellow Trail curves prettily into denser woods, with a sheltering dirt bank on the left.

At the T intersection, turn left onto a wide path toward the Blue Trail, via the White Trail (1.5 miles). The lake is on your right, shining bright through the trees. Enjoy an open view of the water at the culvert pipes. At the next four-way intersection, take a left onto the Blue Trail loop (1.7 miles). In early summer, woods create an intimate tunnel along this wide, grassy path, lined with purple-blooming clover and honeysuckle. Cattails wave and dragonflies sail through the air as the woods thicken, and the path becomes muddy and narrow. The noise of a train suddenly breaks the silence: NJ Transit tracks are a few hundred yards to your left, visible through the trees. But you are hidden from view, like a child playing hooky from school. A black-tea-colored stream of acidic water flows to the right; the color is a natural phenomenon caused by a high content of iron and natural vegetative dyes, such as tannin.

The path morphs to soft moss as you walk between the train tracks on the left and the stream and sloping woods on the right. The path curves to the right, but keep straight on the Blue Trail loop, admiring the fern forest. Old train ties line the way, as well as small rocks thrown from the tracks. The Blue Trail skirts big culvert pipes with an impressive ditch to the left. Go up a small hill onto a narrow, elevated pebble-and-dirt path flanked by trees. The stream deepens to black. The Blue Trail curves right, into a fairy glen of dense skunk cabbage and ferns, along rooty terrain. To the left you can see a field through the trees. To the right are grass-covered hummocks, made of material taken from the lake (dredge spoil). With hills and valleys to burrow in, this area is also a good place to spot foxes, snakes, and minks.

A field flanks the left as you come to a clearing and the lake. A bench sits near birdhouse 77. The trail follows the water's edge (3.1 miles), then cuts to the right and heads into the woods. (You can continue straight and walk a short path along the lake, heading to a little peninsula where you may see turtles; then simply double back.) In the woods, walk a narrow path among dirt hummocks. Cross two small footbridges, still on the Blue Trail, which has some ups and downs. Deer are common here—if you encounter one just keep walking; it will likely bound off into the woods. Walk through a clearing and then the trail splits.

Go left to head back on the White Trail. At the T intersection, segue left onto Maggie's Trail at the sign (3.5 miles), a narrow peninsula jutting into the lake. You'll think you're at the Jersey Shore, given the sand (from mining) and the coastal vegetation. Watch for wildlife: moths, dragonflies, turtles, and frogs. Try to spot a river otter. The path ends at a stone memorial bench, with beautiful views of the lake on three sides. Backtrack and go left onto the White Trail at the Y intersection (4.1 miles) at the wooden footbridge. At the next three intersections, keep on the White Trail toward the parking lot. (You may want to take a quick side trip on the orange-blazed Nature Trail, which is on the left before the parking lot; steps lead down and up a steep gully to a pretty view of the lake.)

## DID YOU KNOW?

Bayberry shrubs have blue-gray nutlets, which provide food for tree swallows and yellow-rumped warblers. In the preserve's American beech forest microclimate, the trees trap air and moisture, causing warmer temperatures in winter and cooler ones in summer. McCormack Lake hosts rare water milfoil, mudwort, and sandplain flax.

## OTHER ACTIVITIES

The preserve is adjacent to the Scotts Corner Conservation Area for hiking and bird-watching. Visit the nearby Cranbury Museum at 4 Park Place East. Hike on the Delaware and Raritan Canal in Princeton. While in Princeton, visit the Princeton University Art Museum in McCormick Hall, and stop by Carnegie Lake and watch the university rowing teams practice. Many eateries are on Route 614 and in Plainsboro and Princeton.

## MORE INFORMATION

Trails are open dawn to dusk. The Rush Holt Environmental Education Center is open Tuesday through Saturday, 9 A.M. to 6 P.M.; Sunday, noon to 5 P.M.; closed Mondays and holidays. Winter hours starting in November are Tuesday through Saturday, 9 A.M. to 4 P.M.; Sunday, noon to 4 P.M. 80 Scotts Corner Road, Cranbury, NJ 08512; 609-427-3052; njaudubon.org/sectioncenters/sectionplainsboro/aboutplainsboropreserve.aspx.

# 20

# MILLS RESERVATION

Score dramatic views of New York City on this rocky hike through woods and along the edges of an exposed quarry.

## DIRECTIONS

From Garden State Parkway, take Exit 154 (Clifton). Bear left after the toll booths, following the sign to Route 46, and travel west on Route 46. In 0.9 mile, take the Valley Road exit. At the bottom of the ramp, bear right onto Valley Road north, but immediately turn left, following the sign for Montclair. Bear left again at the sign "U-Turn, Montclair." Proceed south along Valley Road for 1.0 mile and turn right onto Normal Avenue. Cross the railroad tracks, continue uphill for another 0.3 mile, and turn left into the parking area for Mills Reservation at the top of the hill. The gravel lot has space for about twenty cars, and it can fill up quickly in the summer. *GPS coordinates:* 40° 51.295′ N, 74° 12.526′ W.

## TRAIL DESCRIPTION

The parking lot is not well marked, about 50 yards past the intersection of Normal Avenue and Granite Road. If you go past the fenced-in body of water (Cedar Grove Reservoir), you have overshot. Seven trails totaling 6.1 miles (with a lot of overlap if you want to add length) wind through this woodland and wetland delight, part of First Watchung Mountain. Trail blazes are inconsistent in this 157-acre reservation, so take a moment to walk down the wide, graveled, white-blazed Mills Loop Trail to look at the map and trails kiosk on the left. You might want to snap a photo for reference. (*Note:* The posted trail map does not show all the trails in the park and was upside down at time of this writing, with north at the bottom and south at the top.) There are no bathrooms available. Even

**LOCATION**
Cedar Grove

**RATING**
Easy to Moderate

**DISTANCE**
2.5 miles

**ELEVATION GAIN**
300 feet

**ESTIMATED TIME**
1.5 hours

**MAPS**
USGS Orange;
essexcountyparks.org;
cedargrovenj.org

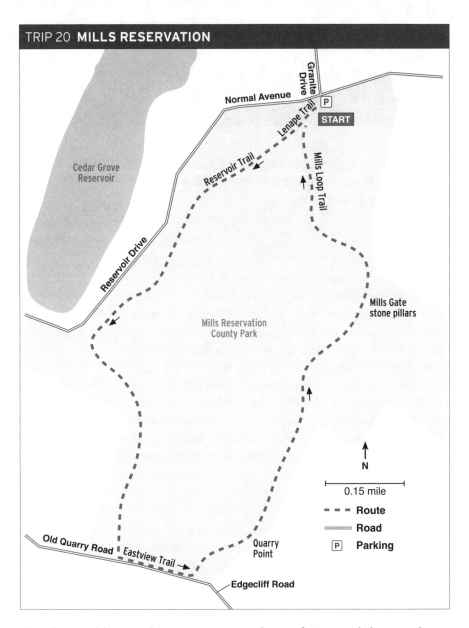

Cedar Grove
Reservoir

Normal Avenue

Granite
Drive

START

Lenape Trail

Reservoir Trail

Reservoir Drive

Mills Loop Trail

Mills Gate
stone pillars

Mills Reservation
County Park

N

0.15 mile

- - - **Route**
——— **Road**
P **Parking**

Old Quarry Road   Eastview Trail

Quarry
Point

Edgecliff Road

though some blazes and intersections are a bit confusing, and the posted map does not show all intersections and trails, don't be afraid to explore. You can always follow Mills Loop Trail—a perimeter path—back to the parking lot.

Start briefly on the yellow-blazed Lenape Trail and take the red-blazed Reservoir Trail south to enjoy excellent New York City views at Quarry Point on the blue-blazed Eastview Trail before winding your way to Mills Loop Trail. Former quarries create steep dropoffs along the exposed Eastview Trail. The highlights here are the views, so visit during leafless season in late fall, winter, or early spring.

Mills Loop Trail is the most popular route (people and dogs), but you'll start on a quieter one: Head for the yellow Lenape Trail marker to the right of the parking lot. The grassy, narrow path invites you into the woods. In season, raspberries greet you on the left. The terrain quickly becomes packed dirt and stone with tricky footing.

In just a few hundred yards, leave the Lenape Trail to veer right on the red-blazed Reservoir Trail. At the next Y intersection, veer right again to stay on Reservoir Trail (pink/purple-blazed Woodland Trail, which is not on the park map, goes to the left). Follow the red blazes downhill. The path is shady and quite rooty. When the path veers to the right, keep straight to remain on the red-blazed trail. At about 0.33 mile, cross a plank footbridge. Note the person-sized flat rocks as you cross them. Go over a ditch. The shady path becomes rockier, with uneven footing over gentle ups and downs. Cross a dry creek bed over more of those eerie flat stones—part of the basalt that forms the Watchung Mountains. Basalt is created when molten lava extruded from Earth's surface cools rapidly.

Four Y intersections are next, and the trail markings are poor. So follow directions closely. At the first Y intersection, go straight and walk through a conveniently cut-out log, near a car-sized boulder on the left. On the right, you can see Cedar Grove Reservoir behind a tall, green fence. Mosses and ferns brighten the forest as you parallel the road. At the second Y intersection, take a left to stay on the red-blazed trail, heading away from the reservoir (0.8 mile). Cross a footbridge and go slightly up into the woods, where another large boulder awaits on the right. At the third Y intersection, veer right. You'll see houses on the right. At the fourth and final Y intersection, turn right as the trail goes slightly downhill and gets rockier. Cross a tiny plank bridge. A large log with carved steps lends a whimsical feel to this part of the hike.

Cross a wide path, where blue-blazed Eastview Trail, yellow-blazed Lenape Trail and red-blazed Reservoir Trail meet (1.2 miles), headed toward a kiosk. After you've oriented yourself, take a right, away from the kiosk, toward the combination of blue and yellow blazes. Reservoir Trail ends here. Almost immediately, turn left and climb a short, steep, basalt hill. (If you go straight, you enter an eight-car parking lot on Old Quarry Road.) Take an interesting walk along an exposed rocky ledge, with the parking lot below. At the Y intersection, turn right—you are still on the blue-blazed Eastview Trail, with a steep dropoff and stellar views of New York City. Watch your footing on the rocks as you enjoy a high ledge-walk around an old quarry. New York City appears through the trees to your right. Go a short distance downhill to an intersection, and take the far right path (still blue) to continue along the bluff. Look below for old quarry formations.

Going uphill is rocky and the footing is tricky, but you are rewarded at the clearing with excellent views of the abandoned quarry and New York City. A few steps farther on is Quarry Point (1.5 miles), a spacious area with a bench where you can sit and look out at New York City and the remains of a concrete

Two stone pillars mark the original 1954 entrance into Mills Reservation.

platform where antiaircraft guns were installed during World War II. The New Jersey Audubon Society hosts its spring hawk count here. You may hear a train whistle mournfully in the distance.

When you are done lingering, walk in front of the bench and turn left to go downhill into the woods. At the bottom of the short slope, take the unnamed pink-and-white-blazed path in the middle that leads straight uphill. (*Note:* These colors do not appear on the park map.) Keep walking on the edge of the bluff on the ledge trail. A small clearing on the right offers the best view yet of New York City, but tread carefully as you gaze—it's a long way down. The path is rocky but flat, with a protective wire fence on the right. Views are spectacular on clear, leafless days and include the colorful houses below in the town of Montclair.

The trail proceeds uphill, following the ledge/bluff, and continues to be very rocky. Go downhill to a three-way intersection with a kiosk to the left (1.8 miles). Take the middle trail (blazed blue). The trail splits around a group of trees but rejoins, so take either split. The flat dirt path loops between the stone pillars of the original Mills Reservation Park (according to the park map, this is the orange-blazed Mills Gate Trail, but there are no discernable orange blazes). The path widens, with a gully to the left, heading toward two unmarked Y intersections At the first unmarked Y intersection, go straight. The cinder path slopes gently downhill. Lovely houses stand on posted property to the right. Keep straight on the cinder path at the second Y intersection. At the T intersection, turn right onto a gravel path (white-blazed Mills Loop Trail, 2.1 miles), and you are almost at the parking lot.

## DID YOU KNOW?

The Lenape word *watchung* means "high hill." Cedar Grove resident Arthur Wynne invented the first crossword puzzle (called "word-cross") in 1913. Famous residents of Montclair include director Steven Spielberg (who lived there from ages 5 to 10), musician/songwriter Joe Walsh, astronaut Buzz Aldrin, late-night host and comedian Stephen Colbert, and makeup artist Bobbi Brown.

## OTHER ACTIVITIES

Hike the easy-to-challenging trails of Cedar Grove's Hilltop Reservation, a 284-acre preserve with a high point of 284 feet. Spend a weekend in Montclair (designated a Climate Showcase Community by the EPA) exploring the art museum and art galleries, live theater, the Yogi Berra Museum & Learning Center (he lived in Montclair for more than 50 years), the 12-acre Van Vleck House & Gardens, and the MLK Peace Garden. There's also a 33-building walking tour through the Historic District.

## MORE INFORMATION

Essex County Department of Parks, Recreation and Cultural Affairs, 115 Clifton Avenue, Newark, NJ 07104; 973-268-3500; essexcountyparks.org/parks/mills-reservation.

# 21

# LENAPE PARK

A mix of urban and rural landscapes—with cozy woods concealing a nearby shopping mall—makes a perfect fit for families with small children and showcases New Jersey's captivating diversity.

**LOCATION**
Cranford

**RATING**
Easy

**DISTANCE**
4.3 miles

**ELEVATION GAIN**
300 feet

**ESTIMATED TIME**
2 hours

**MAPS**
USGS Roselle;
ucnj.org/parks-recreation/
paths-trails-greenways/
lenape

## DIRECTIONS

Take Garden State Parkway to Exit 11, toward Woodbridge; merge onto Garden State Parkway North. Take Exit 136 toward Linden/Roselle/Winfield Park. Keep left to take the ramp toward Cranford/Cranford Shopping District. Turn left onto Centennial Avenue (County Highway 615). After 1.27 miles, turn left onto North Avenue East (NJ 28). Take the first right onto Springfield Avenue (County Highway 615). Turn right onto Kenilworth Boulevard (County Highway 509). Turn left onto County Park Drive, just past Nomahegan Road. In 0.07 mile Lenape Park is on the right. The lot has space for about 50 cars. *GPS coordinates: 40° 40.440′ N, 74° 18.913′ W.*

## TRAIL DESCRIPTION

Lenape Park is intriguing because of its blend of urban and natural settings and also because its trails connect to three other local parks—Nomahegan, Echo Lake, and Black Brook—via the Rahway River Parkway/Greenway. Unfortunately, these connecting trails are not especially well marked.

The entrance to Lenape Park has a kiosk with a map from 1999 (which is not very good for hiking) and an excellent guide to birds by the Friends of Lenape Park. A chemical toilet is near a small, closed-up building. The trails have no names or colors, but not to worry: There is only one main trail, with several optional extensions. Note that Nomahegan Park is right across nearby Kenilworth

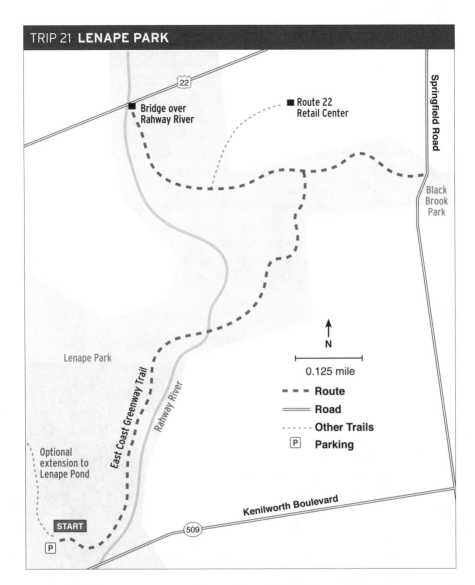

Boulevard, if you care to extend your hike. You'll also approach an entrance to Black Brook Park. Some areas are exposed to sun. Because of the many birds and wildflowers, spring and summer are good times to hike these 400 acres of wetlands, ponds, rivers, creeks, meadows, and forests.

Facing Kenilworth Boulevard, ignore the wide, paved berm to your right (unless you want just a one-mile round-trip hike to Lenape Pond). Instead, take the mowed-grass path to the left that winds around a split rail fence. A gap in a metal fence opens onto a narrow path surrounded by tall phlox with bright purple flowers; on the left is a stream from the Rahway River. The path leads to a wide concrete dike, with Kenilworth Bridge and the Rahway River to your right. It's such fun walking across the dike to the woods beyond. But if you're afraid of heights, simply cross Kenilworth Bridge instead and make your way back to the river.

Take a left at the end of the dike, and follow the barely visible path to the right as it winds slightly uphill over remnants of a stone road, ending in a wide mowed area. After stopping to admire the cattails along the river, go left. The grass path enters the woods and joins the main asphalt trail (be sure to walk on the right as a courtesy to bicyclists). There is a charming red bridge to your right.

Young woods surround you. A stream is on the right. The paved trail is pleasantly elevated. Orange-and-green mile markers (East Coast Greenway markers) plot your journey every quarter-mile.

At about 0.75 mile, learn more about the large sweet gum tree on the right via a sign with a cell phone QR code. Warehouses are on the right, and a grassy clearing pops up on the left. The trail divides at a split rail fence; go left. Enter the woods at a wire fence on the right—bags for dog waste are provided by the park here. On your left is a mounted construction hat, a tribute to Segundo Padilla, a worker who died on-site.

Crossing Rahway River via a concrete dike is a fun start to this hike, a blend of urban and natural.

The trail slopes downhill. Cross a red bridge, admiring the stream below. A sign on an American sycamore tree sports another cell phone QR code. A little path to the left of the sycamore leads to the Model Railroad Club building—take a few minutes to explore and see the model trains (1.4 miles). Back on the main trail, note the contrast of the cattails and ferns to the right with the industrial buildings to the left. Urban and natural, side by side—that is New Jersey!

Marsh, ferns, and cattails continue to the right. A split rail fence hugs the trail, which ends at two-lane Springfield Road in Kenilworth (1.6 miles), with a sandwich bar across the street. Across the street to your right is Black Brook Park.

Turn around and go back the way you came, looking for groundhogs and rabbits. Just before you reach the red bridge again, take an urban side adventure on the dirt path to the right (2.0 miles). Go up a small hill and turn left. To the right is a huge parking lot, and the sloping woods are to your left. The trail narrows and widens through a forest of phlox. A series of telephone wires begin here, with more warehouses to the right, yet the woods are deep to your left. Soon it's apparent you are walking beside a mall. You could step over the low fence and go shopping if you wished. The trail soon ends at Highway 22 East (2.5 miles). Take the narrow path to the left and stop at the "Welcome to the Township of Union, Est. 1667" sign to admire the bridge over the Rahway River. Retrace your steps to the red bridge (3.0 miles).

As you pass the Segundo Padilla memorial, look for a wooded path to the right. This is one of several dirt paths that parallel and intersect the paved main path and can be explored with confidence and safety because they all end up on the paved trail.

The paved trail intersects the mowed-grass path. At the end of the mowed path, turn right through the field. Have fun crossing the dike again. Turn right off the dike and walk to the parking lot (4.3 miles).

*Optional one-mile extension*: Cross the parking lot and continue for 0.5 mile on the unshaded, raised, paved berm toward beautiful Lenape Pond. Note the sign on the right for Project Bluebird, a grassland area set aside in 2002 as a nesting site for eastern bluebirds. Nest boxes provide safe nesting sites, where you can watch the birds raising their young from early April to July. Near dusk, the air is filled with bird sounds. Admire the tiny pond and stream to your left, and watch the bunnies gambol on the green slopes that line the elevated path. A kiosk on the left identifies birds. There's no shade here, so wear a hat or use sun protection. Lenape Pond is to the right of kiosk 4. To the left is Nomahegan Drive (separate from Nomahegan Road).

Walk around the pond, looking for turtles, and note a giant butterfly bush, teeming with life: spiders, butterflies, and bees. Around dusk is a wonderful time to wander here and spy a multitude of mammals (rabbit, woodchuck, muskrat, deer, red fox, and mink). When you are ready, backtrack to your car.

## DID YOU KNOW?

The Friends of Lenape Park hosts an annual Audubon World Series of Birding weekend at Lenape and once recorded 83 different species. The U.S. Army Corps of Engineers installed the concrete dams and berms in the late 1970s as part of a massive flood control project.

## OTHER ACTIVITIES

Visit the charming towns of Cranford, Kenilworth, Mountainside, and Westfield. Also try some of the 36 parks in Union County: scenic Nomahegan, next door; large, multiuse Warinanco; friendly little Briant; Echo Lake, with a dog park, ponds, and dams; and Unami, which offers multiuse trails. Don't forget the Rahway River Parkway/Greenway, part of the East Coast Greenway, which links 25 cities from Maine to Florida (see page 119 and rahwayriverparkway.org).

## MORE INFORMATION

No posted hours. Union County Department of Parks and Recreation, 10 Elizabethtown Plaza, Elizabeth, NJ 07207; 908-527-4000; ucnj.org/parks-recreation.

## EAST COAST GREENWAY

The East Coast Greenway (ECG) links 25 major cities along the eastern seaboard, between Calais, Maine, and Key West, Florida. The ECG's spine will be 3,000 miles long when complete, accompanied by 2,000 miles of alternate routes that link in key cities, towns, and areas of natural beauty. As an urban, shared-use trail, the ECG is right at home in New Jersey, the most densely populated state in the United States.

The New Jersey route is bound on either side by rivers and stretches 98 miles between Pennsylvania and New York. At the northern end in Jersey City, a ferry across the Hudson River carries you to New York City. At the southern end in Trenton, the pedestrian-friendly Calhoun Street Bridge deposits you in Morrisville, Pennsylvania. The rest of the ECG in New Jersey passes through the state's two largest cities, Newark and Jersey City, as well as Trenton, New Brunswick, and a surprising variety of rural landscapes. In fact, there are 45.6 miles of protected greenway in New Jersey, and 54 percent are traffic-free, in large part due to the Delaware and Raritan Canal (see page 40). The canal intersects the ECG for 35.7 miles and is the greenway's longest completed trail.

Other designated ECG trails in New Jersey include portions of the Hudson River Waterfront Walkway in Jersey City (see Trip 24), Lenape Park (Trip 21), Newark Riverfront Trail, Roosevelt Park in Edison, Merrill Park Path in Middlesex County, and Johnson Park Path in Piscataway.

The ECG, spearheaded by the Rhode Island-based East Coast Greenway Alliance, is a testament to collaboration, shared vision, and cooperation among volunteers and officials at the local, state, and national levels. In 1991, eight cyclists met in a room in New York City to plot the vision. In the summer of 1992, ten dedicated cyclists took a month to explore the route from Boston to Washington, D.C., garnering media attention and endorsements from local and state officials. In 1995, the East Coast Greenway name and logo were trademarked. (Consistent signage is still being placed today.) In 1997, the Delaware and Raritan Canal in New Jersey became the first local trail segment to be mapped for public use. In 2000, the East Coast Greenway Alliance partnered with Amtrak. (Since the route generally follows the Amtrak East Coast corridor, many trailheads are accessible by public transportation. In New Jersey, contact

East Coast

Greenway®
ALLIANCE

NJ Transit for details, njtransit.com.) In 2005, cyclists Jenny and Wil Hylton traveled the entire ECG without sponsorship, which garnered tremendous national publicity for the greenway. The project steamrolled, and more funding, partners, and segments were added. Today, tens of millions of dollars in state and federal funds go toward closing key gaps in the ECG.

In New Jersey alone, many volunteers and more than 30 partners support the trail, including the Outdoor Club of South Jersey, the Adirondack Mountain Club (North Jersey Chapter), Recreational Equipment, Inc. (REI), and the New Jersey Transportation Planning Authority and the New Jersey departments of environmental protection and transportation. Honor their efforts and hike it today.

The East Coast Greenway Alliance in Wakefield, Rhode Island, heads the project with partners at the local, state, and national levels. Check greenway.org to find updates, maps, and directions for navigating the ECG.

# 22

# CHEESEQUAKE STATE PARK

Walk through a hardwood forest and Pine Barrens and over freshwater streams. Cross an Atlantic white cedar swamp on boardwalks. Visit the excellent interpretive center.

## DIRECTIONS

From north or south, take Garden State Parkway to Exit 120 and make a right at the end of the exit ramp onto Matawan Road. Follow Matawan Road to the first traffic light and turn right onto Morristown Road. At the next light, make a right onto Gordon Road. The parking lot on your left holds 30-plus cars. *GPS coordinates:* 40° 26.200′ N, 74° 15.926′ W.

## TRAIL DESCRIPTION

Cheesequake State Park comprises 363 acres of varied hiking environments, from a coastal salt marsh habitat to upland forests, and it is just minutes from Garden State Parkway. You'll see vegetation representative of both southern and northern New Jersey. Cheesequake typifies the charm of so many of the state's parks, quickly winding from urban to suburban to rural.

Because of the well-marked trails, this is a good beginner's hike, with one caution: There are lots of steps. Fortunately, there are also lots of benches. You'll follow the Green Trail to the park's highlight: an Atlantic white cedar swamp, where great horned owls live. Look for nature markers near sweetbay magnolias, swamp azaleas, and sphagnum moss. Every season brings visual delights, but avoid hot weather when the bugs thrive (generally May to October).

Your first stop is the park office, to the right of the admissions tollbooth, which provides flush toilets and maps. Cheesequake is part of the New Jersey Coastal Heritage

**LOCATION**
Matawan

**RATING**
Moderate

**DISTANCE**
3.3 miles

**ELEVATION GAIN**
370 feet

**ESTIMATED TIME**
2 hours

**MAPS**
USGS South Amboy; nj.gov/dep/ parksandforests/

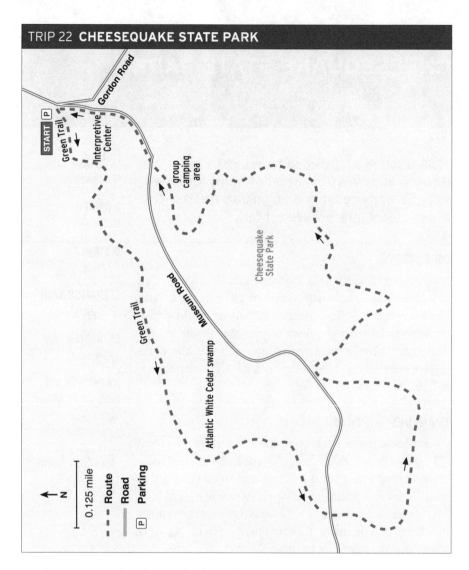

Trail (see page 170). Take a right from the parking lot, and almost immediately the paved trailhead lot appears on your left. All five color-coded trails leave from here; you can even string together different loops for a longer hike. A water fountain is on one side of the lot, and there's a talking kiosk at the other.

Walk beneath the trailhead arch, and head toward the Green Trail marker on the wide, shaded dirt path, which is sure to contain a dog or two. Right away the trail forks; turn left to follow the green blazes. A dramatic stepped boardwalk leads down through oak, sassafras, and sweet pepperbush. Turn left at the bottom, toward the shared Red, Green, and Blue trails, ignoring the Yellow Trail entrance to the right. You are headed toward the not-to-be-missed interpretive center (listed as "Nature Center" on the map). Cross a bridge over freshwater wetlands and climb up wooden steps on a long and rooty dirt path. At the top of the hill to your left are dozens of birdhouses. This is the interpretive center's backyard. Inside the center, find live turtles, taxidermy, bones, and wonderful wall displays that explain cedar swamps, freshwater and saltwater wetlands, second-growth forests, and more. An auditorium hosts educational programs for grades K–12.

At the interpretive center, turn right on the combination Blue, Green, and Red trails, following the split rail fence. Read the educational signs about plants and trees. The dirt path is rooty but flat and winds charmingly through the forest, with a sloping hill to your right. At about 0.2 mile, go slightly downhill through a lovely fern-filled hollow. Walk along a slight ridge, with gentle ups and downs, surrounded by sheep laurel shrubs that bloom in June and July. (*Caution:* Sheep laurel is toxic if eaten.) The trail opens up to a meadow vista, which you can appreciate from the cool, secluded woods. Turn left to go downhill (no trail markers here), over steps and a long boardwalk that covers a seasonally wet area. Take a seat on one of the three benches to admire the deep-green views.

At 0.3 mile, enjoy 42 steps up a hill to an intersection where you turn left onto the Green Trail. Walk among slender young trees on a path that winds like a circling cat. At the next intersection, veer right to stay on the Green Trail, gazing into the huge gully on your left (at the 0.5-mile marker). Descend steps and observe the pitch pines at the nature marker. These trees, a hallmark of the Pine Barrens, are ambiguous. Their thick bark allows them to survive forest fires, yet intense heat is necessary for the cones to open and release their seeds. Cross a wooden bridge over a stream, and then trek up and down rooty hills surrounded by blueberry bushes. Walk in the shade, up steps, past a beautifully shaped sassafras tree with a nature marker at 0.6 mile. Cross the gravel Perrine Road and turn right on the tree-lined Green Trail. Watch out for poison ivy as you admire the lovely hollow and field visible through the woods to the right.

You are walking through what was once a thriving Atlantic white cedar swamp. The swamp has transitioned into wetlands with red maple, birch, and sweet pepperbush. After ascending a slight hill, turn left to stay on the Green Trail at the fork (follow the arrow). Down the hill, a field opens up to the right before more steps down to a long boardwalk. Walk slowly through an immense cedar swamp, noting the copper waters gleaming against the emerald-green grasses and ferns. Easily the trail's highlight, the swamp hosts many varieties of flowers, goldenrods, red-berried American hollies, and eastern red cedars. Sit on a bench and meditate on the artistic, gigantic root balls of overturned trees. Hurricane Sandy in October 2012 closed this section for a year. You'll wonder where the dinosaurs are in this *Jurassic Park*–like setting. The boardwalk zigzags, interspersed with small areas of rooty ground, until finally a dirt path leads uphill and then down.

At 1.3 miles, go under a trail arch and cross the wide dirt Museum Road (turn left on Museum if you want to head back.) Veer left onto the Green Trail. Enjoy the flat dirt trail with no roots as you walk through a forest of eastern white

Dozens of birdhouses behind the interpretive center invite many species, from cardinals to goldfinch.

pines. (White sand occasionally replaces the dirt.) The narrow path takes you up a hill and steps. At 1.6 miles, cross a series of three bridges, watching for darting chipmunks and butterflies. The path is flat and wide, then slopes downhill, banked by green moss and ghostly Indian pipes. At 2.1 miles, veer right to stay on the Green Trail, with a park road to your left. Note the verdant marsh and ferns. Quite soon, take a right at a fork. The area is sometimes muddy, but well-placed logs allow for safe crossing. You'll quickly reach a 100-year-old oak felled by Hurricane Sandy, with hillocks on the right adding drama. Traverse another boardwalk and bridge. At the 2.4-mile marker, turn left to stay on the Green Trail. The hillocks and marsh render the tiny, winding path secluded yet oddly comforting. An observation platform juts over the water. Linger here to watch dragonflies, hear frogs, and appreciate the river birches.

Continue on the boardwalk, climbing steep steps at about 2.6 miles. Then head downhill to a large broken tree and a charming copper-colored stream to the left. Fluffy green grass flanks the path, which goes over steps and a bridge.

Note the smooth brown pebbles on the sandbar. Pass a stand of American beeches, and then go under a trail arch to arrive at Group Campsite East, part of the Gordon Field Group Campgrounds, where you can use the flush toilets and the picnic tables (2.7 miles). Turn left onto the paved campground road. Just past the campsite, turn right as the Green and Red trails arch onto a rooty path into the woods. A series of ups and downs ends at another trail arch, where you turn right onto paved Museum Road (3.1 miles). Note the black birch tree at the nature marker before following Museum Road back to the parking lot.

## DID YOU KNOW?

Migratory hawks and waterfowl, including snowy egrets, black ducks, and northern harriers, flock here in the fall. In spring and summer, ospreys live on the park's nesting platforms. Perrine Pond on the Blue Trail has a bird blind for viewing.

## OTHER ACTIVITIES

Canoers and kayakers will enjoy Cheesequake Creek's self-guided water trail, and more water-related activities can be found at Old Bridge Waterfront Park. Dining is available on Routes 34 and 516, as well as in the tiny town of Old Bridge Township. Drive a race car at Raceway Park, a fabled American drag strip in Englishtown. Search for the foundations of a Cold War Nike missile site in a pine forest on Jake Brown Road, heading west off US 9 South.

## MORE INFORMATION

Seasonal fees from Memorial Day weekend through Labor Day. Weekdays: $5 New Jersey residents, $10 nonresidents. Weekends and holidays: $10 New Jersey residents, $20 nonresidents. Motorcycles: $5 New Jersey residents, $10 nonresidents. Open 8 A.M. to 6 P.M. Mailing address: Cheesequake State Park, 300 Gordon Road, Matawan, NJ 07747; 732-566-2161; state.nj.us/dep/parksandforests/parks/cheesequake.html.

# 23

# RAMAPO MOUNTAIN STATE FOREST

More than 20 miles of trails spiderweb this 4,269-acre park, providing something for everyone: giant boulders, lakes, castle ruins, and views of New York City.

## DIRECTIONS

Take Exit 57 off I-287. Turn left off the exit at the light onto West Oakland Avenue. Go 0.5 mile on West Oakland Avenue (which becomes Skyline Drive, passing under I-287) and make a quick left into a gravel parking lot at the brown wooden park sign. The lot has room for 30 to 40 cars. *GPS coordinates:* 41° 01.951′ N, 74° 15.119′ W.

**Public Transportation:** From the Port Authority Bus Terminal in Manhattan (operated by the Port Authority of New York and New Jersey), take NJ Transit bus 197 to Ringwood Avenue at Burnside Place in Wanaque. Walk to Back Beach Park, traveling east on Burnside Place, then to Decker Road and to Fourth Avenue (15 minutes, 0.8 mile).

## TRAIL DESCRIPTION

Where to start with this delicious 4,269-acre hunk of woods that borders the Ramapo Mountain Reservation? A flat 3-mile stroll around sparkling, island-dotted Ramapo Lake? A rugged trek on red-blazed Cannonball Trail to cross the footbridge over I-287? A short journey to the "balanced boulder" on purple-blazed Tamarack Trail? Those are all great options, but on this hike, you'll take blue-blazed MacEvoy Trail to white-blazed Castle Point Trail for dramatic and rocky views of the lakes and mountains, and explore the romantic ruins of Van Slyke Castle. Autumn brings fiery color to the leaves; spring astonishes with flowers. Winter makes footing tricky on the rocks, but the unobstructed views are spectacular. Cool woods refresh in summer.

**LOCATION**
Oakland

**RATING**
Strenuous

**DISTANCE**
5.4 miles

**ELEVATION GAIN**
650 feet

**ESTIMATED TIME**
3 hours

**MAPS**
USGS Wanaque; state.nj.us/dep/parksandforests/; nynjtc.org; *North Jersey Trails Map*, Eleventh Edition, New York-New Jersey Trail Conference

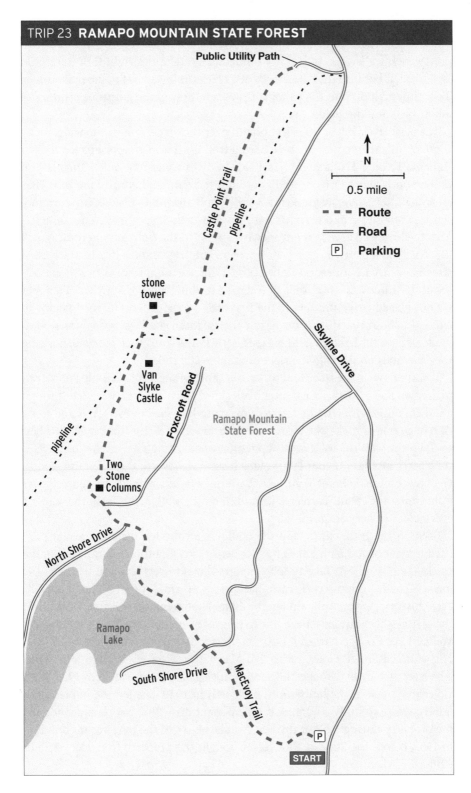

TRIP 23 **RAMAPO MOUNTAIN STATE FOREST**

Public Utility Path

Castle Point Trail

pipeline

N

0.5 mile

- - - **Route**
——— **Road**
P **Parking**

stone
tower

Van
Slyke
Castle

Foxcroft Road

pipeline

Ramapo Mountain
State Forest

Skyline Drive

Two
Stone
Columns

North Shore Drive

Ramapo
Lake

South Shore Drive

MacEvoy Trail

P

START

From the gravel parking lot, head toward the two chemical toilets and a trail kiosk, where the blue-blazed MacEvoy Trail starts. The trail goes between two pretty rock walls. The trail forks immediately; take the right fork uphill; do *not* turn left because that dead-ends at a creek. Enjoy a brief boulder scramble. Take time to look into the valley on your left, noting the gorgeous outlines of an off-trail boulder field.

The path levels out as your feet pound over rock face. Follow the wide, rocky route uphill, keeping on the blue-blazed trail until it intersects a paved road at Ramapo Lake, a 120-acre human-made body of water (0.7 mile). Turn left on paved South Shore Drive to walk out onto the dam and admire the lake. (For an easier alternative, just take the 3-mile stroll around the lake.) Turn around, retrace your steps, and turn left onto paved North Shore Drive. The route follows the lovely lake, with many viewing spots. To the right are interesting rock gardens. You'll pass a large private estate on your right, and a dry, boulder-filled streambed. In 1.1 miles, go right at the Y intersection, toward two stone columns. Pass between them on a gravel road (technically, the MacEvoy Trail, but it's not blazed here) and ignore the first trail on the left as the road begins to curve. In about 50 yards, at the next Y intersection, you'll see a big brown-and-white sign on the left for white-blazed Castle Point Trail. Turn left here, noticing the enormous boulders to the right of the sign (1.2 miles).

You are now on the steep and rocky, but short, white-blazed Castle Point Trail to the Van Slyke Castle ruins. After a brief level patch, the trail veers left through another rugged climb up to a narrow dirt path hemmed in by shrubs and trees. At a huge pile of rocks and trees, veer left and scramble up. Take one more hop to the right onto the rock outcropping for a rewarding view of the forest. Two rock outcroppings on your left provide beautiful views of the lakes and woods. Get back on Castle Point Trail, go left around a boulder, and hoist yourself over a charming rock wall. Turn around and sit on the wall, drinking in the scenery, spectacular in fiery autumn.

Back on the trail, climb atop the boulders on the left for an excellent panoramic vista of Ramapo Lake and Stephens Lake. Continue up the trail to the castle site (1.4 miles). Take time to explore the old fireplaces and mantels. The former "castle," now an eerie ruin that springs up amid the trails, has a complicated history. As you walk among the dilapidated remains, imagine what life in the early 1900s must have been like in this mansion built by Wall Street tycoon William Porter, who named it Foxcroft. Porter died in a traffic accident in 1911. His widow, Ruth A. Coles, remarried Manhattan attorney Warren Van Slyke, who later died from complications following a gallstone operation in 1925. Ruth Coles remained in the house until her death in 1940. She left the home to her family, who promptly sold it. A couple bought it in 1942 but then abandoned the property during a bitter divorce. Vandals burned the long-vacant building in 1959, before the State of New Jersey bought the property from the estate of Clifford F. MacEvoy.

The water tower on the Van Slyke Castle grounds. Large portions of the castle, including a swimming pool, chimney, furnace, and crumbling stone walls, can still be explored today.

Keep to the left of the ruins, and at the Y intersection, go left on white-blazed Castle Point Trail. Pass a concrete structure that was once a swimming pool. As the trail levels out, note the outcropping of rocks on the left with gorgeous views of the lake. Climb uphill now, over rocks and through a boulder field, to a stone tower (1.7 miles) that used to hold the mansion's water cistern; metal pipes still lead from it. Walk around the tower and peer in before heading back to Castle Point Trail and going north

The uphill trek on Castle Point Trail heading north is rocky. Climb the outcropping to the left for good views of the forest and lake. Go down a rugged hill. The trail intersects with a mowed public utility path (2.7 miles).

With a detailed topographic map, you can explore this area further. This hike ends at the public utility path. Turn around and go back the way you came, past the tower and castle, and over the stone wall, following white-blazed Castle Point Trail all the way downhill. Once down, turn right onto the gravel path at the intersection, pass between the stone pillars, then turn left onto North Shore Drive. At the intersection of North Shore and South Shore drives, go left, then take a quick right onto blue-blazed MacEvoy Trail. At the Y intersection, go right to stay on the blue-blazed trail back to parking lot.

## DID YOU KNOW?

The Ramapough Mountain Indians are descended from the Lenni-Lenape. Several thousand still live in New Jersey. The Ramapough Lenape Nation was recognized in 1980 by the State of New Jersey but has never been federally recognized. Two movies have been made about the Ramapough: *Mann v. Ford* (2011), which documents the tribe's lawsuit against Ford Motor Company for a toxic waste landfill located near affordable housing for tribal members, and *American Native* (2013), which details the Ramapough Lenape Nation's efforts to gain federal recognition.

## OTHER ACTIVITIES

Go south (turn right out of the parking lot) on Skyline Drive (Lakeside Avenue) to Pompton Lakes for both food and ice cream at the Ice Cream Station. About 5 miles away are Ringwood State Park (visit Ringwood Manor) and New Jersey Botanical Garden in Ringwood. Within 10 miles are the 107-acre freshwater wetlands at the Celery Farm in Allendale, administered by the Fyke Nature Association, and the 81-acre wildlife sanctuary at J.A. McFaul Environmental Center in Wyckoff.

## MORE INFORMATION

Open sunrise to sunset. Mailing address: c/o Ringwood State Park, 1304 Sloatsburg Road, Ringwood, NJ 07456-1799; 973-962-7031; state.nj.us/dep/parksandforests/parks/ramapo.html.

# 24

# LIBERTY STATE PARK

Enjoy an easy-to-access trail with trees, flowers, birds, green grass, and the immense Hudson River, all in the lap of New York City.

## DIRECTIONS

Take the New Jersey Turnpike to Exit 14B toward Liberty State Park/Jersey City. Bear left toward Liberty State Park and Science Center/Port Liberte. In about 100 feet, turn left onto Bayview Avenue, travel 0.25 mile, enter a roundabout, and take the first exit of the roundabout to Morris Pesin Drive. Park at the end of the road in the clearly signed lot on the right, with space for about 100 cars. *GPS coordinates: 40° 41.673′ N, 74° 03.528′ W.*

**Public Transportation:** *By rail:* NJ Transit's Hudson-Bergen Light Rail stops at the Liberty State Park Station near the Liberty Science Center, which is on the north end of the park (park office is on the south end). Walk five minutes to the Liberty Science Center, go through the parking lot, and take a left on Phillips Street toward the water and path.

*By water:* From the North Cove Marina, directly in front of the World Financial Center in New York City, take the Liberty Landing Ferry to the Liberty Landing Marina. Walk east, away from the marina, toward the Central Railroad of New Jersey Terminal, and walk to any section of the waterfront to get on the Hudson River Waterfront Walkway.

## TRAIL DESCRIPTION

Start in the park office at 200 Morris Pesin Drive and pick up a map and other information, such as ferry schedules for Ellis and Liberty islands, Battery Park, and Manhattan. A map is not strictly necessary for directions but lets you know what landmarks you're

**LOCATION**
Jersey City

**RATING**
Easy

**DISTANCE**
5.2 miles

**ELEVATION GAIN**
20 feet

**ESTIMATED TIME**
2 hours

**MAPS**
USGS Jersey City; state.nj.us/dep/ parksandforests/

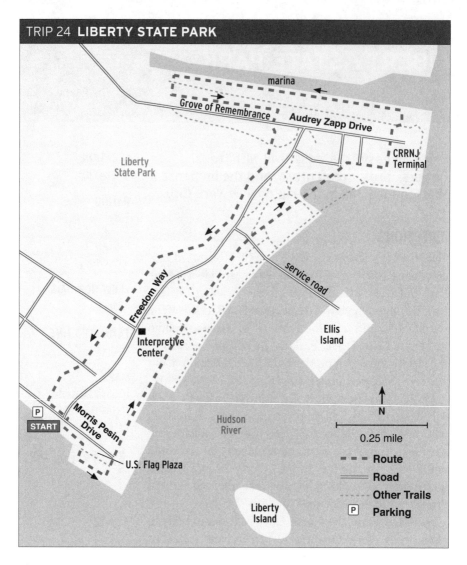

marina

Grove of Remembrance

Audrey Zapp Drive

CRRNJ Terminal

Liberty State Park

service road

Freedom Way

Interpretive Center

Ellis Island

Morris Pesin Drive

P

START

Hudson River

N

U.S. Flag Plaza

0.25 mile

Liberty Island

- - - Route
—— Road
········· Other Trails
P Parking

observing. On this hike, you follow the red-hexagonal-tiled path of the Hudson River Waterfront Walkway toward the Statue of Liberty, turn left at Liberty Landing Marina, and make your way back along any of the footpaths that cut through the green. Liberty State Park is a verdant, flower-and-tree-filled, 1,212-acre space, surrounded by water on three sides. You will enjoy the following south-to-north route, which takes you past Liberty Island, Ellis Island, the Central Railroad of New Jersey (CRRNJ) Terminal, the 9/11 memorial, Liberty Landing Marina, the Grove of Remembrance, Christopher Columbus Plaza, and the Liberty State Park Nature Interpretive Center. Damage from Hurricane Sandy in 2012 closed the center, but a nature walk, tidal marsh, and pier are still there, all peaceful and pleasantly surprising in this urban setting. You can turn around at any time for a shorter stroll.

In spring, the park is alive with cultivated flowers and blooming trees. Summer brings crowds, concessions, festivals, fireworks, and activity. Fall slows into a quiet and serene winter, with many varieties of ducks and birds.

From the park office, make your way through U.S. Flag Plaza to the path along the water (New York Harbor and the Hudson River), and head north (away from the park office) for an up-close-and-personal sighting of the Statue of Liberty. This 2-mile promenade is beautiful, with excellent city views. Walk toward New York City, with Lady Liberty on your right, perched atop Liberty Island. (You can take a ferry to Liberty and Ellis islands from the CRRNJ Terminal.) Look closely at the rocks along the water; you may spot a sunning harbor seal. The Verrazano-Narrows Bridge, which connects Staten Island and Brooklyn, shines in the distance.

On a park sign, read about Morris Pesin. Frustrated with a three-hour trip by car and ferry to visit Liberty Island, Pesin made a well-publicized eight-minute canoe trip from Jersey City to Liberty Island in 1958. This trip sparked Pesin's eighteen-year crusade to create an urban state park that offered easier access to the Statue of Liberty. On June 14, 1976, his dream came true.

Admire the grandeur of the next famous sight: the Renaissance revivalist immigration station perched atop the 27-acre Ellis Island in the harbor. Twelve

Liberty State Park in spring brings daffodils, tulips, and stunning views of the New York City skyline.

million immigrants passed through Ellis Island. Two-thirds of them landed at the CRRNJ Terminal, where trains took them to their destiny. Ferries to Ellis Island run daily, except for December 25. For a good view of Ellis Island, pause at the bridge that runs to the island (1.3 miles). You can't hike the bridge; it's only for authorized personnel. But you can always take the ferry. Interestingly, 90 percent of the island is in New Jersey; the other 10 percent belongs to New York, or so ruled the U.S. Supreme Court in 1998. Since 100 percent is federal property, state ownership is merely a point of pride. When you visit, try to discover which state "owns" which part.

Sightseeing and news helicopters buzz through the sky as you enjoy the spring tulips and daffodils; nascent tree blooms soften the horizon. Head to the Victorian-style CRRNJ Terminal and enter through the wide doors. Here, you can buy ferry tickets to the Statue of Liberty and Ellis Island. Bathrooms and snack shops are available, as well as information on the terminal's history. Use peaked in 1929 (21 million passengers), but times changed, and the terminal ceased railroad operations on April 30, 1967.

The "Empty Sky" 9/11 monument is next on the walkway (2.2 miles). This is New Jersey's official memorial to honor the 749 state residents who died in the September 11, 2001, attacks. The two 30-foot tall, 210-foot-long structures are stunning. Walk the 12-foot-long alley of bluestone with the names of the deceased etched in its walls. You are also allowed to take a rubbing with pencil and paper.

Head past the water fountain on the left and you are at Liberty Landing Marina (2.6 miles), with its gorgeous boats and views of terraced apartments across the water in Jersey City. There are several restaurants near the marina. In spring, the cherry trees are beautiful. Pass the Marine Center building on the left; the path changes to black asphalt, then ends. Go left and walk through the parking lot for boats, cross the cobblestone road, and turn left onto the paved path (3.1 miles). You'll walk through the park's greenery back toward the park office.

Explore the landscaped Grove of Remembrance on your right, but watch out for cyclists. Turn right on the path with the one-way sign, across from the Marine Center building. Then turn left and go through circular Millennium Park. Cross two paved roads and turn right on the second path after the road. In spring, the pine trees are yellow with pollen. Go left at the Y intersection toward Christopher Columbus Plaza. Playgrounds and restrooms appear. Go right at the Y intersection, carefully cross road that is open to traffic, and pass the bridge to Ellis Island (4.0 miles). This lovely green section of the park is called the "Green Ring" (4.4 miles). Flags from many nations line Freedom Way to the right.

Bear left toward a fitness station and climb the hill to the right for benches if you need a rest.

Don't miss the interpretive center on the left (4.6 miles). Although the building is closed courtesy of Hurricane Sandy, the nature walk is lovely. Stroll on the dock stretching across the tidal pond; hear the *konk-a-ree* of the red-winged blackbird and the "trickling" song of the marsh wren. Lady Liberty peeks through the reeds.

When you leave, note the Daily News building to the right as you head toward the Verrazano-Narrows Bridge and the park office.

## DID YOU KNOW?

The waterfront path is part of a longer route: the official Hudson River Waterfront Walkway. When complete, the walkway will cover 40 miles (18.4 as the crow flies) and span nine New Jersey municipalities, from the George Washington Bridge in Fort Lee to the Bayonne Bridge in Bayonne. For updates and access points, visit hudsonriverwaterfront.org.

## OTHER ACTIVITIES

Take a two-hour kayak ecotour of the Hudson River Estuary; call 201-915-3400, extension 202, for details. Explore the Liberty Science Center at the north end of the park, where you can enjoy films, laser shows, the biggest planetarium in the Western Hemisphere, and much more. Chow down at the reasonably priced Liberty Park Diner on Morris Pesin Drive. Visit Boxwood Hall, an American Revolution site, in nearby Elizabeth (908-282-7617). And there's always the ferry into Manhattan.

## MORE INFORMATION

Open daily from 6 A.M. to 10 P.M. The park is partially ADA accessible. Call the park office for details. Liberty State Park administration office: 200 Morris Pesin Drive, Jersey City, NJ 07305; 201-915-3400; state.nj.us/dep/parksandforests/parks/liberty.html.

# JERSEY SHORE

The Jersey Shore region, part of the Atlantic Coastal Plain, is home to pinelands, beaches, and marshes. Also known as the Outer Coastal Plain, here the soils are nutrient-poor compared with the fertile, loamy earth of the Inner Coastal Plain, which earns New Jersey its nickname of the Garden State. But the Shore's sandy soil supports many rare plant species, such as yellow-flowered bog asphodel, white milkweed, seaside buttercup, and sphagnum moss, and also provides mineral riches. The pure quartz sand was once heavily used for glassmaking and the finer silica sand for producing cosmetics and silica gel. Visitors will see remnants of industrial factories while wandering the lowlands and rolling hills.

This region has four major coastal rivers: Manasquan, Shark, Navesink, and Shrewsbury. You'll get a good overview of the Navesink and Shrewsbury rivers at Hartshorne Woods Park (Trip 27), as well as an education on World War II coastal defenses as you explore the old bunkers. The Jersey Shore's beaches (see Trips 29 and 30) are crowded with vacationers in summer, but off-season hiking is rewarding, peaceful, and beautiful. Lighthouses, seaside towns joined by sandy beaches, county parks, state parks, and wildlife management areas round out "the Shore" experience.

The hikes in this section cover a good sampling of the region. You'll walk in the woods, wander the Pine Barrens (see Trip 26), roam along rivers, pound the sands and boardwalks along the ocean, and enjoy learning some history.

Facing page: A ship's outline seen offshore from Ocean Grove.
Photo by Dorian Wallender, Creative Commons on Flickr.

# 25

# CLAYTON PARK

Spring flowers, cozy trails, and mountain laurels make this park a wonderful refuge close to the madding crowd milewise yet mentally far from it.

## DIRECTIONS

From I-95, traveling east or west, take Exit 11 (Imlaystown/Cox's Corner). If westbound, turn left. If eastbound, turn right. Get on Route 43 (Imlaystown/Hightstown Road). At the first intersection, turn left onto Route 526, then immediately right to continue on Route 43 (Davis Station Road). Follow for 1.0 mile. Turn left onto Emley's Hill Road and follow to the park on the left. GPS may say Cream Ridge, New Jersey. The gravel parking lot holds about 30 cars. *GPS coordinates:* 40° 09.362′ N, 74° 30.286′ W.

## TRAIL DESCRIPTION

Clayton Park is a bit off the beaten path, but the road signs to get there are clear, and you'll enjoy the drive past rolling farmlands, tree farms, and horse farms. You'd never know that Six Flags Great Adventure is less than 10 miles to the west, off I-95. Such are the contrasts of rural and urban in the great state of New Jersey.

The 438-acre park is known for its wildflowers in spring. In April and May, discover jack-in-the-pulpit, trout lily, spring beauty, purple hepatica, wild geranium, trillium, and wild ginger. Trees include large American beech, black oak, and the tulip poplar, with its orange-centered blooms. Ferns line many sections of the trail, layered beneath spicebush and viburnum. Lyme ticks are also prevalent in season, so take precautions.

**LOCATION**
Imlaystown

**RATING**
Easy

**DISTANCE**
4.2 miles

**ELEVATION GAIN**
490 feet

**ESTIMATED TIME**
2 hours

**MAPS**
USGS Allentown, USGS Roosevelt; co.monmouth .nj.us/documents/130/ clayton_brochure_ june_2017.pdf

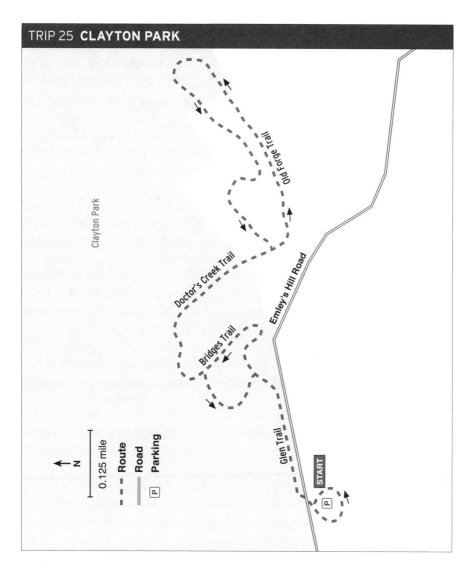

The 6-mile network has signposts at intersections but can still be a bit confusing because the colors on three separate trails are similar or the same. Dark-blue square blazes mark two trails (Bridges Trail and Old Forge Trail), and a somewhat lighter blue square blaze marks a third (Doctor's Creek Trail)! But don't let that keep you from this enchanting adventure. The park is small, so it's hard to get lost for long, especially if you remember where you came from. Additionally, the kiosk at the parking lot has a posted map as well as printed maps you can stick in your pocket. The parking lot also has a chemical toilet and picnic tables. Trails can be slippery in wet conditions and are popular with mountain bikers and horses. This hike uses four routes: green-blazed Glen Trail to blue-blazed Bridges Trail to light-blue-blazed Doctor's Creek Trail and then to blue-blazed Old Forge Trail.

Start on green-blazed Glen Trail, a packed-dirt path. At the intersection, where a chemical toilet is conveniently located, veer left to continue on Glen Trail. Within 50 yards, veer right onto blue-blazed Bridges Trail (0.1 mile), which is still flat, but can be leaf-strewn and slippery. Head downhill and note the two small trees growing in the middle of the path, which becomes rooty and flattens out as the valley slopes to the left. The trail widens and gets smoother as you go down a steep curve on red dirt. Cross a wooden bridge over a deeply rutted ravine (0.5 mile). At the junction just past the bridge, veer right, still on blue-blazed Bridges Trail (*Note*: Bridges Trail also goes to the left.) The path heads slightly up and may be muddy.

Keep straight, ignoring the two unmarked trails to the right at the "Caution" fences. The dirt path heads downhill. Stay straight, ignoring two more unmarked trails, this time to the left. At the intersection, take a right onto the light-blue-blazed Doctor's Creek Trail at a double-trunked tree. Go downhill, where the path levels out, and veer right on Doctor's Creek Trail (0.9 mile), which also goes left. Note the "Restricted Area" sign to the left. Take a rooty downhill trek to a beautiful stream. The dirt path widens, and a house is on the left. Cross a wooden bridge over a stream and admire the phalanx of skunk cabbage (1.0 miles).

At the Y intersection, turn right onto dark-blue-blazed Old Forge Trail (Doctor's Creek Trail goes to the left, 1.1 miles). The narrow, muddy trail is at first flanked by high banks, but as they diminish, the bare tree shapes become more fancifully shaped. Look for "the lovers" tree: two trees entwined in an embrace. The banks reappear as the trail heads steeply uphill and becomes worn and uneven. The reward is a spreading green meadow behind a slatted wooden fence, with a valley sloping dramatically to the right. The path is sandy here and tracks the curve of the meadow.

At the Y intersection, go right on blue-blazed Old Forge Trail (1.4 miles), which also goes to the left. Head uphill, following the fence on your right. Then start downhill on a hard dirt path—go straight to continue on Old Forge Trail, ignoring an unmarked trail to the right. The path levels and hills slope to the left. Continue straight, ignoring an unmarked trail to the left. The fence ends, and the woods path slopes downhill. Water shines from a unnamed pond to the right. Head down a steep bank, where you can see geese and ducks in the water. (*Caution:* The footing is uneven here.) Mountain laurels line the way, and hundreds of skunk cabbage proliferate in the watery valley to the right.

The route heads gradually up, following the valley to the right. Admire the magnificent swelling land contours as you wander up and down past wildflowers.

At a three-way intersection, turn left to continue on Old Forge Trail toward the white parking lot sign (2.4 miles). (You aren't very near the parking lot yet, but "P" signs appear.) The meadow is ahead. Take a right at the next "P" sign. Enjoy the wildflowers, butterflies, and the field and valley to the left. As the path winds, a field, road, and house appear on the right, and a valley and hills on the left. At the Y intersection, turn left toward parking lot signs, still on blue-blazed

Skunk cabbage abounds in wet areas throughout Clayton Park.

Old Forge Trail, which eventually merges with Doctor's Creek Trail. Detour to the right toward the house for a view of the water and perhaps some amphibians and soaring red-tailed hawks. Once on the marked trail again, go over a bridge (3.0 miles) that crosses a stream and head uphill.

At the Y intersection, go left on blue-blazed Bridges Trail (3.1 miles) toward the white parking lot sign. At the next few junctions, continue following the white "P" signs. Go over a bridge and a steep hill. At the bottom of the hill, head toward the "P" sign and take green-blazed Glen Trail (3.8 miles) back to the parking lot.

On the drive out, stop at the educational Clayton Park Activity Center on Davis Road. Just beyond, admire the beautiful stained glass windows of a restored private home that was formerly a Baptist church.

## DID YOU KNOW?

In 1720, the great-great-grandparents of Abraham Lincoln donated land where the Old Yellow Meeting House was built (70 Yellow Meeting House Road, Imlaystown). This private land and old cemetery is open during the day. Tours upon request: Friends of Old Yellow Meeting House, P.O. Box 23, Cream Ridge, NJ 08514, oymh.org.

## OTHER ACTIVITIES

Visit the Imlaystown Historic District. Hike 1,500-acre Crosswicks Creek Park in Allentown. Explore Colliers Mills Wildlife Management Area, a National Audubon Society Important Bird Area, in New Egypt (no blazed trails). In Jackson, stroll easy paths at Bunker Hill Bogs. Robbinsville, to the north, is the geographic center of New Jersey and home to the 6,300-acre Assunpink Wildlife Management Area. There are no blazed trails, but see the online topographic map at the New Jersey Division of Fish and Wildlife website, nj.gov/dep/fgw/pdf/wmamaps/colliers_mills.pdf.

## MORE INFORMATION

Open 7 A.M. to dusk. Monmouth County Park System, 805 Newman Springs Road, Lincroft, NJ 07738; 732-842-4000; monmouthcountyparks.com.

# 26

# WELLS MILLS COUNTY PARK

Well-maintained trails, bogs, hills, and an excellent nature center make this a scenic Pine Barrens primer and a good workout in cooler, bug-free months.

## DIRECTIONS

From Garden State Parkway southbound or north-bound, take Exit 69 (Waretown) and turn left (west) onto Wells Mills Road (Route 532). Proceed approx-imately 2.5 miles to the park entrance on the left. A large parking lot holds at least 50 cars. *GPS coordinates:* 39° 47.761′ N, 74° 16.589′ W.

## TRAIL DESCRIPTION

With more than 900 acres, Wells Mills is the largest park in Ocean County and is part of the Pine Bar-rens (see page 148). Pine and oak forests predominate on 16 miles of hiking trails. Habitats include Atlantic white cedar and maple-gum swamps, a freshwater lake, streams, and bogs. Blueberry bushes abound, as well as curly grass ferns, pitcher plants, sundews, turkey beards, and large swaths of sphagnum moss. Wildlife includes deer, foxes, Fowler's toads, and eastern box turtles. The well-marked trails roll up and down over dirt and sand paths, with boardwalks over marshes. This trip uses only the white-blazed Macri Trail (also called Penn's Hill), which makes a big circle through the park. Sev-eral trails connect, making it easy to design longer or shorter routes. It's best to hike during cooler weather to avoid the bugs; Lyme ticks are also prevalent, so use pre-cautions. The boardwalks, bridges, and steps can be icy in winter, and they may be slippery in wet conditions. In fall, beautiful tundra swans float on Wells Mills Lake.

**LOCATION**
Waretown

**RATING**
Moderate

**DISTANCE**
8.3 miles

**ELEVATION GAIN**
750 feet

**ESTIMATED TIME**
4 hours

**MAPS**
USGS Brookville;
njhiking.com/best-hikes-in
-nj-wells-mills/

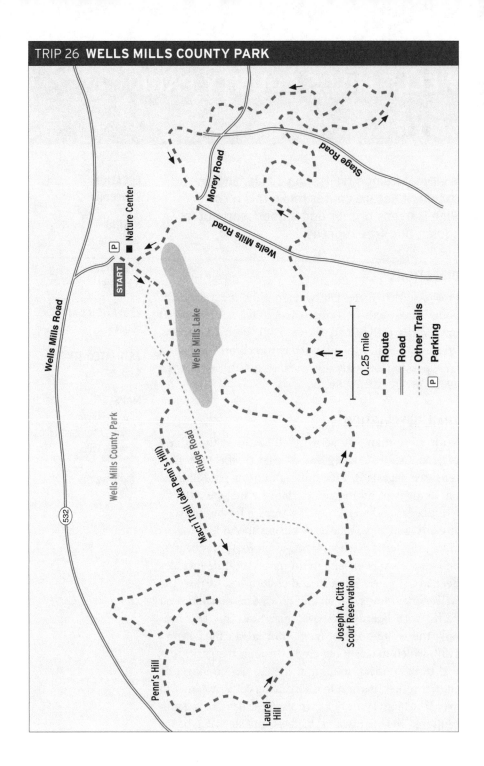

**Legend:**
- - - Route
— Road
······ Other Trails
P Parking

0.25 mile

N

Wells Mills Road

532

Wells Mills County Park

Penn's Hill

Macri Trail (aka Penn's Hill)

Ridge Road

Laurel Hill

Joseph A. Citta Scout Reservation

Wells Mills Lake

Wells Mills Road

Morey Road

Stage Road

Nature Center

P

START

Make your way to the three-story Wells Mills Nature Center, which has indoor toilets. Look around at the exhibits, grab a map, and climb to the third-floor observation deck for a good view of Wells Mills Lake. Sign in at the trailhead to the right of the nature center at the edge of the lake. Then start your journey on the white-blazed Macri Trail, where you'll see a green "7" sign. All elevation, such as it is, occurs at the beginning of the hike.

Walk past pretty, human-made Wells Mills Lake—there are no natural lakes in the Pine Barrens. The path is rooty here, but after traversing a wooden board-walk, it softens with pine needles, and pine trees line the way. Stay on white-blazed Macri Trail (blue-blazed Conrad Trail goes to the right).

Walk through a small swamp with coppery, tannic cedar water. The soft dirt path leads through narrow trees. Admire the islands in the lake from one of the many picturesque bridges and inviting benches. Continue straight on white-blazed Macri Trail at the Estlow Trail/All Terrain Bike Trail junction, heading downhill. Go straight over a dirt road, then uphill on a pine straw–strewn path that muffles your footfalls. The texture and color of the tree bark is extraordinary: thick brown slabs like floating islands, rimmed with green lichens and dusted with colorful fungi. Feel the trees' skin and marvel at the myriad colors. Cross a dirt ditch and keep following the signs for Macri Trail. Logs block some side trails—a sign to stay off them. Short bushes line the trail as it winds through black-barked trees. Traverse a long, serpentine boardwalk and head up a slight hill (1.0 mile), then go downhill through the pines.

Go uphill (the white-blazed trail is now called Penn's Hill) and cross a ditch on flat terrain before the path begins to roll. Spring-green bushes lighten the woods. You are walking on a ledge with a dropoff below. Some bare hardwoods on the right observe your passage (2.0 miles). Cross an unmarked trail and descend; cross a wooden bridge at the bottom of the hill. Admire the mountain laurels as you climb 126-foot Penn's Hill. The trail winds to the left and reaches sandy Laurel Hill at a lofty elevation of 130 feet. (2.8 miles).

Head down and cross a footbridge; the path begins to level out. Note the expanse of sphagnum moss. After another footbridge, the path goes up, and you are rewarded by a boardwalk spanning mossy water. The bank slopes to the left of the pine straw–covered path, which heads toward a grove of mountain laurels. Walk up and down some fun wooden steps. The forest thickens, and the path becomes rooty and wet from the Wells Mills Lake tributaries. More boardwalks and upward steps lead to a fence. Step over the bottom rail and turn right onto a wide path to continue on white-blazed trail, now called Macri Trail, passing briefly through the Joseph A. Citta Scout Reservation (3.4 miles). You'll come face-to-face with a "Do Not Enter" sign on a gate. Take a hard left here, staying on Macri Trail.

Walk on a bridge over Oyster Creek (3.8 miles), and go uphill. At a big inter-section with a dirt road, all-terrian bike trail, and green trail, go left (3.9 miles), following white blazes onto a wide, sandy path (get out your beach ball). At the

Plank bridges span the swampy areas of Wells Mills County Park; use caution.

sign for Ocean County Park, turn left onto Macri Trail, blanketed with pine straw. Admire the tunnels of mountain laurels, enjoy a long boardwalk, and look for toads before heading uphill. Enter a field of miniature trees covered with ghostly white lichens. From here on out, the trail is flat. At 5.7 miles, cross a dirt road, Morey Road, for the first time.

A long boardwalk and a bridge cross the muddy, watery bogs of Oyster Creek (6.4 miles). Tread an angled boardwalk that leads to a beach of white sand, pine straw, and sphagnum moss. Cedar chips on the path give way to a fairy-tale-like narrow, sandy ribbon lined with moss. At a road (which is probably a firebreak, a gap in vegetation to slow or stop the progress of a fire), go straight to continue on the white-blazed trail. Enter a controlled-burn area with a huge firebreak trench to the right.

The winding path crosses several unnamed dirt roads and all-terrain bike trails; follow the white blazes. Enjoy another boardwalk. Go straight across Morey Road, which has a gate to the right (7.3 miles) A pretty valley with a sometimes-dry streambed is to your right on this wide, white sand path. At the next road, turn right to stay on the white-blazed Macri Trail, which becomes a cinder path. Cross another bridge and watch for amphibians. To your right is the pink-blazed, 0.7-mile Shrub ID Trail (8.1 miles), which you can explore. Otherwise, keep straight and go left at the Y intersection, continuing to follow white blazes. The lake is on your left now, and there are benches here if you need a rest. Return to the nature center and parking lot, remembering to sign out at the trailhead before you leave.

## DID YOU KNOW?

Every October, Wells Mills County Park hosts the annual Pine Barrens Jamboree, a day of music, hiking, food, and crafts. The short Visually Impaired Persons' (VIP) Trail starts near the nature center. The VIP Trail has a guide rope and a tape player that indicates special objects to be heard, felt, or smelled.

## OTHER ACTIVITIES

Go northeast on Wells Mills Road to Bryant Road and visit the Candace McKee Ashmun Preserve, a 4,000-acre semi-wilderness in the Forked River Mountain Wildlife Management Area. Check out folk, blues, and country music on Saturday nights at the nonprofit, volunteer-run Albert Music Hall on Wells Mills Road. Run by the Pinelands Cultural Society (PCS), it's one of the best deals around: $5 for adults and $1 for children 11 and younger. For information, call 609-971-1593.

## MORE INFORMATION

Hours are 7 A.M. to dusk. Wells Mills County Park, 905 Wells Mills Road, Waretown, NJ 08758; 609-971-3085. Administered by Ocean County Department of Parks and Recreation, 1198 Bandon Road, Toms River, NJ 08753; 1-877-627-2757; oceancountyparks.org.

## THE PINE BARRENS AND THE PINELANDS

What's the difference between the Pine Barrens and the Pinelands—formally the Pinelands National Reserve? Quite simply, New Jersey's Pinelands is a political area, and the Pine Barrens is a geographic region within the Pinelands. A pine barrens is any area of sandy, acidic soil where pines, oaks, cedars, blueberries, cranberries, and other acid-loving plants predominate. Early settlers called places with this nutrient-poor soil "barren" because traditional crops did not grow well there.

John McPhee's 1967 best-selling book *The Pine Barrens* ignited the public campaign to save the Pinelands. His accounts of the Pinelands' natural resources and the effects of water and fire on this region hold true today.

The Pinelands National Reserve (PNR) was created by Congress in 1978 with the passage of the National Parks and Recreation Act; it was the first national reserve in the country. The PNR is huge: It includes 1.1 million acres and covers portions of seven counties and all or part of 56 municipalities in central and southern New Jersey. To help protect the Pinelands from development and manage growth, the New Jersey Pinelands Commission was created in 1979. The commission includes representatives from state, county, and federal agencies. Today the Pinelands Commission, the National Park Service, the New Jersey Department of Environmental Protection, Division of Parks and Forestry, and nonprofit groups work together to protect the PNR.

The water of the shallow, slow-moving surface streams in the Pine Barrens is filtered by sandy underground layers of earth. Within these layers, separated by silt and clay, lies a huge natural reservoir: the Kirkwood-Cohansey aquifer system, which extends more than 3,000 square miles. The contents, an estimated 17 trillion gallons of water, could cover the entire state of New Jersey in a lake 10 feet deep. This aquifer is the Pinelands region's primary source of drinking water and provides approximately 90 percent of all the water to streams, wetlands, and rivers in the Pinelands region. The brewed-tea color of the surface water stems from a high iron content and natural vegetative dyes, such as tannin. The water's high acidity helps produce some of the distinctive flora of the Pinelands, such as carnivorous sundews and pitcher plants, orchids, and Pine Barrens gentians.

Water helped support New Jersey's industries as far back as the 1700s, from shipbuilding, paper mills, sawmills, charcoal kilns, and bog iron smelters to glassmaking. Once-thriving villages and factories are now ghost towns that fascinate visitors today. Ghost towns in the Pine Barrens include Martha, Ong's Hat, and Harrisville, all in Burlington County. Other deserted villages in the Pine Barrens are Estell Manor (Trip 32), Atsion (Trip 42), and Whitesbog Village (Trip 50). (See *Ghost Towns and Other Quirky Places in the New Jersey Pine Barrens*, by Barbara Solem-Stull, Plexus Publishing, 2005.) Also curious are the countless perfectly round, 20- to 30-foot-wide circles sprinkled throughout the pine forests; these are remnants of charcoal kilns and are especially striking beneath a thin coating of snow. Abandoned sand quarries hold pristine lakes and ponds, with beaches of quartz sand and miles of surrounding sugar-sand trails. In fact, water—be it wetlands, bogs, streams, or cedar swamps—covers 35 percent of the PNR.

Despite all that water, wildfires are common in the Pinelands due to the seasonally dry ecosystem. Fires have shaped the PNR's ecology over the centuries. Prescribed burning began in the late 1930s to manage tree-stand composition and wildlife habitat. Today's controlled burns help prevent wildfires, but fire is actually a friend to pine tree survival. The intense heat causes the pine cones to "pop," allowing the seeds to sprout and new trees to grow. The Forest Resource Education Center in Jackson (Trip 31) holds a public burn every October. Scientists predict that wildfire suppression over the next several decades will eventually encourage oaks to grow in place of pines. Whether caused by fires wild or controlled, the acres of blackened trunks in the Pinelands lend a surreal quality to the landscape.

Native cranberries and blueberries have continued to adapt to the Pine Barrens' conditions and are a major component of New Jersey's agricultural industry. In fact, the blueberry was first cultivated by a Pine Barrens resident, Elizabeth White, in 1916. Educational cranberry tours are available today (see Trip 50). Flooded cranberry bogs bring a watery beauty to the Pine Barrens and provide homes for tundra swans and many varieties of amphibians. In fact, the Pine Barrens tree frog, a state endangered species, needs the acidic waters of the Pine Barrens' swamps and bogs to survive, and its range is primarily restricted to this area.

Whether called the Pinelands or the Pine Barrens, this wide expanse of natural beauty and preternatural quiet remains an extraordinary region that must be experienced to be believed. Follow the footsteps of John McPhee.

*I was in the pines because I found it hard to believe that so much unbroken forest could still exist so near the big Eastern cities, and I wanted to see it while it was still there.*
John McPhee, *The Pine Barrens*, 1967

For more information about the Pinelands, contact:

New Jersey Pinelands Commission, P.O. Box 359, New Lisbon, NJ 08064; 609-894-7300; nj.gov/pinelands.

Pinelands National Reserve, 389 Fortesque Road, P.O. Box 568, Newport, NJ 08345; 856-447-0103l; nps.gov/pine.

New Jersey Department of Environmental Protection, Division of Parks and Forestry, P.O. Box 404, Trenton, NJ 08625; 800-843-6420; njparksandforests.org.

Pinelands Preservation Alliance, 17 Pemberton Road, Southampton, NJ 08088; 609-859-8860; pinelandsalliance.org.

## 27

# HARTSHORNE WOODS PARK

Water, woods, and history meet in 794 acres of hills, deep forests, beaches, and World War II heavy artillery bunkers.

## DIRECTIONS

From Garden State Parkway, take Exit 109 toward Red Bank/Lincroft. After 0.23 mile, merge onto Half Mile Road. After 0.54 mile, turn right onto West Front Street. In 1.12 miles, turn left onto County Highway 13. After 0.12 mile, turn left onto NJ 35. In 0.47 mile, turn right onto Navesink River Road, which becomes Locust Point Road. After about 1 mile, turn right onto Hartshorne Road. In about 0.5 mile, Hartshorne Woods Park is on the left (Buttermilk Valley Entrance). The paved parking lot holds about 20 cars. *GPS coordinates: 40° 24.014' N, 74° 00.803' W.*

## TRAIL DESCRIPTION

Hartshorne Woods was a former coastal defense site and now has 15 miles of trails over 794 acres, with three main hiking sections. The Buttermilk Valley section goes through a beautiful forest of oaks, mountain laurels, and wildflowers. The Monmouth Hills section becomes more rugged and uneven as you venture deeper into the forest. The Rocky Point section (Navesink Military Reservation Historic District) is hilly, exposed to sun, and has a mix of paved and dirt paths. Here are two World War II bunkers, a Cold War radar surveillance site, and fantastic views of Navesink River and the towns of Sea Bright (located on a barrier peninsula) and Rumson.

Many turnaround points can shorten this hike, which starts at the Buttermilk Valley entrance and rounds the perimeter of the park on Laurel Ridge, Grand Tour, Rocky Point, Bunker Loop, and Cuesta Ridge trails.

**LOCATION**
Locust

**RATING**
Strenuous

**DISTANCE**
9.3 miles

**ELEVATION GAIN**
1,600 feet

**ESTIMATED TIME**
5 hours

**MAPS**
USGS Sandy Hook East, USGS Sandy Hook West; monmouthcountyparks .com

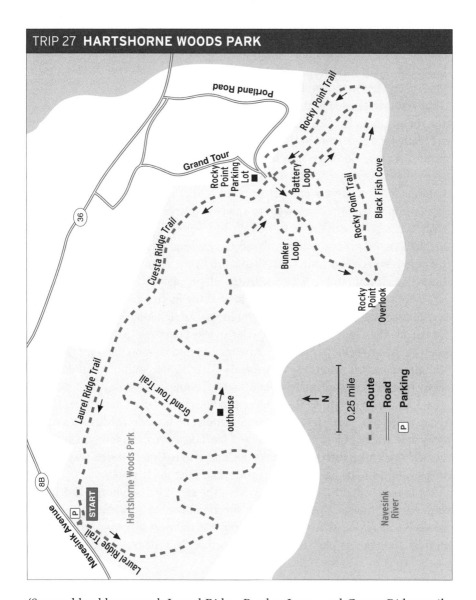

(Square blue blazes mark Laurel Ridge, Bunker Loop, and Cuesta Ridge trails, so you must read the trail names to distinguish among them.) Look for egrets, barred owls, woodpeckers, and hummingbirds. The twisted branches and triple-trunked trees are fantastic. In summer, the area is gorgeous with phlox and blueberries. In fall, the trees glow, and goldenrods and glimmering berries shimmer.

Pick up a map from the parking lot kiosk to the left of the chemical toilets; there is a water fountain here as well. Face the woods and go to the very far right of the parking lot for blue-square-blazed Laurel Ridge Trail. The trail starts in the woods on a wide dirt path. Go uphill over water bars and past mountain laurels galore. Step carefully around big rocks and roots on the rolling path. Pass a ranger residence before heading into a wooded valley. Walk slowly to admire the fabulous tree bark. At 0.4 mile, a path on the right leads down to Hartshorne Road, but go left to stay on Laurel Ridge Trail.

The trail bends sweetly at a wooden fence on the right. At the intersection, go straight as Laurel Ridge Trail winds up and down, with a valley to your right. Get ready for a steep downhill with tricky footing. Look out for mountain bikers in this part. Go down into deep woods and, in summer, a forest of ferns. An uphill section of sand and dirt leads to a wooden "Hopes and Dreams" box (handmade by an 8-year-old girl named Charlie) where you can leave a note about a hope or dream if you want to and read others' notes as well.

You'll see a wooden fence to the left just before Laurel Ridge Trail meets the challenging black-diamond-blazed Grand Tour Trail. Take a sharp right (1.9 miles) onto Grand Tour Trail (shared briefly with blue-square-blazed Laurel Ridge Trail; if you want to head back, turn left on Laurel Ridge Trail here). Walk past laurels and fern forests. Veer left toward the fence (ignore a rogue path to the right that leads to a house). At the maintenance sign, turn left. (If you need to use the facilities, take a right down a narrow 50-yard path to a chemical toilet.) Smell the honeysuckle as Navesink River comes into view on the right. The river is a tidal estuary flowing into Shrewsbury River at Sea Bright, continuing into Sandy Hook Bay and ultimately the Atlantic Ocean.

At 3.1 miles, you are at the midpoint connector of the Grand Tour Trail's figure-eight loop. Turn right at this intersection and head downhill into a sunny, rocky area where phlox, goldenrods, and blackberry bushes bloom in summer. (For a shorter hike, turn left and take the blue-square Cuesta Ridge Trail back to the parking lot.) The path widens as you reenter the shady woods.

At the next junction, go left, away from the sign for Hartshorne Road. Traverse another rugged open area with flowering bushes and plants before the woods begin again. At 3.6 miles, turn right at the next junction, which is not marked. Note the "triplet" tree on the left before the wide trail heads slightly up past a fern garden to the right.

Arrive at an intersection with a paved road and two stone pillars on the right. Go across the road into the black diamond Rocky Point Trail's wooded area (trash can on right of trail entrance). The steep downhill is a biker's delight, so be alert. A rocky uphill leads to a chain-link fence on the left. Carefully step down onto a cute footbridge.

Go right at the paved path onto Bunker Loop Trail (marked on the park's trail map but not on the actual trail, 4.0 miles). The huge hill to your left is the back of a World War II bunker. Explore the two bunkers here, then return to where you started and take a right into the woods to continue on Rocky Point Trail. Wind and weather have twisted the laurels into an enchanted forest.

Don't miss the side trail loop to the Rocky Point Overlook. Take a right onto the side trail at 4.7 miles. Keep to your right for a loop-around view (better in

The fishing pier at Black Fish Cove on tidal Navesink River.

leafless seasons) of Navesink River (4.9 miles). Continue the circle and arrive back at the intersection to continue on Rocky Point Trail. Take a right where the path soon splits.

At 5.7 miles, you'll reach a paved road. Turn right on it to reach Black Fish Cove with a pier, picnic table, and chemical toilet. Linger to enjoy a spectacular view of Navesink River.

Return via the paved road and take a quick right onto a dirt path at a tree with a metal black-diamond marker for Rocky Point Trail. In the woods, you'll see a wooden fence on your right. Stay on this narrow trail; do not take side paths. Look to your right to see the town of Sea Bright, on a barrier peninsula, bordered to the west by the convergence of the Navesink and Shrewsbury rivers and to the east by the Atlantic Ocean, which you can see and smell. Cross a paved road to stay on Rocky Point Trail. Go over a bridge in the woods and enjoy a cardio workout uphill.

At about 7.4 miles, you'll reach another paved road and the Rocky Point parking lot. Turn left to walk blue-squared Battery Loop Trail (and use one of the chemical toilets if needed), keeping the parking lot on your right. At the junction, go left. You'll come to two big bunkers, one with a huge gun; a sign explains the gun's construction, use, and significance.

Between these bunkers is a gravel road to the right—take it to climb a big hill (actually the top of one of the bunkers) and sit on the bench for a spectacular water view. Explore further or head back down to the Rocky Point parking lot.

With the Rocky Point parking lot on your left, cross the road, heading toward two stone pillars with an "Authorized Vehicles Only" sign. A water tower is on your right. Go between the pillars onto a paved road, keeping straight. In a few hundred yards, you'll see the blue-blazed Cuesta Ridge Trail on your right. Take this dirt road into the woods, straight to the Buttermilk Valley parking lot. Don't turn left or right on any side paths. Cuesta Ridge Trail becomes Laurel Ridge Trail. It's a pretty woods walk, mainly flat but with some rocky, rutty areas. Go straight at the "Dismount Area" sign and head toward the water fountain, kiosk, and chemical toilets.

## DID YOU KNOW?

Water views and hills appealed to many nineteenth-century artists. A simple online search of Hartshorne Woods Park art history reveals nineteenth-century paintings that prove true the novelist James Fenimore Cooper's statement that this is one of the most beautiful combinations of land and water in America.

## OTHER ACTIVITIES

Less than 1 mile north off NJ 36, view the New York City skyline from Mount Mitchill Scenic Overlook and Monmouth County's 9/11 memorial. Keep going southeast to the nonoperational Twin Lights Lighthouse, a unique lighthouse built in 1862 with two non-identical towers linked by keepers' quarters and storage rooms; one beacon flashed and the other remained fixed (call 732-872-1814 for hours). Five minutes farther is Sandy Hook, a popular beach for swimming and hiking, which is linked to history with Fort Hancock and is the oldest continuously operating lighthouse in the United States. To the south, find 8 miles of trails and river views at Huber Woods Park in Locust.

## MORE INFORMATION

Open 7 A.M. to dusk. Monmouth County Park System, 805 Newman Springs Road, Lincroft, NJ 07738; 732-842-4000; monmouthcountyparks.com.

# 28

# BARNEGAT BRANCH TRAIL

Take an educational stroll through the past and the present with this easy walk on a flat asphalt-and-crushed stone path past water, through suburbs, and by a pitch pine forest.

## DIRECTIONS

The access point at William J. Dudley Park is at the intersection of Atlantic City Boulevard (Route 9) and Sycamore Street. From I-195 East, take US 9 South. In 22 to 23 miles, the park will be on your right. The parking lot holds about 50 cars. *GPS coordinates:* 39° 52.190′ N, 74° 10.231′ W.

**Public Transportation:** Take the train or bus to Toms River, then take the 559 local bus, which drops you off across the street from Cedar Creek Campground, 1052 Atlantic City Boulevard (Route 9). Walk 0.1 mile south on Route 9 to reach the park. For information and schedules, visit njtransit.com.

## TRAIL DESCRIPTION

The Barnegat Branch Trail is a flat "rail-to-trail" project that follows the abandoned Barnegat Branch Division of the Central Railroad of New Jersey. When complete, it will stretch northward 15.6 miles from Barnegat Township to Toms River. Currently, it is 10.4 miles long and begins on Memorial Drive in Barnegat Township and ends at Railroad and Maryland avenues in Berkeley Township, with a 1-mile municipal trail extension from Railroad Avenue to Atlantic City Boulevard. Several road crossings (trail entrances) intersperse the route, but all are extensively marked to ensure pedestrian safety. Choose from several access points with parking for cars and bicycles. (See the park map for details.)

**LOCATION**
Bayville

**RATING**
Easy

**DISTANCE**
6.2 miles

**ELEVATION GAIN**
100 feet

**ESTIMATED TIME**
2.5 hours

**MAPS**
USGS Forked River; oceancountyparks.org

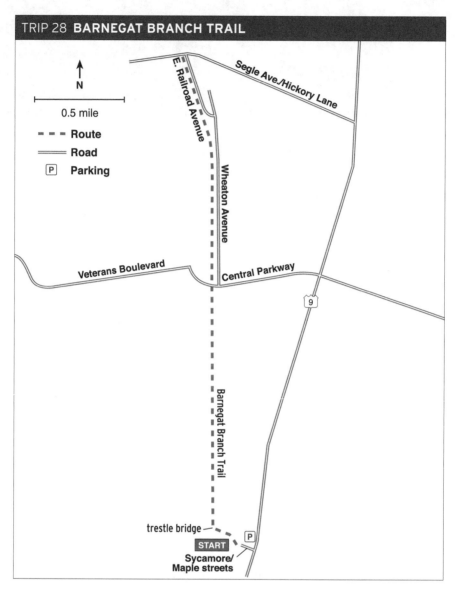

This hike travels the newest section of the trail, near the planned midpoint at William J. Dudley Park, which has a lovely small beach (no dogs allowed) with swimming, a playground, picnic tables and grills, a covered pavilion, volleyball nets, and flush toilets. The trail has many historical markers that explain this interesting area. You'll pass through sites of former villages supported by the sawmill and cranberry industries. You'll go by a nursing home that was formerly the grand Royal Pines Hotel, which was not completed until after the stock market crash; its grand opening was November 18, 1929. The hotel struggled on through two winter seasons. The building was abandoned, and bootleggers later erected a 2,500-gallon still nearby. Walk through Barnegat Park, designed in

1887 to be a retirement community for Civil War veterans. Stroll past a striking forest of pitch pines, once used to make charcoal on-site.

To begin, follow the clear signage for Barnegat Branch Trail into the woods on a shaded gravel path, bordered by copper-colored Cedar Creek on the left and by ferns, bushes, and trees all around. Shade is sporadic, so wear a hat for sun protection. Soon, a small clearing appears on the left, and you can examine the tannic waters of the creek. A picturesque boardwalk zigzags through a cedar grove to a beachy expanse of water crossed by a tall wooden railroad bridge to nowhere (an abandoned trestle), inviting you to linger. On the other side of the creek, a dirt road eventually leads to a township sports field.

Follow the concrete gridwork across the dirt and turn right onto the flat gravel path that is part of the Barnegat Branch Trail (with a nearby chemical toilet). The entire trail is flat and easy, and you can turn around at any time. Goldenrods shimmer. A mix of cedars and deciduous trees (including blackberry and catalpa) stretch greenly to the right, while industry and suburbia twinkle behind the fences on the left. The trail is a mix of rural and suburban, narrowing through communities, industrial parks, woods, and pineland. It's fun to see the cutoff paths kids have made from their backyards to the trail. Guardrails begin to run on the right, probably to keep ATVs from accessing the woods. The first educational marker appears on the right, welcoming you to the Cedar Creek Cut, a carve-out required to make the railroad trestle operational. As you stroll, gazing at the sandy terrain, consider that the soil is actually the remains of the Atlantic Ocean floor, from a time when ocean elevations covered New Jersey.

Banks on the left disappear, offering a clear view into suburban backyards. In fall, the trees are glorious. Princeton Avenue, on the left, parallels the trail. Butterflies flit among purple, yellow, and white wildflowers. There is a bench next to bike racks and an information marker (1.7 miles). Note the trail sign as you cross the 15-car parking lot and Serpentine and Princeton avenues. On the other side of the road, the trail resumes. Read about nearby Double Trouble State Park at the marker on the right. Cardinals zoom across the path, which is now shady, elevated, and boggy on the left.

Make another road crossing (Central Boulevard and Wheaton Avenue) and read about bootleggers (2.1 miles). Suburban homes line the left and right of the trail. Soon another 15-car parking lot appears, at the old Barnegat Park location at Maryland and Railroad avenues (2.4 miles). Cross the lot and the road. Now the grass stretches like an English lawn behind a split rail fence to the right. A marker on the left informs you of the roadside oddities to the north on Route 9 in Bayville, such as a 20-foot plastic dinosaur named Ruggles, a 25-foot Renault champagne bottle, and a 1950 Fiat, airborne over a salvage yard. More houses, hammocks, and vegetable gardens appear on the right. A two-lane paved road begins to parallel the trail on the right, while the left gives way to some fire-scorched pineland with a marker explaining this postindustrial forest. Soon you'll reach the end of the 10.4-mile Barnegat Branch Trail; (Hickory Lane and

The copper-colored waters of Cedar Creek gleam along the trail.

East Railroad Avenue) at the Ocean County Utilities Authority building, with a marker explaining the county's wastewater reclamation system (3.1 miles). (*Note:* If you want to walk the trail from this end and go south, be aware there's no official parking lot here; two to four cars could squeeze alongside Hickory Lane.)

Turn around and walk back to the parking lot the way you came.

## DID YOU KNOW?

*Barende-gat* is Dutch for "inlet with breakers." The area was named by Henry Hudson around 1609. In the early 1900s, Barnegat became known for "sneak boxes," lightweight duck-hunting boats that can sneak in on their prey through New Jersey's marshes and bays. Still manufactured today, they're also used for racing.

## OTHER ACTIVITIES

Go south on the trail for the remaining 6.75 miles, stopping at Waretown for the railroad history display. Get in your car and visit several nature spots within 10 to 15 miles away: Lochiel Creek Park, Forsythe National Wildlife Reserve, Enos Pond Park, Double Trouble State Park, Forked River Mountain Wildlife

Management Area, and Jakes Branch County Park. Head north on Route 9 for dining and miniature golf, passing Ruggles, the iconic 20-foot plastic dinosaur, on the left. Drive to Millcreek Park at 111 Chelsea Avenue in Bayville to see gorgeous boats up and down Toms River.

## MORE INFORMATION

Trail open dawn to dusk. Many road crossings have buttons to activate warning lights, handy for a large group. The logo for the Barnegat Branch Trail features a ghost locomotive and the Statue of Liberty, a nod to the historic Central Railroad of New Jersey in Liberty State Park (see Trip 24), a terminal that many immigrants passed through. Ocean County Department of Parks and Recreation, 1198 Bandon Road, Toms River, NJ 08753; 1-877-627-2757, extension 5954; oceancountyparks.org. For updates on trail extensions, visit planning.co.ocean .nj.us/frmTPBarnegatBranch

# 29

# MANASQUAN TO ASBURY PARK

Hike 10 miles of boardwalk traversing eight northern New Jersey beaches. Sand dunes, surf, seabirds, and shells make this a winner.

## DIRECTIONS

**To Manasquan train station:** Take NJ 34 South heading toward Sea Girt/Manasquan. Take a right onto County Road 524 Spur (Atlantic Avenue). Turn right on North Main Street. Turn right after the 7-Eleven on the left. The Manasquan train station is on the left. Buy a ticket ($3.50) at the self-service terminal and enjoy the short one-way ride to Asbury Park, the fourth stop. Trains run about every hour. From Asbury Park, walk along the boardwalks and beaches and return to your car at Manasquan Station.

　　**Public Transportation:** If leaving from New York's Penn Station or New Jersey terminals, take the New Jersey Coast Line train to Asbury Park and back. See njtransit.com for more information. *GPS coordinates:* 40° 07.001′ N, 74° 02.435′ W.

## TRAIL DESCRIPTION

In this unique hike, you'll start at the Manasquan train station, ride the rails to Asbury Park, then tread the boardwalks and beaches along the Atlantic Ocean back to Manasquan. It's a brilliant way to get the most out of eight fabulous beach towns in one day without arranging a car shuttle at either end of the hike. At any point, you can leave the oceanfront and explore the towns of Asbury Park, Ocean Grove, Bradley Beach, Avon, Belmar, Spring Lake, Sea Girt, and Manasquan. You can even cut the hike short and take a train from Bradley Beach, Belmar, or Spring Lake back to Manasquan. You'll be on boardwalks and sand and probably in the

**LOCATION**
Manasquan

**RATING**
Moderate

**DISTANCE**
9.8 miles

**ELEVATION GAIN**
50 feet

**ESTIMATED TIME**
4 hours

**MAPS**
USGS Asbury Park; newjerseyshore.com; DeLorme *New Jersey Atlas & Gazetteer*

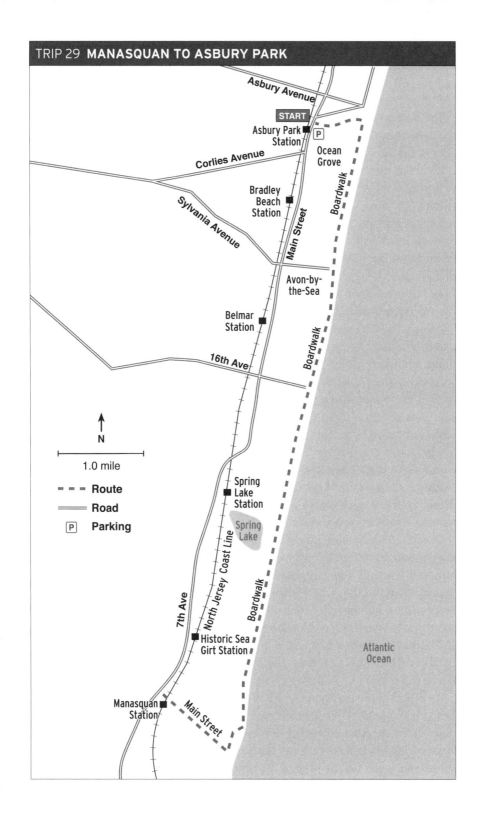

Asbury Avenue

START

Asbury Park
Station

P

Ocean
Grove

Corlies Avenue

Bradley
Beach
Station

Main Street

Boardwalk

Sylvania Avenue

Avon-by-
the-Sea

Belmar
Station

Boardwalk

16th Ave

N

1.0 mile

- - - Route
——— Road
P Parking

Spring
Lake
Station

Spring
Lake

North Jersey Coast Line

Boardwalk

7th Ave

Atlantic
Ocean

Historic Sea
Girt Station

Manasquan
Station

Main Street

water, so don versatile footwear. If you plan to stay and swim, you must buy a beach badge, which range from $5 to $10 a day and are usually discounted for seniors and members of the military, and often free for children 11 and younger. (See newjerseyshore.com/beach-badges.shtml for details.)

The beaches are fine in any season. Crunch frozen sea-foam in winter; enjoy the calm in spring before the summer crowds; walk respectfully past sea turtle eggs in summer; relish the scarlet Virginia creeper on the sands in fall.

It's about three blocks from the Asbury Park train station to the beach. Head to Springwood Avenue and go left (east) to the next intersection at Main Street (Route 71). Cross Main Street to Lake Avenue (Springwood becomes Lake Avenue). Stay on Lake Avenue and pass Emory Street and Grand Avenue (both are on your left, Wesley Lake is on your right); pass the colorful Asbury Park paddleboats. At Heck Street (on your left) turn right onto a bridge (0.6 mile). Immediately after the bridge, take a left on a path through Founders Park. Wesley Lake is now on your left. After the park, the path goes along Beach Avenue and intersects the boardwalk. Turn right onto the boards, heading south (0.9 miles).

Asbury Park is one of New Jersey's northernmost beaches (Deal, Sea Bright, and Sandy Hook are farther north) and perhaps most famous for the Stone Pony nightclub, where Bruce Springsteen began playing in 1974. (The Stone Pony is still open.) The 1-mile boardwalk was built shortly after the town was founded in 1871 by manufacturer James Bradley. The Great Depression and the postwar years slammed this and other shore towns, but revitalization began in 2007, with restoration of the Paramount Theatre and Convention Hall. There is even a Yappy Hour for dogs at the Wonder Bar. Asbury Park also has a thriving LGBTQ community. But it's best known as a destination for fun and sun.

Keep walking on the boards, smelling the salty air, maybe stopping for a cold drink, until you reach Ocean Grove (1.3 miles). Ornamental signs proclaim each town as you hike the boardwalk.

Ocean Grove, besides having a laid-back beach and an adorable main street, is a permanent camp meeting site for the United Methodist Church. Since 1869, hundreds of tents (now attached to wooden structures, whose ownership is passed down through generations) have housed worshippers from May through September. Churchgoers gather in the Great Auditorium, built in 1894. The acoustically acclaimed auditorium is used for worship and concerts and holds 10,000 people. Take a seat and a break from the sun in the large Boardwalk Pavilion. Then walk, enjoying the absence of parking meters, on to Bradley Beach (1.8 miles).

It's said that the notorious pirate William Kidd anchored his ship at Bradley Beach back in 1679. His treasure is rumored to be buried between two large pines in the area that is now Brinley Avenue. Bradley Beach is known as a quiet, family-friendly shore town. Stroll the boardwalk made of honeycomb-patterned stone, and linger on the bright-blue benches and watch the surfers; the beach

A happy pair of bikes along the boardwalk.

between Third and Fifth avenues is reserved for these daredevils. Take a shade break in the gazebo on Fifth Avenue, then head toward Avon (2.5 miles).

Avon, or Avon-by-the-Sea, has a short boardwalk, about eight blocks long, but some swear it's the prettiest stretch of sand on the Jersey Shore. The Victorian homes are certainly gorgeous and are visible from the oceanfront. You may want to stop and eat at the enclosed Avon Pavilion restaurant. Avon's boardwalk ends at the jetty, where the water is calmer and you can see crabs scuttling at low tide.

Next, hoof it to Belmar (French for "beautiful sea"), where the 1.3-mile boardwalk is made of Trex, a wood alternative constructed from recycled materials (3.1 miles). Belmar offers wheelchair and stroller access to the beach via Mobi-Mats, hard surface ramps. Playgrounds every few blocks, with water-bottle filling stations, make Belmar truly child-friendly. Quench your thirst and satisfy your hunger at the Fifth Avenue Pavilion. Belmar has lovely sand dunes—but be careful not to walk on them! Dunes provide shore protection and a habitat for plants and animals.

Watch seagulls dive as you enter Spring Lake, which has a 2-mile stretch of Trex boardwalk and is a true rarity: It's noncommercial, so it has a great ocean view (5.4 miles). Lack of boardwalk storefronts also allows you to admire the Victorian homes, a leftover from the 1800s when barons of industry vacationed here. Bed-and-breakfasts are abundant in this laid-back, upscale community. Natural springs feed into the town's largest lake, hence the name.

Sea Girt is small, only 1 square mile, with 0.5 mile of Trex boardwalk. Wind-swept cedars from boardwalk to water give the town a wild, unexplored feel. Visit the 1896 lighthouse at the mouth of the boardwalk (Nine Ocean Avenue), which marks the inlet leading to Wreck Pond (6.7 miles). (The lighthouse put an end to the wrecks.) Look for ducks in this tidal pond.

On to the finish line—Manasquan (8.2 miles). Elks Beach is devoted entirely to those with limited mobility, offering a platform and beach wheelchairs. The 1-mile asphalt boardwalk is also accessible. Walk over the Glimmer Glass Bridge, a drawbridge that spans the tidal inlet. The beach part of the hike ends here.

There is an ice-cream shop on Ocean Avenue if you feel like rewarding your-self. Then make your way along Beach Front Road, which parallels the ocean until it intersects Main Street (8.8 miles). Turn right on Main Street and stroll a pleasant mile through town to the Manasquan train station on the left.

## DID YOU KNOW?

The sand dunes at Bradley Beach were constructed using snow fences and dis-carded Christmas trees. Inlet Beach at Manasquan has one of the finest surfing beaches on the East Coast. The knobbed whelk, found along the beaches, is the New Jersey state seashell. Italian restaurants at the Jersey Shore serve it under the name *scungilli*.

## OTHER ACTIVITIES

Hike Manasquan Reservoir, a 1,204-acre expanse of woods, wetlands, and fields. An easy 5-mile perimeter trail showcases waterfowl. The reservoir's 1-mile Cove Trail leads to the educational Manasquan Reservoir Environmental Center (331 Georgia Tavern Road, Howell, NJ 07731; 732-751-9453). On a rainy day, play pinball at the Silverball Museum in Asbury Park (1000 Ocean Avenue) or visit the Paranormal Museum (621 Cookman Avenue).

## MORE INFORMATION

The boardwalks are open 24/7. State of New Jersey, Department of State, Division of Travel and Tourism, P.O. Box 460, Trenton, NJ 08625; 1-800-VISITNJ (847-4865) for free publications. For other inquiries, call (609) 599-6540; visitnj.org/nj/beaches/boardwalks and newjerseyshore.com.

# 30

# ISLAND BEACH STATE PARK: JOHNNY ALLEN'S COVE TRAIL AND BARNEGAT INLET TRAIL

Choose between a short hike or a long one (or do both!) on a unique barrier reef that separates Barnegat Bay from the Atlantic Ocean. Experience green thickets of fauna, sugary dunes, towering osprey nests, and a beckoning lighthouse.

## DIRECTIONS

Take Garden State Parkway to Exit 82A. Go east on NJ 37 for about 6 miles to NJ 35. Turn right and follow signs on NJ 35 through town to the park, where you can pay at one of two kiosks (See "More Information" for rates). The most accurate address is Intersection of Route 35 South and 24th Avenue. GPS coordinates: 39° 45.968′ N, 74° 05.807′ W.

## TRAIL DESCRIPTION

### Johnny Allen's Cove Trail (Lot 16)

Island Beach State Park is a jewel in the crown of the Jersey Shore. With 3,000 acres of sand dunes, beaches, tidal marshes, freshwater wetlands, and maritime forests, this 10-mile-long, undeveloped barrier island is worth the entrance fee. The park is divided into three sections—northern, central, and southern—and this two-part hike explores the southern section, which includes Johnny Allen's Cove (a self-guided nature trail) and beach walks. The northern and central sections are worth exploring on your own for the pretty beaches, short nature trails, ocean swimming, and Fisherman's Walkway boardwalk. Beach wheelchairs are available for the swimming area and Fisherman's Walkway and for surf fishing; check at the pavilion at Lot 7 during the season or call the park office in the off-season.

**LOCATION**
Seaside Park

**JOHNNY ALLEN'S COVE TRAIL:**
**RATING**
Easy

**DISTANCE**
1.2 miles

**ELEVATION GAIN**
100 feet

**ESTIMATED TIME**
30 minutes

**BARNEGAT INLET TRAIL:**
**RATING**
Moderate

**DISTANCE**
4.1 miles

**ELEVATION GAIN**
200 feet

**ESTIMATED TIME**
3.5 hours

**MAPS**
USGS Seaside Park;
state.nj.us/dep/
parksandforests/

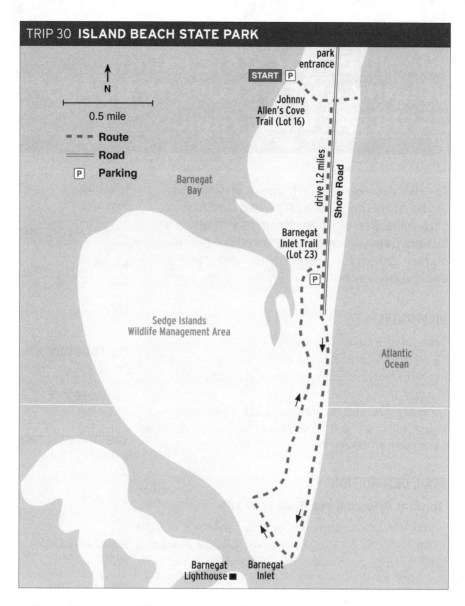

↑ N

0.5 mile

- - - Route
——— Road
P Parking

park entrance

START P

Johnny Allen's Cove Trail (Lot 16)

Barnegat Bay

drive 1.2 miles

Shore Road

Barnegat Inlet Trail (Lot 23)

P

Sedge Islands Wildlife Management Area

Atlantic Ocean

Barnegat Lighthouse ■   Barnegat Inlet

If possible, go on a fall day, free from the summer crowds and entrance fees. (Park officials restrict access when all of the almost 2,000 parking spots are full.) Part of the New Jersey Coastal Heritage Trail route (see page 170), Island Beach State Park has nine easy-to-moderate trails that show off dunes, beach plums, shadbush, bayberry, fiddler crabs, and osprey nesting platforms. (The park is home to the state's largest osprey colony.) In winter, red foxes are stunning against the stark landscape, along with harder-to-see snowy owls. In fall, surf anglers dot the shores. Spring brings festivals, flowers, and birds.

Pay your entrance fee at one of the two kiosks. The building attached to the kiosks has maps and flush toilets, so be sure to grab a map before setting out. The paved road bisects the barrier reef, with the Atlantic Ocean on the left and Barnegat Bay on the right. Common reeds, wind-twisted pines, and beach heather (a lovely golden color in May) border the road, along with "Turtle Xing" and "Do Not Feed Fox" signs (foxes love beach plums). In September, yellow goldenrods, red-budded prickly pear cacti, and silver-gray bayberries catch the eye.

Numbered parking lots dot both sides of the road. Drive past lot 7, for Fisherman's Walkway Trail (the only universally accessible trail). For a sneak peek at the ocean, pull in at lot 9 and walk a narrow, sandy path that's shaded by dense sea shrubs before it opens onto a wood-railed boardwalk. Stroll past the blooming ocean goldenrod to the white sand and azure sea. You may see surf anglers, whose cars are parked legally if they have a Mobile Sport Fishing Vehicle Permit.

Return to your car and drive past the canoe and kayak access point at lot 13 on the right. You'll soon reach the interpretive center and the nature center at lot 16 on the left, 7.0 miles from the park entrance. Staffed by the volunteers from Friends of Island State Park, the centers do not have regular hours; call 732-793-1315 to find out hours of operation. But you can still hike the trails and admire Janet's Garden, a living herbarium. Flush toilets and water fountains are available here. If it's late August or early September, sit on the blue benches between the two buildings and try to count the wind-pushed migrating monarch butterflies feeding in the flowerbed. Check out the pathways, painted with the outlines of turtles, squid, and seals. Head about 100 yards down the sand and crushed-shell path toward your first trail of the day: Johnny Allen's Cove Trail.

At the T intersection, the posted sign tells you that you can walk 0.3 mile left to Barnegat Bay on the Johnny Allen Cove Trail, or 0.2 mile right to the Atlantic Ocean. Turn left down the sandy path, stopping to read the many educational nature signs. Pass a lovely grove of cherry and holly trees. Blackbirds fly into an "anchoring" thicket of American holly, pitch pine, shadbush, black cherry, red cedar, and blueberry. The thicket "anchors" the sands of the barrier island and also provides food and cover for numerous birds. Look for the sassafras tree's slate-blue berries on stems that turn crimson in autumn.

Cross Ocean View Trail, which is the paved road you drove in on (there's only one road on the barrier reef, so you can't get lost, 0.2 mile) and continue on the path to enter Johnny Allen's Cove Trail. Feel the cool bay breezes as you crunch along the narrow trail of crushed shells that look like uncooked oatmeal, but don't kneel for a better look—the shells are sharp! The blueberries here flower in the spring; 8-foot-tall reeds with tiny purple flowers at their base stand guard. A carpet of yellow and purple asters leads to a dainty wooden bridge. Beyond are the salt marsh and Barnegat Bay (0.4 mile). In the distance, to the left, is an osprey nesting platform. Look for fiddler and horseshoe crab shells. Turn around and head back, going straight at the sign for the Atlantic Ocean and Barnegat Bay (nature center on your right); head toward the ocean.

Hear the surf as you walk down a sunny, sandy path, reading nature signs. Pass through a magnificent coastal thicket, which tapers off into fantastic windblown

Barnegat Lighthouse, known as "Old Barney," is across the inlet on Long Beach Island.

shapes that give way to white sand, crimson-leaved Virginia creeper, and green Japanese sedge grass. Follow the wooden fence to a bench, noting pointy bird tracks in the sand. (*Note:* Be sure to stay off the dunes.) Dip your toes in the ocean before heading back to parking lot 16 and your car.

### Barnegat Inlet Trail (Lot 23)

For this longer (4.1 miles) part of the hike, drive 1.2 miles south to parking lot 23 (space for 50 cars) at the literal end of the road. Head toward the Barnegat Inlet Trail sign at the beginning of the parking lot. Travel a short footpath and turn right onto the beach (0.1 mile). You are walking toward the Barnegat Inlet. Keep walking, admiring the dunes and distant Barnegat Lighthouse to the right, watching the ocean and anglers to the left. Wet seashells shine; birds stalk the water for dinner. Keep walking until you reach the inlet, with a great view of the lighthouse (1.6 miles). Curve right around the inlet along the rock seawall; if you go straight, you'll be swimming in the Barnegat Inlet. Enjoy the passing sailboats. The seawall path here has a different feel, quieter, as the waves lap the stones. Partially buried sandbags at the path's end remind you of the ocean's force. Backtrack, taking a left in about 300 yards to read the nature marker about birds; you are in a circular sand parking lot. An unmarked trail leads from the circular sand parking lot; take it to the winter anchorage canoe and kayak access area (3.6 miles). The trail runs between dunes and passes houses and fishing shacks. Walk to the road (3.8 miles) and take a right to your car. Catch the sunset before you leave.

## DID YOU KNOW?

The town of Seaside Park measures only 0.77 square miles and has a year-round population of about 2,200 residents. In 1945, scientists from Johns Hopkins University tested the world's first supersonic antiaircraft missile here as part of Operation Bumblebee.

## OTHER ACTIVITIES

To the north is the borough of Seaside Heights with amusement parks, arcades, rides, and a boardwalk. To the south is South Seaside Park. Less than 5 miles away are Barnegat Lighthouse State Park and the Barnegat Light Museum, Double Trouble State Park, and William J. Dudley Park (see Trip 28). Lots of dining options are on NJ 35 and 37. Red Fox Beach Bar & Grill is in Island Beach State Park.

## MORE INFORMATION

Open 8 A.M. to sunset. Fee per car from Memorial Day weekend to Labor Day ranges from $6 to $20, according to the day of the week and state residency. There's a reduced fee for motorcycles, and no fee for bicycles or walk-ins. When all parking spots are full, no more vehicles are allowed in. Text telephone users can call the NJ Relay Service at 800-852-7899. Mailing address: Island Beach State Park, P.O. Box 37, Seaside Park, NJ 08752, 732-793-0506, state.nj.us/dep/parksandforests/parks/island.html.

# NEW JERSEY COASTAL HERITAGE TRAIL

The 300-mile New Jersey Coastal Heritage Trail (NJCHT) joins areas of maritime heritage, coastal habitat, wildlife migration, relaxation and inspiration, and historic settlements. Congress authorized the NJCHT in October 1988 so the public could access, understand, and enjoy the resources associated with coastal New Jersey. The trail links five regions along the Atlantic seaboard: Sandy Hook, Barnegat Bay, Absecon, Cape May, and Delsea. Even though it was originally designed for vehicular travel, the NJCHT does connect many walkable areas of interest to hikers. In fact, at least six hikes in this book follow parts of the NJCHT: Cheesequake State Park (Trip 22), Island Beach State Park (Trip 30), Belleplain State Forest (Trip 35), Thompson's and Moore's Beaches (Trip 36), Cape May Point State Park (Trip 37), and Bivalve Wetlands Walk (Trip 40).

Put your hiking shoes in the car and start at the top with the Sandy Hook Unit of the Gateway National Recreation Area. Stop in at the visitor center in the Lighthouse Keepers Quarters at the north end of the park. (The center is open seven days a week from 9 A.M. to 5 P.M.; 732-872-5970; nps.gov/gate/planyourvisit/index.htm). Visit the lighthouse and the lighthouse museum. Take a walking tour of Fort Hancock, a coastal defense fort from 1895 to 1974. Drive to and tour the nearby Nike Missile Radar Site at Horseshoe Cove, guided by Nike veterans. Drive south to visit the Barnegat Bay region, with its attractive ribbon of barrier islands. Walk Long Beach Island's 18 miles of sandy shore. Climb the 217-step Barnegat Lighthouse for an osprey's-eye view of the barrier island known as Island Beach State Park (Trip 30). Head south on Garden State Parkway to County Road 539 and drive toward Tuckerton and the Great Bay Boulevard Wildlife Management Area. A road to nowhere, this narrow, 4-mile spit of land is the best bird-watching area in Ocean County.

In the Absecon and Cape May regions, drive to North Wildwood and visit the unique 1874 Victorian-design Hereford Inlet Lighthouse (also called Swiss carpenter Gothic and stick style). Hike Corson's Inlet State Park in Ocean City and wander Cape May Point State Park (Trip 37).

Drive to the Delsea region and visit the 400-year-old white oak in Salem, owned and maintained by the Religious Society of Friends, or Quakers, since 1681. Check out nearby Fort Mott in Pennsville, part of a postbellum three-fort defense system. (The two other forts were Fort Delaware and Fort DuPont.) The easy Nature Interpretive Trail is universally accessible. An NJCHT welcome center provides more information about the ecosystem and Fort Mott's history. Don't forget Belleplain State Forest (Trip 35).

New Jersey's Coastal Heritage Trail is more than just hiking: It's an environmental, cultural, historical, and educational journey.

Due to a sunset clause, the National Park Service is no longer the legislative authority managing the NJCHT, which is now maintained by many private entities working alongside local, state, and federal agencies. For guides to the trail's five regions, contact:

National Park Service, New Jersey Coastal Heritage Trail Route Headquarters, 389 Fortescue Road, P.O. Box 568, Newport, NJ 08345-0568; 856-447-0103; nps.gov/neje.

State of New Jersey, Department of State, Division of Travel and Tourism, P.O. Box 460, Trenton, NJ 08625-0460; 609-599-6540; new-jersey-leisure-guide.com/coastal-heritage-trail.html.

New Jersey Department of Environmental Protection, Division of Parks and Forestry, P.O. Box 404, Trenton, NJ 08625; 800-843-6420; njparksandforests.org.

# 31

# FOREST RESOURCE EDUCATION CENTER

Enjoy a flat pineland walk, a seedling nursery, the headwater of Toms River, and viewing the nests of ospreys, eagles, and hawks.

**LOCATION**
Jackson

**RATING**
Easy

**DISTANCE**
5.4 miles

**ELEVATION GAIN**
300 feet

**ESTIMATED TIME**
2.5 hours

**MAPS**
USGS Lakehurst; state.nj
.us/dep/parksandforests

## DIRECTIONS

Take I-195 East toward I-95/Belmar for 21.44 miles. Take Exit 21 toward Jackson, and merge onto County Highway 527 South. In 4.81 miles, turn right just past Skylark Drive. In 0.6 mile, turn left onto Don Connor Boulevard. In 0.23 mile, the center is on your left. The parking lot has room for 50 to 60 cars. *GPS coordinates:* 40° 05.715′ N, 74° 19.298′ W.

## TRAIL DESCRIPTION

This hike is a pretty, educational route through the only forestry education center in New Jersey, which distributes more than 300,000 seedlings annually. Children are especially welcome.

You'll walk 4.2 miles, mostly on flat, yellow-blazed Pine Acres Trail, and then walk behind the interpretive center to explore the educational bounty, such as the nurseries and Sensory Awareness Trail, for another 1.4 miles. The center has 8 miles of trails that are fairly well marked; as of April 2018, there were plans to improve trail signage and blazes.

Grab a map from inside the interpretive center, and view the impressive taxidermy and a wealth of information on forest stewardship. Note the many educational programs for children. Exit and cross the parking lot, moving away from the center, and head out on the red-blazed Firewise Trail. Very soon, at a kiosk, turn left and then go straight, still on the red trail, heading toward the yellow Pine Acres Trail. Take a right at the circle near beautiful chestnut oaks. Then cross Don Connor

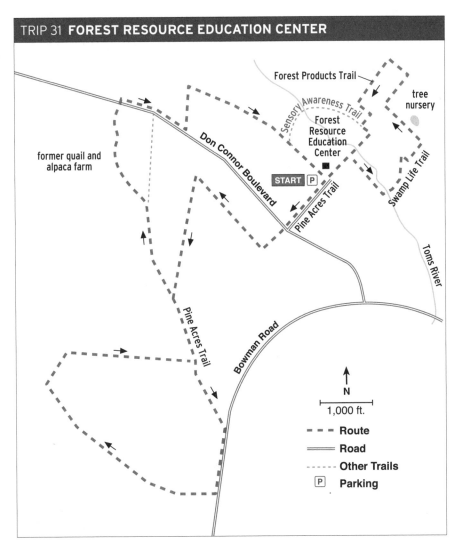

Boulevard (0.2 mile) and enter yellow-blazed Pine Acres Trail, surrounded by pitch pines and short-leaf pines. Go straight at the junction (ignore any random blue blazes) to stay on Pine Acres Trail. Be careful of potholes.

At the T intersection, go left, following yellow blazes, where the sandy trail widens. Cross paved Bowman Road (1.2 miles), then turn right and walk for 0.2 miles on the shoulder of the road (1.4 miles). At a wooden fence, cross Bowman Road again (because the shoulder is not safely walkable) and go straight. A map kiosk is on the left; however, use the map from the interpretive center because the kiosk can be misleading. Just stay on the yellow trail at every intersection until you reach the interpretive center again. At the Y intersection with an unmarked trail, go left at the yellow blazes. The pretty woods are a good example of the Pinelands region (see page 148). At the next Y intersection with an unmarked trail, go straight on the yellow-blazed trail as it narrows through the bushes and shrubs. In late fall, the ground crunches with leaves underfoot. At the T intersection, turn right. At the next Y intersection, you'll see a bench to your left and a bridge over the Maple Root Branch. Make a right at the Y intersection, away from the water. The trail is quiet, and footfalls are muffled by thick pine straw; tall, thin pines soar into the blue sky. At the dirt road, take a left (at about 2.5 miles), and at the next Y intersection, go left, still on yellow-blazed Pine Acres Trail.

Enter a clearing with broomstraw and several abandoned buildings. This was once a quail production farm. An alpaca farm was also here. Explore the ruins and field, then continue into the woods on the other side of the field onto a sandy path typical of the Pinelands. At the Y intersection, go right. At the gate, cross Don Connor Boulevard again (3.3 miles). Take a right to road walk, noting the fire ditch to the left.

Pass a drainage grate in the road. Then turn left at a big dirt path (3.5 miles), with yellow blazes on some trees a few yards in. At the Y intersection, go right (3.7 miles). Fire ditches are on the left. At the T intersection, go right. The trail is still sandy, and the woods slope to left. Ignore the path with birdhouses to the left. Ramble up and down gentle hills, and veer left at the next Y intersection. Go around or over an orange-and-white-striped wire across the path. The Sensory Awareness Trail (4.0 miles) is to the left if you'd like to explore it (a guide rope leads through tactile signs and "talking trees"), and then you're back at the parking lot (4.2 miles).

The next loop is more a saunter than a hike, past tree nurseries and seedling fields, and allows the unique opportunity to see trees being grown by a state forestry service. Alfred Gaskill, New Jersey's first official state forester, started a nursery here in 1907, growing seedlings of jack pine, western yellow pine, Scotch pine, and locust. In 1926, the nursery produced 6 million evergreen seedlings. In 1981, it moved to Jackson and now distributes more than 300,000 seedlings annually (growing many more). Seedlings include hardwoods, Atlantic white cedars, oaks, white pines, Norway spruces, shrubs, and pines (loblolly, shortleaf, pitch, and pitch-loblolly hybrids).

Go behind the interpretive center. Take a left on the wide dirt road toward the gate. The trails are mostly unmarked. You'll see a sign for the Water Shed Project and Swamp Life Trail (4.3 miles), but save those journeys for another day. Instead, walk over the bridge, stopping to look at the headwater of Toms River, only 200 feet wide at this point. A pretty, mossy, rooty unmarked trail leads you to trout-stocked waters (fishing is permitted). Near some benches, note an owl box high above, and see if you can spot the beaver damage prevalent here. Turn right to walk along the river. Then head left on an unmarked trail into the woods onto a corduroy road and walk over another bridge, past blueberry bushes. At the irrigation pond for the tree farm, go right, toward more benches. The duck blind and pump house are visible.

This flat walk passes a seedling nursery, a former quail farm, and Sensory Awareness Trail.

Turn right on the wide path flanked by firs at the top of the pond. At the T intersection, go left, following the wire fence to the right. Walk through a plantation with rows of pines and firs. The tree nursery is ahead, where employees collect cones for seeds. Every April, 40,000 trees are sold or given away. Note the growing fields for seedlings. Turn right at the dirt road, following the fence. Take the next left to the nursery, which was part of the old quail farm (4.5 miles). Examine the huge, perhaps 18-by-15-foot, wooden watershed map, which is erected horizontally on the ground like a wooden dance platform, outside the nursery. Turn left toward the greenhouses (where there is more parking). Now you are on Forest Products Loop Trail, blazed light green, a wide dirt trail.

Follow Forest Products Loop Trail as it curves left. At a T intersection, go right through a metal gate and down a wide dirt road. Cross the bridge where you were before. After the bridge, turn right and go up some steps. Go straight at the fork onto Nature Trail, marked with a sign. A kiosk on the right shows an impressive crosscut Indian oak; read the fascinating history of dendrochronology (tree-ring dating). Duck behind the signage for a pretty lookout over water; note the yoga platform. The Forest Products Loop Trail goes on, but turn left at the Indian oak tree kiosk to a staged display of osprey, eagle, and hawk nests. Head to the "talking tree" kiosk (yes, it speaks; 4.9 miles). Go right at the pavilion to another large wooden watershed display platform, this one of Barnegat Bay—note the numbered rivers. Here, you are back at the interpretive center.

## DID YOU KNOW?

New Jersey is 42 percent forested. One acre of forest absorbs 6 tons of carbon dioxide and emits 4 tons of oxygen. Laboratory research shows that visual exposure to settings with trees produces significant recovery from stress within five minutes, as measured by changes in blood pressure and muscle tension. See "Forest Bathing, or *Shinrin-Yoku*," page 17.

## OTHER ACTIVITIES

On the first Saturday of October at the Forest Resource Education Center, attend the Fall Forestry Festival, which includes a controlled burn, with flames as high as 20 feet; a helicopter does a water drop. In August, take the Full Moon Hike, an interpretive hike through the pine forest. For details, call the interpretive center at 732-928-2360 or see state.nj.us/dep/parksandforests. Explore 9 miles of trails at Turkey Swamp Park, located on 2,226 acres with a 17-acre lake (200 Georgia Road, Freehold). Tour Howling Woods Farm, a rescue and placement center for domestic-bred wolves, wolf dog hybrids, and northern breeds (1371 W. Veterans Highway, by appointment only, 732-534-5745). Visit Monmouth Battlefield State Park, an American Revolution battle site (16 Business Route 33, Manalapan). Enjoy Six Flags Great Adventure (One Six Flags Boulevard) and Jackson Premium Outlets (537 Monmouth Road).

## MORE INFORMATION

Open dawn to dusk. 495 Don Connor Boulevard, Jackson, NJ 08527; 732-928-2360; state.nj.us/dep/parksandforests.

# GREATER ATLANTIC CITY

Atlantic County is located in the Atlantic Coastal Plain. A coastal plain is a flat, low-lying piece of land next to an ocean. The entire Atlantic Coastal Plain is the largest geographic area of New Jersey and covers more than half the state. Beaches, dunes, lagoons, meadows, tidal salt marshes, brackish bays, and river estuaries characterize the landscape.

The topography is mainly low and flat, with the highest elevation approximately 150 feet above sea level. Atlantic City, in the eastern portion, sits on Absecon Island, which is known as a "drumstick" barrier island: fatter in the updrift direction (the direction from which the sand comes), like the meaty end of a drumstick, and thinner on the other end (the direction in which the sand is going). Absecon Island is artificially stabilized with human-made seawalls, breakwater installations, and jetties. Even so, at 8 P.M. on October 29, 2012, when Hurricane Sandy made landfall near Atlantic City, the effects were devastating. The storm had the widest gale diameter ever observed and hit during the highest tide of the month, creating a record storm surge. (The last similar surge was in 1821.) Wind and water damaged or destroyed oceanfront properties and homes and covered the roads with sand. After the storm, many beaches were 30 to 40 feet narrower. Fortified beaches fared better, as did those with sand dunes. Still, the devastation was immense: 70 to 80 percent of the city was underwater.

Surprisingly, the salt and tidal marshes of the Atlantic Coastal Plain remained remarkably stable, proving much more resilient than the land mass. Recovery to vegetation, artificial bird nests (such as osprey platforms), and mammal population was unexpectedly quick. Experts conclude that for ecosystem resilience, large disturbances to wetland stability may be less important than long-term preservation strategies. In short, during Hurricane Sandy, the coastal marsh system functioned as nature designed. Visit the marshes at Edwin B. Forsythe National Wildlife Refuge (Trip 33) and see for yourself.

The Pinelands National Reserve absorbs several inland municipalities in Atlantic County (see page 148). The Pinelands is known for sandy, acidic soil and a preponderance of pine trees, Atlantic cedar swamps, marshes, migratory birds, and water-filled cranberry bogs. It also contains mining pits (see Trip 34) and interesting industrial ruins (see Trip 32) and is considered the birthplace of the Jersey Devil (see page 189 and Trip 33).

All wildlife is important in the Atlantic Coastal Plain, but the New Jersey section includes sixteen species federally recognized as endangered or threatened, including the piping plover and northeastern beach tiger beetle. State endangered species include the bald eagle, black skimmer, peregrine falcon, and short-eared owl. Regional protective priorities include the eastern box turtle and northern diamondback terrapin. The hikes in this section, especially at the Edwin B. Forsythe National Wildlife Refuge (see Trip 33), afford a first-rate education on the wildlife in this area.

# 32

# ESTELL MANOR PARK

This hike includes a swamp walk on a 1.8-mile boardwalk, paths through the historic ruins of World War I munitions productions, and lookouts over the majestic South River.

## DIRECTIONS

From I-295 South, take Exit 60A toward Camden. In 24.0 miles, merge onto NJ 73 South on Exit 36A, toward Berlin. In 22.0 miles, keep left at the fork to go onto Mays Landing Road. In 6.0 miles, turn slightly right onto Eighth Street, go 0.08 mile, and turn left onto Black Horse Pike (US 322 East). Go 5.0 miles and turn right onto Weymouth Road (County Highway 559). Go another 5.0 miles and turn right onto Old Harding Highway (County Highway 606). In 0.5 mile, take the second left onto US 40 East (Harding Highway). Go 0.76 mile and take the first right onto Boulevard Route 50. In 1.75 miles you will reach Estell Manor Park (109 Boulevard Route 50). *GPS coordinates: 39° 23.908′ N, 24° 44.547′ W.*

## TRAIL DESCRIPTION

The informative Warren E. Fox Nature Center (with flush toilets) awaits in the Estell Manor Park parking lot (50-car capacity), resplendent with butter-yellow ginkgo trees in autumn. Enter the center and pick up trail maps and a nature trail guide, then explore the exhibits of live turtles and snakes, dioramas, impressive taxidermy, and historical artifacts. The knowledgeable rangers will probably recommend spending an extra hour to take the 2.2-mile driving tour on Purple Heart Drive before hoofing the easy and universally accessible Swamp Trail Boardwalk to the Bethlehem Loading Company History Trail (BLCHT) and returning to the parking lot. Pick up a free guide to

**LOCATION**
Mays Landing

**RATING**
Easy

**DISTANCE**
5.6 miles

**ELEVATION GAIN**
150 feet

**ESTIMATED TIME**
2.5 hours

**MAPS**
USGS Dorothy,
USGS Mays Landing;
atlantic-county.org/parks/
estell-manor-parks-trails
.asp

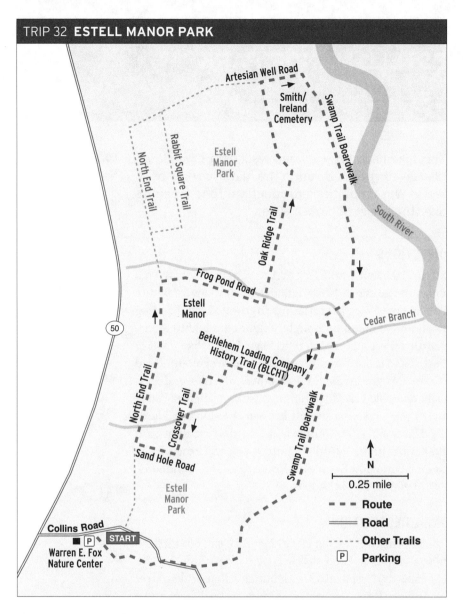

the 18 stops along the BLCHT and learn about this once-expansive World War I munitions plant and administration buildings.

It's better to drive (versus walk) the paved 2.2-mile loop. Pull over and exit your car to visit the ruins of the Estellville Glassworks, an early nineteenth-century glass factory. Next is the humbling Veterans Cemetery, with more than 5,000 interments. Walk the short, unnamed hiking trail on the right at the beginning of the cemetery to reach a platform with 180-degree views of Stephen's Creek. Drive to the next parking lot and get out of the car to visit a playground and a curious floating dock. At the far right corner of the lot, near the water and a smoker's corner, is a paved walking path to the right that leads to Steelman's Creek Burial Ground, a small 1700s cemetery that is worth a visit. Get back in the car and drive to the nature center parking lot.

Now strap on your hiking shoes, head to the back of the nature center, and follow the sign to the Swamp Boardwalk Trail, listed simply as "boardwalk" on the sign. (The trails in this park are marked, not blazed with a color.) The elevated, universally accessible 1.8-mile nature trail features streams, a cedar swamp, a coastal forest (a wild palette of color in autumn), ruins of the Bethlehem Loading Company, and two overlooks of the South River. There are more than 27 miles of trails, so be sure to pick up a trail guide at the nature center.

The boardwalk begins with a tree ID game—take the handy map and pencil the park provides in a box and walk the short trail to the right to test your knowledge. Now proceed, crossing over the loop you just drove, stepping carefully on the sometimes slippery leaf-covered boards. In 0.1 mile at the intersection, go right at the boardwalk sign (to the left is a sign for Greenbriar Trail). Red holly berries shine in the woods. At the T intersection (0.5 mile), take a left to stay on the boards (Mistletoe and Center trails are to the right). Veer right, ignoring Sand Hole Road to the left (0.7 mile). An army of cedar trees crowd the boardwalk. Soon a bench and swamp observation area appear on the right. At the next bench and a kiosk (1.2 miles), take the fork on the left, which puts you on the Bethlehem Loading Company History Trail (BLCHT). Explore the ruins of the Bethlehem Loading Company, a World War I munitions plant where explosives were mixed and loaded into shells mainly 155 mm.

Red arrows provide accurate guidance along this history trail, which consists of many crisscrossing dirt paths, which can be uneven and wet as they wind through the woods. But the bold red arrows and posted maps make the BLCHT easy to follow. Numbered signage at the 18 stops explain the significance of each ruin. You'll visit five stops on this hike. Follow the red arrows to marker 14, and see part of the 30.5-mile railroad bed that delivered 75 carloads of building supplies daily. Go straight to cut over Crossover Trail (glance left at the beautiful clearing); trees and shrubs hem the path. Marker 15 shows remains of the large two-story pouring/filling building. Turn left to follow the next red arrow. As you walk, note the concrete hole on your left, part of the footings for an elevated piped-steam heat system. Take a right at the next red arrow, passing a pretty field on the left. Follow the arrows to marker 16, admiring the lovely swamp to the right, and view the site of the receiving building, where components used to make 8-inch Howitzer shells were unloaded. Continue to marker 17, and see what's left of the buildings where the 8-inch shells were poured. Heavy concrete walls that separated the extruding machines from each other still stand, eerily overgrown with vines and trees. Continue through the quiet woods to marker 18, the foundations of the 8-inch-shell finishing building, where shells were packed with everything but the fuse—that operation was performed on the battlefield. Fifty percent of munitions workers were women.

In operation from 1825–1877, Estellville Glassworks, the ruins of which you'll pass on this hike, was the first of its kind capable of producing both hollowware (bottles) and window glass.

To exit the BLCHT, take a right at the next red arrow onto dirt Sand Hole Road; a kiosk (#11) is on the right (1.9 miles). Sand Hole Road ends at a T intersection with North End Trail (2.0 miles). (If you want to head back now, turn left toward the nature center. Or, if you have time, explore more of the BLCHT.) Take a right on wide North End Trail, watching for bicyclists, toward Artesian Well Road. Keep straight and ignore all side paths. Ruins of the BLC water tower are on your left. Take a right at the kiosk (2.5 miles) onto Frog Pond Road. The Swamp Boardwalk Trail appears at 2.8 miles; take a left away from the boardwalk to Oak Ridge Trail. Oak Ridge Trail becomes a very pretty, if a bit rooty, dirt path, moss-lined and shaded by trees. Cross Eagle Bridge, and turn right on Artesian Well Road (3.5 miles), toward the chemical toilets and lovely Great Egg Harbor River/South River straight ahead. Turn right toward the kiosk and visible Swamp Boardwalk Trail. BLCHT marker 12 (ruins of the power plant) pops up (3.6 miles). The boardwalk soon splits. Take a right for a 30-second walk to the Smith-Ireland Cemetery, surrounded by an unlocked iron fence. You're only 1.7 miles from the nature center.

Backtrack to the boardwalk and follow it all the way back to the nature center; ignore side trails. You'll go through a small, pretty section of marshes and

South River. Near dusk, each step flushes birds from the tall grasses edging the boardwalk, their wings like silk sheets rustling. Continue to enjoy the magic at the second South River lookout, admiring the broad, cloud-reflecting ribbon that curls toward civilization. The boardwalk ends at a paved path that leads to the nature center.

## DID YOU KNOW?

This is headquarters for Atlantic County's parks and recreation division. In winter, vultures roost near the park entrance, a primordial sight with wings spread in the thin sun. An artesian well (nondrinkable water) is north of the main entrance; go 1.0 mile down Artesian Well Road and look for it.

## OTHER ACTIVITIES

Visit the Atlantic County Veterans Museum (adjacent to the park and Veterans Cemetery), featuring military artifacts from the American Revolution through today. Hike 11-acre Weymouth Furnace on Route 559, north of Route 322 (Black Horse Pike), a former iron furnace and paper mill on Great Egg Harbor River. Explore 4,867-acre Maple Lake Wildlife Management Area, south on Route 557.

## MORE INFORMATION

Open 7:30 A.M. until a half-hour after sunset. Part of the Atlantic County Park System. 109 Boulevard Route 50, Mays Landing, NJ 08330; 609-645-5960; atlantic-county.org/parks/estell-manor-park.asp.

# 33

# EDWIN B. FORSYTHE NATIONAL WILDLIFE REFUGE

Explore a birder's paradise, with mystical marshes, a cozy woods trail, and stunning views of Atlantic City.

## DIRECTIONS

From Garden State Parkway, take Exit 48 for US 9 (toward Port Republic/Smithville). Continue onto US 9 South (New York Road). After 5.7 miles, the sign for the entrance is on the right; turn right at the sign onto East Lilly Lake Road to reach the parking lot (800 E. Lilly Lake Road). The large paved lot has space for more than 60 cars. *GPS coordinates: 39° 27.902′ N, 74° 27.026′ W.*

## TRAIL DESCRIPTION

This refuge is immense, stretching nearly 50 miles (and 47,000 acres) from around Oceanville to Holgate, Manahawkin, Forked River, and Mantoloking. It was created to protect migratory birds, and 82 percent is wetlands. Predictably, tens of thousands of migrating ducks, geese, wading birds, and shorebirds linger here in spring and fall, feasting on the rich resources. Many species spend the winter here, and peregrine falcons and ospreys use the nesting platforms. Trees (pitch pines, oaks, and white cedars) dominate 5,000 acres, providing homes for deer, box turtles, and foxes. Be prepared from mid-May through mid-October when ticks and biting insects abound. Winter brings a calm, meditative feel. Fall and spring are riots of color from leaves and flowers.

This hike is in the Brigantine Unit, with five well-marked routes to choose from. You'll travel the popular Songbird Trail through a variety of upland habitats, coming back on Wildlife Drive, where you can either explore other trails or end the hike.

**LOCATION**
Galloway

**RATING**
Easy

**DISTANCE**
5.3 miles

**ELEVATION GAIN**
300 feet

**ESTIMATED TIME**
2.5 hours

**MAPS**
USGS Oceanville; fws.gov/refuge/Edwin_b_forsythe/

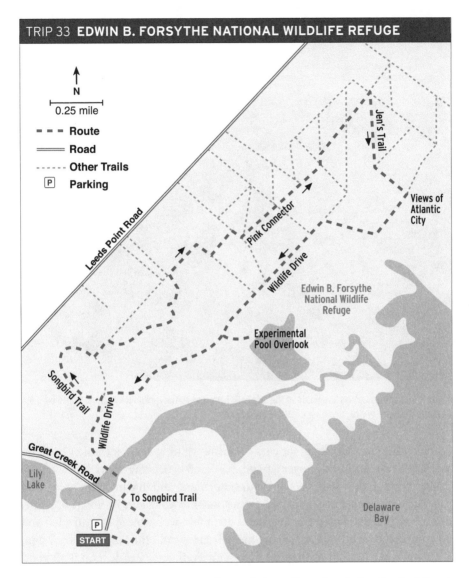

## TRIP 33  EDWIN B. FORSYTHE NATIONAL WILDLIFE REFUGE

**Legend:**
- - - Route
=== Road
····· Other Trails
P Parking

N
0.25 mile

Leeds Point Road

Jen's Trail

Pink Connector

Wildlife Drive

Views of Atlantic City

Edwin B. Forsythe National Wildlife Refuge

Experimental Pool Overlook

Songbird Trail

Wildlife Drive

Great Creek Road

Lily Lake

To Songbird Trail

Delaware Bay

P

START

---

Stop at the visitor contact station beyond the self-pay kiosk (no fee for hikers) for an informative journey through impressive exhibits on the value of barrier islands, salt marshes, and more. There is an educational film in the station about the birds of the refuge. Orient yourself to the area via a wooden floor map and a viewing guide to points north, south, east, and west. Flush toilets are available at the station, and there is a fountain to fill water bottles.

Head to the left of the outdoor toilets, where you'll find a posted trail map and signs to the Songbird Trail loop. A cinder path leads through a picnic area to some wooden steps. Take a left at the bottom of the steps onto the gravel road. The way to blue-blazed Songbird Trail is well marked. Turn right at the gate (blue arrow) onto Wildlife Drive, a one-way dirt road that circles the entire

Atlantic City shines across the fields of the Edwin B. Forsythe National Wildlife Refuge. Photo by U.S. Fish and Wildlife Service, Creative Commons on Flickr.

refuge. (*Caution:* Watch out for cars—you are walking against traffic.) Walk on Wildlife Drive on a bridge over a pond, bordered by waving reeds. Pause on the bridge to watch the swans (get out your binoculars) and in winter, try to identify the blue and red berries. Private homes sprawl to your left. At about 0.7 mile, at a metal gate and small parking area with a few accessible spots, turn left and go around the metal gate, following the blue arrow and the Songbird Trail sign. (You could go straight at the gate onto Jen's Trail, a 0.75-mile loop with good views of the refuge.) The blue-blazed trail enters the woods.

The white sand trail is pretty in the green pine forest. Take a right at the blue arrow onto a narrow, curving path with rolling ups and downs, surrounded by the fresh scent of pine. Watch for roots and slippery moss. At the next blue arrow, turn right; a wire fence is on your left. Follow the fence and turn left where it ends at a bench and blue arrow. (Wildlife Drive is straight ahead if you want to return.) A graceful path leads up a gentle slope to another blue arrow, where you take a right. The woods close in; look for triple- and even quadruple-trunked trees. The path opens up into a small clearing with soft grasses beneath your feet.

At the Y intersection, go left at the blue blaze, back into the woods. Songbird Trail becomes a narrow dirt trail that undulates past 10-foot high, red-berried American holly trees. At a field, the trail splits; simply follow the blue arrow to the right. In this open area with low bushes, pause and look up—you may spot an eagle. A field on your right, lined by stately pines, contains milkweed pods and berries that are colorful in winter. Blue arrows lead you left and then right, back into the woods. The trail slopes down past more fantastic tree shapes and holly. At the same wire fence as before, blue arrows lead to the right, and then right again, before pointing left. Emerald-green moss shines against white sand just before a T intersection with an unnamed trail; blue arrows indicating Songbird Trail lead you to the right. Cross a wide unnamed road that cuts through the woods. (At 2.0 miles, you'll see pink blazes that lead back to Wildlife Drive, if you want to shorten the hike.) Proceed to the next blue arrow and take a left there, which puts you on a narrow, rolling dirt trail, with a bench on the right. Continue following the blue arrows through an area with lovely foliage in autumn. (*Note:* Because of ticks and insects, this trail is not recommended from mid-May through mid-October unless you take precautions.)

At the intersection with an unnamed trail, continue right on blue-blazed Songbird Trail. Periodic patches of white sand highlight the brown and green woods. A metal bench perches on the left atop a slight rise at a T intersection with an unnamed trail. Keep to your left to continue on Songbird Trail; white-blazed Jen's Trail feeds in here. Another blue arrow directs you to curve to the right onto a wide, sandy path. Stop to look for deer and red fox tracks. A bench beneath two fir trees makes for a peaceful rest overlooking a pond.

Suddenly the trail intersects Wildlife Drive, the 7-mile road that circles the refuge (3.2 miles). Turn right, but pause for views of Atlantic City, shining straight ahead across the marsh and bay. The city glimmers with its own personality, changing from hour to hour. The road is unshaded. Watch for cars. An open field stretches to the left, and a "scrub-shrub" area is to the right (a habitat in between a meadow and a forest, which eastern meadowlarks, cottontail rabbits, butterflies, and some other animals prefer). Turn left at the sign for Experimental Pool Overlook (3.9 miles) and linger on the viewing platform with spotting scope. You may see snow geese and Atlantic brants (geese). Enjoy another view of Atlantic City to your right.

Continue on Wildlife Drive, heading to the parking lot. The private homes on the right signal that the lot is close. Cross a bridge over a pond, looking for resident swans. You can recycle your brochure in the mailbox on the trail. Then turn left at the metal gate. Turn right at the headquarters sign, then go up the steps and through the picnic area to your car.

## DID YOU KNOW?

The Jersey Devil is rumored to have been born in the small town of Leeds Point. Tales of this ferocious creature have terrified New Jersey children of all ages for years (see page 189). Leeds Point is about 3 miles away and worth the trip. While there, drive to the end of Oyster Creek Road for dinner at Oyster Creek Inn Restaurant and Boat Bar and a magnificent sunset overlooking Great Bay.

## OTHER ACTIVITIES

The Wildlife Drive auto tour at Edwin B. Forsythe National Wildlife Refuge on 800 E. Lilly Lake Road, especially near sunset, is worth the $4 entrance fee. (Pay and get a dashboard tag at a self-service kiosk near the visitor contact station. Park employees do check for tags.) Park and walk Leeds Eco-Trail over the tidal salt marsh. Climb Gull Pond Tower. See osprey nesting platforms and dozens of swans. Visit historic Smithville a few minutes away on Route 9, with many shops and restaurants.

## MORE INFORMATION

Mailing address: Edwin B. Forsythe National Wildlife Refuge, P.O. Box 72, Oceanville, NJ 08231; 609-652-1665; fws.gov/refuge/edwin_b_forsythe. Mailing address: Friends of Forsythe National Wildlife Refuge, P.O. Box 355, Oceanville, NJ 08231; 609-652-1665; friendsofforsythe.org.

# THE JERSEY DEVIL

Deep in the tall, unmoving pines, on a sugar-sand path, mysterious footprints appear. Larger than those of a horse, the footprints are cloven and made by a creature with two legs. As you step cautiously on the path, deeper into the Pine Barrens, thick pine straw muffles your footfalls. The preternatural quiet of the Pine Barrens transforms to an eerie hum; the silence achieves a presence, an actual tangible quality. As you creep past fire-blackened trunks and mysterious deep holes of cold, blue water, you hear it before you see it: an inhuman scream of rage and hatred, an unearthly cry. You freeze, as a breeze lifts your hair—not a breeze of refreshment, but a hot, acrid wave, made by a devil with large, leathery wings. The red-eyed creature with a dragon-like tail, sharp, glittering teeth, and talons of steel begins its attack. The Jersey Devil has struck again.

More than 2,000 sightings of the Jersey Devil have been reported since 1735, when Jane Leeds of the Pine Barrens in South Jersey gave birth to an unwanted thirteenth child. At the end of her rope, Leeds reportedly screamed, "Let this one be a devil!" And it was. Lore has it the beautiful baby sprouted wings, a thick coating of body hair, and ferocious hooves, claws, and teeth. The story goes on to tell of the creature demolishing the mother and the midwives, and maiming and killing onlookers before flying from the house to live forever in the desolate Pine Barrens.

This 10-foot-tall, kangaroo-like creature with the face of a horse, the head of a dog, and the wings like a bat, plus claws and a pointed tail is seen to this day by travelers on Garden State Parkway and the Atlantic City Expressway and by hikers in the Pine Barrens. But Jersey Devil phobia reached its peak in January 1909. Hundreds of sightings were reported throughout the Delaware Valley area, even in the cities of Camden and Philadelphia. Livestock was slaughtered, footprints traipsed across snow-covered rooftops, schools in lower New Jersey and Philadelphia closed or suffered poor attendance, and mills shut down when workers refused to leave their homes.

The Jersey Devil, as depicted in the *Philadelphia Post* in 1909.

Variously described as "a large, flying kangaroo," "an ostrich-like creature," and "a deer with wings," the reported monster terrorized trolley car passengers, fire fighters, and dogs. Bloodhounds refused to track it. A thousand eyewitness accounts were reported that year.

In 1820, Joseph Bonaparte, Napoleon's older brother, claimed he saw the Jersey Devil near his home in Bordentown, New Jersey. In the early 1800s, the Revolutionary War hero Stephen Decatur claimed he saw the creature fly across the sky within firing range and shot it with a cannonball, but the beast kept going. Other reports have come from forest rangers, fishermen, foragers, taxi drivers, campers, and paddlers.

Some say the Jersey Devil's supernatural origins boil down to politics, plain and simple, beginning in 1677, with Daniel Leeds's arrival from England. Leeds settled in Burlington, New Jersey, and published an almanac that relied on astrology. His Quaker neighbors deemed this evil and thus began a feud in which Leeds was labeled "Satan's Harbinger." Leeds's son Titian took over the almanac and came up against competing almanac publisher Benjamin Franklin. A publicity battle ensued, and Franklin won. Daniel Leeds became a target of anti-British fervor (his family sided with Great Britain), and by the time of the American Revolution, the "Leeds Devil" symbolized sedition. The fervor eventually faded, as it often does, until the early twentieth century, when T.F. Hopkins, a Philadelphia publicist, opened a 10-cent museum at Ninth and Arch streets. There, Hopkins displayed the "Leeds Devil," captured "after a terrific struggle." The poor caged and chained creature was simply a kangaroo upon which Hopkins had slapped wings. Being promoted as a living dragon that "Swims! Flys! Gallops!" catapulted the creature into lasting lore.

Strange things happen in the Pine Barrens. Counts build castles on isolated islands, and famous aviators crash (for both stories, see Trip 49). Dyslexic forest rangers fight the evil of man (see *Idiot!*, a novel by Christopher Klim, Hopewell Publications, 2007). In a sparsely populated land of crumbling walls and rusted machinery, remnants of once-thriving factories and towns, the quietness of the Pine Barrens can unnerve the average person accustomed to clamor. Is it any wonder that imagination begins to fill the gaps of quietude with tales of the supernatural?

(For more on the Jersey Devil, see *The Secret History of the Jersey Devil*, by Brian Regan and Frank J. Esposito, Johns Hopkins University Press, 2018, and the online magazine *Weird N.J.*, weirdnj.com/stories/jersey-devil).

# 34

# EGG HARBOR TOWNSHIP NATURE RESERVE

Enter a world of water and pines on this unique and dog-friendly hike through a former quarry.

## DIRECTIONS

Get on Atlantic City Expressway East. Take Exit 12 toward US 40/Mays Landing/Smithville. Keep right to take the ramp toward Mall/Race Track/Atlantic Cape Community College. Merge onto County Highway 575. Turn right onto English Creek Avenue (County Highway 575). Turn left onto School House Road. Take the first left onto Zion Road (County Highway 615). The reserve will be on your left. The paved parking lot holds about 50 cars and has a few accessible spots. *GPS coordinates:* 39° 21.530' N, 74° 39.111' W.

## TRAIL DESCRIPTION

The reserve is like a two-story building. The bottom (created by a former mining operation) consists of a 45-acre human-made lake, filled by subterranean springs, dotted with islands and anglers. Trails run along the lake's sandy beach. The top is a 125-acre oak-pine forest, with miles of flat trails, and affords a striking view into the reclaimed water-filled mining pit.

Fall and spring are wonderful, bug-free times to visit. Winter snow brings crowds to one of the best sledding hills in the state. Birders will enjoy watching the wading and migratory birds, including ospreys, peregrine falcons, and bald eagles. An environmental center has educational programs, an interactive trail (via smartphone app), and a monarch butterfly habitat restoration project. There are several pet waste bag dispensing and disposal receptacles.

At the parking lot (with chemical toilet), head toward the lake, passing through a metal gate, and stop at the trail map sign. The map shows three trails: the blue-blazed

**LOCATION**
Egg Harbor Township

**RATING**
Easy

**DISTANCE**
3 miles

**ELEVATION GAIN**
100 feet

**ESTIMATED TIME**
1.5 hours

**MAPS**
USGS Marmora;
sites.google.com/site/
ehtnatres/trailmap

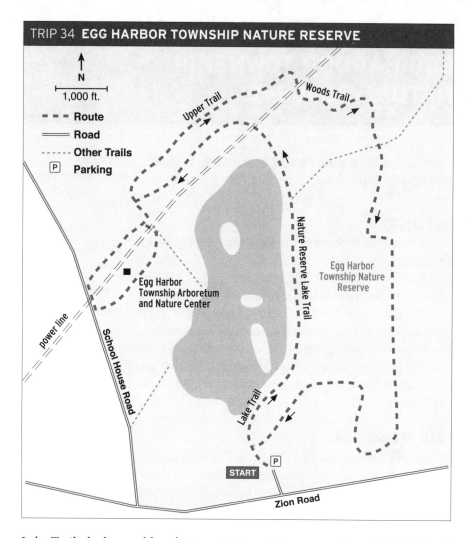

N

1,000 ft.

- - - **Route**
===== **Road**
········ **Other Trails**
P **Parking**

Upper Trail

Woods Trail

Nature Reserve Lake Trail

Egg Harbor
Township Nature
Reserve

Egg Harbor
Township Arboretum
and Nature Center

power line

School House Road

Lake Trail

START

P

Zion Road

Lake Trail, the brown-blazed Upper Trail, and the orange-blazed Woods Trail. Be aware that the Lake Trail is the only trail that is consistently blazed. Once you reach the beginning of Upper Trail, the route dissolves into ribbons tied around trees. Obviously, as of this writing, the trails in this Reserve were still being blazed, despite what is indicated on the posted trail map. On this hike, you will take the blue-blazed Lake Trail to the environmental center, loop back, to the lake, and head to the "second story," where the Upper and Woods trails are still being blazed.

At the trail map sign, look down into the old quarry. Veer right to descend into the quarry and begin the hike around the lake on blue-blazed Lake Trail. Blue ribbons mark the trail, as well as some wooden guideposts with blue arrows. The lake is now on your left. An interesting watery pit is to your right, flanked by high banks (old quarry walls) on Upper Trail. Also to your right are the long wooden steps to the top of the sledding hill.

You are hiking on wide, sandy paths in the quarry pit, a unique sensation of being in the bottom of a very large hole. Walking down to the edge of the lake is permitted in areas where the signs allow. Look for animal tracks in the sand, perhaps even spotting some cloven footprints by the Jersey Devil (see page 189). Find the bog iron formations along the water's edge. (Bog iron is an iron oxide that precipitates from spring water and forms deposits in wet areas.) An otherworldly atmosphere prevails; you are definitely in the Pine Barrens (see page 148).

Just past the power-line tower, at the "toe" of the lake, turn right to continue on Lake Trail, which is flanked by tall reeds (0.8 miles). Turn left on the blue-blazed Lake Trail at the unnamed intersection, moving away from the first power-line tower, and walk under the power lines. In about 100 yards, guideposts appear at an unnamed intersection; turn left here into the woods, at the blue tape on a tree, marking the Lake Trail (0.9 mile).

This area of the trail is popular with dog lovers, so expect to see many canine hikers on this path. In a few hundred yards, take a right at the Y intersection, away from the lake, continuing on blue-blazed Lake Trail. Woods are now on either side of you. Birds chatter in spring, and eagles have been seen here.

A smartphone QR code is affixed next to a black oak. In winter and early spring, the environmental center, where you are heading, is visible on the left through the woods. At the Y intersection with an unnamed trail go straight, continuing on blazed Lake Trail. Read about pitch pines and red-backed sal-amanders on nature signs. Spring creates vernal pools in this area. The path is now soft, dark dirt and leads to a graveled area with a couple of benches. Con-tinue the brief walk to the environmental center (no bathrooms). Benches at the center provide opportunity for a rest near the monarch butterfly restoration sta-tion (1.0 mile). If possible, time your visit for October, when monarch butterflies swarm by the thousands to southern New Jersey.

Get up from the bench and walk through the small meadow on the path (not trail) that heads away from the environmental center. In 100 yards, note the per-simmon trees and birdhouses on the right. At the meadow's end, go left toward another birdhouse, and in 50 yards, you intersect the blue-blazed Lake Trail you came in on. Soon the trail takes a right toward the lake, visible ahead. Turn left at the lake to head north to the brown-blazed Upper Trail. At an intersection with an unnamed path, follow the brown arrow to go straight. To the left are a wire fence and private homes.

At the junction with a power line, go left. This turn and the following ones are not on the map posted at the preserve. You are on a sandy path with the lake below. Take a left at the next power-line tower toward creatively painted con-crete pipes, large enough for a child to crawl through (1.6 miles). Past the pipes, the trail heads left into the woods, and for some reason is marked by a blue rib-bon. The path is lined with a row of pine trees. At the plain wooden guideposts and blue ribbons, turn right, following the blue ribbons into the piney woods.

Most of this hike is in the pines that frame the former mining pit.

Here, you feel as if you are on a totally different walk than you were just minutes ago: now in the comfort of pines and not in the bottom of a quarry pit. Turn left at the Y intersection, at the double green ribbon tied on the tree, heading away from the lake, even deeper into the woods. On the map posted in the park, this should be the orange-blazed Woods Trail, and perhaps will be when the trail-blazing is complete. It's a pretty, flat walk through the pines, and a real trail-blazing adventure! You are not in the wilderness so are in no danger; simply have fun wandering from ribbon to ribbon. Your footfalls are muffled by soft dirt and pine straw; the path meanders, giving way to oak trees. At the unnamed T intersection (1.9 miles), go right (there is very little distance between turns on this hike). At the next unmarked four-way guide post, go straight.

The path narrows, lined by mountain laurels and blueberry bushes. At the unnamed T intersection, go right; the trail here is marked with deep-pink ribbons. At the next unnamed T intersection, go left at the orange ribbon. When you reach another unnamed T intersection and plain wooden guidepost, go right, staying on the wide trail that is marked with an orange ribbon—what is, or will be, Woods Trail.

At the next unnamed intersection, go straight at the double pink ribbons on the trees. At the Y intersection, go right, still following double pink ribbons, and you'll hear the sound of cars (2.4 miles). Soon you will see Zion Road to the left. At the next T intersection, take a left at the orange ribbon onto a sandy path. Shortly, you'll see the lake stretching in the distance, like a hologram. Walk out of the woods to the bank for a wonderful view, noting the long wooden steps at the sledding hill. Turn left and rest a while on the bench overlooking the lake. Then continue on for half a mile to the parking lot.

## DID YOU KNOW?

Bog iron, which is naturally rust resistant, was mined here and used for tool and wrought iron rail production. Colonial Americans used bog iron for cannonballs during the American Revolution.

## OTHER ACTIVITIES

Enjoy the area's dining cornucopia: seafood, Mexican, and some of the famous Jersey diners. Start exploring on Route 615. Visit Storybook Land (6415 E. Black Horse Pike), established in 1955, where children's classics come alive. Kitsch lovers must tour the six-story Lucy the Elephant, billed as America's oldest roadside attraction (9200 Atlantic Avenue, Margate City). Estell Manor Park (Trip 32) and Edwin B. Forsythe National Wildlife Refuge (Trip 33) are nearby.

## MORE INFORMATION

Hours are dawn to dusk. Egg Harbor Township Municipal Building, 3515 Bargaintown Road, Egg Harbor Township, NJ 08234; 609-926-4000; sites.google .com/site/ehtnatres/home.

# SOUTHERN SHORE

The Southern Shore is part of New Jersey's Outer Coastal Plain. You won't stub your toes hiking here, because much of the region is flat and covered with sandy soil, especially in the area of the Pinelands that bleeds briefly into the northern part of the Shore, and on the Atlantic Ocean beaches themselves.

Cape May County has the distinction of being the southernmost county in New Jersey and is almost completely surrounded by water. The county's western coastline meets Delaware Bay, and its eastern and southern coastlines embrace the Atlantic Ocean. With 30 miles of beaches, Cape May County attracts many vacationers. Tourism is the county's single largest industry, although lima beans once covered 5,000 acres. The town of West Cape May still calls itself the lima bean capital of the world and hosts an annual lima bean festival. Growing vineyard grapes is more common now than in years past.

Cape May is a very popular destination for birders—one of the world's most celebrated migratory junctions. Every autumn, the county's unique wind patterns and geography bring millions of migrating hawks, seabirds, shorebirds, and songbirds, not to mention butterflies and dragonflies. Cape May and Cumberland counties are a natural stopover for more than 120 different species of birds.

On the Delaware Bay side, which includes the entire coastline of Cumberland County and the western coastline of Cape May County, the region changes to salt marshes, mudflats, and wetlands. Located on 6,000 acres of coastal wetlands, the nonprofit Wetlands Institute, based in the town of Stone Harbor, provides a wonderful overall education on life in the salt marshes and the marshes' importance (see page 208 and Trip 40).

Facing page: Migrating monarch butterflies can be seen by the thousands in October, this one off Thompson's Beach in southern New Jersey.

The Delaware Bay side—also known as the Bayshore, with 42 miles of beach-front coastline—is quite a different animal from the Atlantic Ocean side. Usually bypassed by beachgoers headed to the ocean, the communities here are smaller; some are even disappearing due to rising sea levels. Cumberland County, where the shore is entirely on the Delaware Bay side, is served only by state and county routes. In contrast, the Atlantic City Expressway takes you directly to Cape May County, via Exit 0.

But what the Bayshore lacks in people, it more than makes up for in wildlife (see outdoors.org/DEbays for more information). In May and June, millions of Atlantic horseshoe crabs come to Delaware Bay to spawn (see Trip 36). Tens of thousands of red knots, a type of migratory bird, depend on the horseshoe crabs' eggs for refueling on their flight from South America to the Arctic. Other migratory shorebirds that rely on these eggs are the ruddy turnstone, semipalmated sandpiper, sanderling, dunlin, and short-billed dowitcher.

The Bayshore is also prime oystering grounds. The wetlands in the community of Bivalve (see Trip 40) in Cumberland County were once known as the oyster capital of the world.

Also impressive is the Southern Shore's preponderance of wildlife management areas—according to the New Jersey Department of Fish and Wildlife, 23 in Cape May and Cumberland counties combined. It follows that there are fourteen conservation organizations with offices in the Bayshore.

The ecologic importance of the Southern Shore and its sandy, marshy beauty is undisputed.

# 35

# BELLEPLAIN STATE FOREST

Lose yourself in this long woods walk, with tunnels of mountain laurel, soothing lakes, and interesting wetlands.

## DIRECTIONS

If going south, take Garden State Parkway to Exit 17 to Route 9 and then to Highway 550. If going north, take Exit 13 to NJ 55 South, to Route 47, to Route 347, and then to Highway 550. Follow signs to the forest (One Henkinsifkin Road). The parking lot holds about 30 cars. *GPS coordinates: 39° 14.908′ N, 74° 50.549′ W.*

## TRAIL DESCRIPTION

Belleplain is 21,254 acres of pine-oak and Atlantic white cedar forest, interspersed with lowland hardwoods, plantations of evergreens, swamps, three ponds (Hands Mill, Pickle Factory, and East Creek), and one lake (Nummy). The Civilian Corps of Engineers created Lake Nummy from a cranberry bog in 1933. At this National Audubon Society Important Bird Area, you can see bald eagles, barred owls, Cooper's hawks, and many songbirds, including a proliferation of yellow-throated warblers. Choose from more than 40 miles of trails. On this hike, you'll get a good leg-stretch and an overview of the forest by taking North Shore, Goosekill, and East Creek trails and coming back to North Shore. In April, enjoy white and purple wood violets, twittering birds, and the blooming golden club in East Creek Pond. In May and June, a profusion of mountain laurels burst into clouds of white and pink, and the aquatic, carnivorous, yellow floating bladderwort appears on ponds, as well as bullhead pond lilies. In midsummer, pick highbush blueberries. Belleplain is part of the Pinelands but not the Pine Barrens (see page 148),

**LOCATION**
Woodbine

**RATING**
Moderate

**DISTANCE**
10.3 miles

**ELEVATION GAIN**
300 feet

**ESTIMATED TIME**
5 hours

**MAPS**
USGS Tuckahoe; state.nj .us/dep/parksandforests/

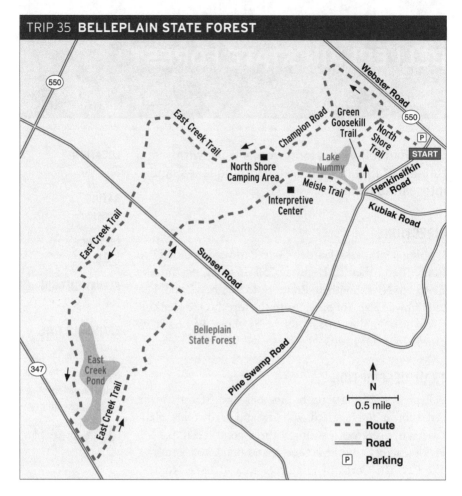

which allows for richer soil conditions and more growth. Belleplain is also part of the New Jersey Coastal Heritage Trail (see page 170).

Start directly from Belleplain State Forest headquarters on Henkinsifkin Road. Be sure to grab a map (the free New Jersey Audubon Belleplain State Forest Birding Map is the most detailed) from the ranger's station. Facing the headquarters building, walk to the right onto orange-blazed North Shore Trail, a lovely, narrow dirt path through the woods. Read about lichens on the nature signs that line the path. Continue on North Shore Trail and take a right at a circle to get on green-blazed Goosekill Trail (unmarked here, but the square yellow marker soon appears as the trail widens to a surface made of tiny stones, 0.3 mile). Walking on these root-free flat trails is a delight. Turn right at the green blaze toward the two-lane, paved Highway 550. Turn left on the road for a short walk across a small culvert. Turn left at the "Gypsy Moth Killed Oak Salvaged 1988" sign and a guardrail, at the metal sign for the yellow-and-white-blazed Champion Trail (0.8 mile).

Champion Trail, a dirt trail, turns off almost immediately to the left, but don't take it. Instead, walk straight onto the paved, shady road (called Champion Road) that's closed to cars You'll feel like you're on the Avenue des Champs-Élysées. On the left is the North Shore Camping Area, with a few picnic tables, restrooms, and a drinking-water pump, open in season, Memorial Day to Labor Day (1.6 miles). On the right is Ballfield Pavilion and a large athletic and recreation field. Turn left here at the stop sign and head toward a 60-car parking lot, playground, picnic tables, swimming beach, and restrooms, fronted by glistening Lake Nummy. Take a moment to look around at this impressive complex. Side trip completed, walk back to the stop sign, turn left, and in a few yards, just before the bridge, turn right onto white-blazed East Creek Trail (2.0 miles). (You can drive to Lake Nummy and park there if you want to start here and make the hike 2.0 miles shorter.)

Head into the woods on the white-blazed, shaded dirt path. Take a right at the fork; be careful of roots and admire the mountain laurels. Soon a short boardwalk leads over a primordial-feeling swamp. In winter, all is quiet as you walk into the sun past moss and large, red-berried American holly trees. Cross the one-lane paved New Bridge Road (2.7 miles) onto white-blazed East Creek Trail on the other side. Pine straw hushes your footfalls. At the four-way intersection in the forest of mountain laurels and tall pines, keep straight on East Creek Trail. A footbridge spans a stream. Cross a dirt road, keeping straight on the white-blazed trail (orange-blazed Cedar Trail is to your right). Two overlapping trees caress the path. At another dirt road, keep straight to stay on the white-blazed trail. A fire ditch is to the left. Cross the one-lane paved Sunset Road (3.7 miles) and pick up white-blazed East Creek Trail on the other side, still nestled deep in the woods. Some patches of the trail can be muddy and flooded here in spring, but a nine-trunked tree on the left is your reward. This peaceful spot makes a perfect opportunity for forest bathing (see page 17).

The shaded trail continues to meander through the woods and understory, eventually crossing a one-lane paved road into the woods on the other side. Mountain laurels begin to crowd the path. Cross a dirt road. Soon two T intersections pop up in quick succession—make right turns on each. Very quickly, the white-blazed East Creek Trail turns left. (In leafless seasons, East Creek Pond peeks through the trees.) Tread a boardwalk over a small swamp, and head straight. The quiet here is pervasive, despite the faint murmur of cars. The trail begins to follow East Creek Pond on the left (4.9 miles), and becomes a bit rooty and muddy. Enter a small tunnel of mountain laurels as the path eventually winds to the pond and follows the water's edge. You can walk to the shore at periodic inroads. A fuchsia-colored metal bench, the only one on the trail, allows full enjoyment.

Back on the white-blazed trail, enter the gravel parking lot at the East Creek Pond boat ramp on Route 347 (5.5 miles) at the south end of East Creek Pond. Walk down the ramp and look for April-blooming golden club along the water's

A super moon in December rises above Lake Nummy in Belleplain State Forest.

edge, as well as bald eagles, ducks, and turtles. To begin the loop back, turn left on busy Route 347 and road walk across a bridge (shoulders are ample), stopping to admire the expanse of the creek below. Pass East Creek Group Cabins on the left. Look closely as you pass a telephone pole and you'll see a white arrow guiding the way. About one minute (750 feet) past the group cabins, the trail sign points to the left, back into the woods, on East Creek Trail again (5.9 miles).

Soon the traffic sounds fade on the flat path, framed by huge mountain laurels (make that mental note about spring again). Keep straight. The trail can be very muddy and often flooded in spring, but there are walk-around paths. Footbridges and boardwalks cross serene swamps. At the T intersection, go left, following the white arrows. The path is flat, lined with moss, and hugged by trees. Go left to follow the white arrow at the overgrown field on the right. Walk by a pretty field before popping back into the woods at the white arrow and fire ditch.

Cross paved Sunset Road (7.9 miles) onto the path on the other side. Traverse a cute footbridge. At the Y intersection, go left at the white arrow. At the next Y intersection soon after, go left to follow the white arrow, admiring the carpet of green moss. A recycling center for campers appears on your right just before the trail ends in a T intersection at a paved road. Take a left, then a quick right onto paved Deans Branch Road/Meisle Road. Lake Nummy is on your left, and the interpretive center is on your right (8.9 miles). If the center is open, go in and explore. Otherwise walk down the road, keeping the center on your right. Sit on the benches, stroll on the dock, and admire the lake, beautiful at any time. Look for yellow pond lilies and floating bladderwort in season.

Go straight, still on the paved Meisle Road, past the nature markers. Toward the end of the lake, turn left at the orange blaze on a tree; although not marked as such, this is Meisle Trail. A pretty, gentle path pads through the Virginia pines, with the lake on the left. (A footbridge helps with the muddy parts.) At the T intersection, go left onto a dirt road called Green Goosekill Trail (green metal square, 9.4 miles). Then continue straight on the green-blazed trail, ignoring yellow-blazed Nature Trail that crops up on the left. Admire the highbush blueberries, sheep laurel (which has a unique "spring-loaded" pollination system—when an insect lands, the anthers pop out and shower it with pollen), and the common greenbrier (with gorgeous blue or red berries in fall). (*Caution:* Sheep laurel is toxic if eaten.) In summer, inhale the perfume of sweet pepperbush blooms. Walk over a culvert pipe in a few hundred yards, then take a right onto orange-blazed North Shore Trail (10.0 miles). Look for frogs as you pass a muddy swamp, with a stream flowing to your right. At the Y intersection, go right, which takes you back to the headquarters parking lot.

## DID YOU KNOW?

There's a beaver dam not far down Tom Field Road (or Narrows Road), which is a dirt trail leading left off East Creek Trail (before East Creek Pond), about 0.5 mile after Sunset Road.

## OTHER ACTIVITIES

Thirty minutes away in Millville is Wheaton Arts and Cultural Center (1000 Village Drive), known for glass creations, and Millville's arty Glasstown Arts District. To the south, in Dennis, is 8,000-acre Dennis Creek Wildlife Management Area; farther west in the town of South Dennis is Beaver Swamp Wildlife Management Area on Beaver Dam Road, with bald eagles (off Route 47). About 15 miles north, in Heislerville, are East Point Lighthouse (call 856-785-0349 for hours) and Heislerville Wildlife Management Area.

## MORE INFORMATION

Open dawn to dusk. Mailing address: P.O. Box 450, Woodbine, NJ, 08270; 609-861-2404; state.nj.us/dep/parksandforests/parks/belle.html.

## 36

# THOMPSON'S AND MOORE'S BEACHES

These secluded beaches are horseshoe crab spawning areas, home to a large diamondback turtle population, and a haven for migrating birds and monarch butterflies.

**LOCATION**
Heislerville

**RATING**
Easy

**DISTANCE**
2.4 and 1.4 miles

**ELEVATION GAIN**
20 feet

**ESTIMATED TIME**
2 hours

**MAPS**
USGS Heislerville;
state.nj.us/dep/fgw/pdf/
wmamaps/heislerville.pdf

## DIRECTIONS

*Thompson's Beach*: Take NJ 55 South to Exit 13 toward Glassboro/Vineland. In 41.0 miles, stay straight to go onto NJ 47 South. In about 5 miles, take a right onto Highway 616 (Glade Road). In less than 2.0 miles, turn right onto Thompson's Beach Road. There's parking space for about eight cars. *GPS coordinates:* 39° 12.169′ N, 74° 59.611′ W.

*Moore's Beach* (from Thompson's Beach): Take a right off Thompson's Beach Road onto Glade Road (Route 616). After 1.6 miles, take a right on Route 47 at a sign for Pine Barrens Byway, toward Wildwood. After 0.4 miles, turn right at the sign for Moore's Beach. (*Caution:* This is a rough gravel road with big potholes and flood potential.) There is no parking lot, but limited parking is available along the roadside. *GPS coordinates:* 39° 11.368′ N, 74° 57.067′ W.

## TRAIL DESCRIPTION

In 1950, these salt marsh beach areas were hit hard by an unpredicted tidal wave that swept away businesses, boardwalks, and human lives. A storm in 1980 virtually finished the remaining beach communities, and in 1998, Maurice River Township bought what was left and demolished it. The once-thriving horseshoe crab population, and the bird population that depended on the crab eggs, suffered badly. Hurricane Sandy in 2012 hammered what was left. But the good news is that major restoration is ongoing and the beaches are now a popular destination for birders, especially in May during mating season and in fall during

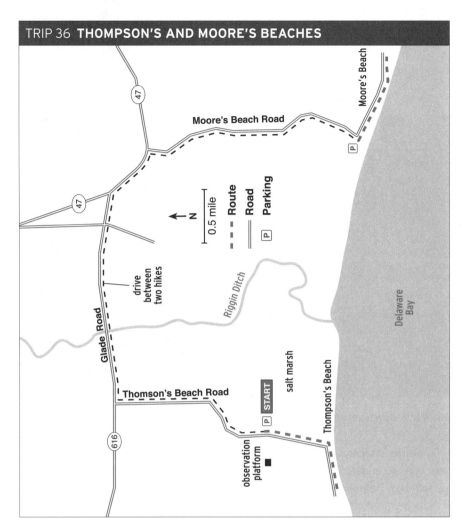

shorebird migration. And as a result of a cooperative initiative (see "Did You Know?") the important horseshoe crab spawning ground is being revitalized.

In spring, warblers, sparrows, and other songbirds join the shorebirds, waders (especially red knots), waterfowl, ospreys, peregrine falcons, and eagles. As many as a million birds can pass through during the second week in May. Watch for cormorants spreading their large wings to dry. In summer, snowy egrets and great blue herons are particularly lovely. At low tide, clapper rails cackle distinctively. Look for diamondback terrapins. Fall brings monarch butterflies, red knots, and raptor migration. Winter is quietly beautiful, especially if you spot an eagle perched on a snag (a standing dead tree). Summer is buggy, but the swimming is nice and the days are long. At any time of year, it's best to walk the beach at low tide. The trail is mainly just the beach; follow the ocean and the occasional nature sign, and use your car to make the 5.0-mile journey from Thompson's Beach to Moore's Beach.

A former New Jersey game warden examines a horseshoe crab.

The hike on Thompson's Beach starts at a large wooden observation station; you may see a bald eagle perched there. Start walking to the ocean on Thompson's Beach Road, a flat gravel road that was built after Hurricane Sandy.

Pass by reeds, cordgrass, and scraggly dead trees (snags) in the eerie and calm salt marsh to the right. Salt marshes are one of the most productive ecosystems on earth: They provide food, shelter, water cleansing, and flood protection (see page 208). As you walk, imagine the homes, schools, shops, and restaurants that occupied this area up until 1998. Look for the last of the monarch butterflies, feasting on the remains of seaside goldenrods before they continue migration to warmer climes. They'll be back in March and April to lay their eggs on milkweed, which the caterpillars eat before their transformation.

Once you reach the ocean (0.8 mile), turn right to walk along the beach. Enjoy the black skimmers from May through October. These large birds have a serious underbite: Their long lower jaw dips into the water, making it easy to skim for fish. Unfortunately, you may see many dead diamondback terrapins. The terrapins crawl into pots put in the water to catch crabs; since the turtles can't escape, they drown, and are discarded on the beach by crab fisherman. A simple plastic device called an extruder is all it takes to keep the turtles out of the crab pots. Note the abundance of horseshoe crab shells left behind after molting.

Look for great blue heron tracks in the sand as the waves lap and the gulls cry. Imagine the biologists "rocket netting" shorebirds from July through September to band them. (After a large number of desired birds have gathered, nets are shot into the air to cover them. Banders work quickly so birds won't overheat or injure themselves in a panic.)

Pretend you are a 10-year-old beachcomber for a while longer, and when you reach the barrier of the salt marsh (1.2 miles), turn around and head back to your car. As you leave the beach, examine the snags for eagles and ospreys. Ospreys nest lower than eagles, but they aggressively battle for the best tree.

Get in your car and take the short drive to Moore's Beach. Park on the roadside and enter the beach. Old board roads (corduroy roads), built for vehicles prior to paved roads, still lie underwater. Hunt in the sand for debris from the former towns. Beach flowers bloom. An oyster bar sits offshore (an oyster bar is a protected area seeded with shells for the pinprick-sized oysters to land on). Periwinkle snails live in the brackish waters of the marsh lining the sand; diamondback terrapins eat them. Look up to spot graceful bird murmurations (unified flight patterns that make shapes in the sky) that will leave you breathless. At 0.7 mile, this section ends; turn around and return to your car.

## DID YOU KNOW?

The "reTURN the Favor" program trains people to rescue horseshoe crabs by turning them off their backs. Thank the American Littoral Society and Conserve Wildlife Foundation of New Jersey, which created conservation partnerships funded by New Jersey Recovery Fund, National Fish and Wildlife Foundation, and New Jersey Corporate Wetlands Restoration Partnership. Additional funding was provided by Public Service Electric and Gas Nuclear LLC (returnthefavornj.org).

## OTHER ACTIVITIES

Tour East Point Lighthouse at 10 Lighthouse Road in Heislerville, built in 1849 and fully restored in 2017. Call 856-785-0349 for hours; there is a small fee. Stroll and drive Matt's Landing for terrific bird-watching; take County Road 616 (Dorchester-Heislerville Road) to Matt's Landing Road, and turn right. For birding, dune viewing, and marine life, visit Corson's Inlet State Park in Ocean City (5898 Bay Avenue), about 45 minutes east of Heislerville, off County Highway 619 (Bay Avenue). Restaurants are on Route 47.

## MORE INFORMATION

Open dawn to dusk. Closed May 7 to June 7 to protect shorebird and crab breeding. Administered by the New Jersey Division of Fish and Wildlife, Mail Code 501-03, P.O. Box 420, Trenton, NJ 08625-0420; 609-292-2965; state.nj.us/dep/fgw.

## SALT MARSH ECOSYSTEMS

Salt marshes are one of the most productive ecosystems on earth. They protect the mainland from flooding and erosion, filter sediment and pollutants, afford a safe nursery for many species of coastal fish and shellfish, provide food and nesting for migratory birds, and house mammals, insects, and diamondback terrapins. As far as ecosystems go, salt marshes rival Iowa cornfields. But instead of pigs, cows, and humans, salt marshes feed muskrats, mink, raccoons, snowy egrets, ospreys, great blue herons, swans, sparrows, and crustaceans. Common cordgrass even supports the air-breathing coffee bean snail as it slowly climbs along the grassy stalk at high tide. Unfortunately for the snail, the birds crunch and eat it, as the shell helps grind up food in their stomachs.

How can an environment so salty support a single living thing, let alone so many? It seems that halophytes (salt marsh plants) love salt, or, to be more precise, they process it well. Plants such as cordgrass manage salt stress, with salt-excreting glands and mechanisms to reduce water loss and promote high water-use efficiency. Salt marsh plants also have the ability to deliver oxygen to below-ground roots, much like the trees in the Amazon do during times of high water.

The tides also promote life. As a transitional habitat between ocean and land, salt marshes receive plenty of tidal water—twice a day, in fact. Water decays the plant life, which creates soft marsh substrate ("pluff mud") and, eventually, dense layers of peat. Fiddler crabs, marsh snails, insects, fish, and mussels further shred the organic material. Bacteria, fungi, and small algae break down what remains. The tide goes out, carrying nutrients back to the sea, where they feed fish and other coastal organisms.

Over time, the buildup of organic material from repeated decay acts like a giant sponge, absorbing and holding water that would otherwise erode the shoreline and flood the coast and all of its inhabitants. The dense organic material also filters pollutants.

The salt marsh is the backbone of the beach, the barrier between sand and land. This is especially important in New Jersey, which has 245,000 acres of salt marsh, mostly along Delaware Bay and the Atlantic coast of Cape May and Atlantic counties.

Outright destruction, such as from farming (mainly salt hay), has been greatly diminished by federal and state legislation. But other dangers exist, such as pollution from overpopulation along the coast and improper mosquito and flood control that either dries up or floods the marshes.

As the sea levels continue to rise, the nurturing, nutritive, protective, and self-sustaining salt marshes will keep pace—as long as we let them.

## 37

# CAPE MAY POINT STATE PARK AND SOUTH CAPE MAY MEADOWS PRESERVE

Enjoy sand dunes, marshes, woods, beaches, birds, and butterflies at the end of New Jersey, surrounded by the sea.

## DIRECTIONS

Take Exit 0 (yes, zero) off Garden State Parkway toward Cape May on Route 109. Turn right onto Bank Street, then left onto Broad Street. Turn right onto Highway 633, which becomes Highway 606. Turn left onto 215 Lighthouse Avenue (Highway 629). A large parking lot is on the left (space for about 200 cars). You'll see the Cape May Lighthouse. *GPS coordinates: 38° 56.060′ N, 74° 56.954′ W.*

## TRAIL DESCRIPTION

Cape May Point State Park is managed by the New Jersey Division of Parks and Forestry. The Nature Conservancy manages the adjacent South Cape May Meadows, a nature preserve. Both are on major migratory routes for seabirds, shorebirds, and songbirds. The Cape May Peninsula acts as a funnel for birds migrating along the Atlantic Flyway. From mid-May to June, the shorebirds and songbirds return. Summer hosts nesting American oystercatchers, least terns, piping plovers, and black skimmers. Magnificent hordes of airy dragonflies and vividly colored monarch butterflies float through in late summer and early fall. In fall, hundreds of hawks power past this premier migration route, headed south. Horseshoe crabs lay eggs here in May and June during their annual migration.

All year long, visitors can enjoy the dunes, ocean, freshwater wetlands, woods, meadows, and ponds.

Take blue-blazed Plover Trail and red-blazed Duck Pond Trail through the highlights of the park, using a connector trail to South Cape May Meadows. Enjoy a

**LOCATION**
Cape May Point

**RATING**
Easy

**DISTANCE**
3.4 miles

**ELEVATION GAIN**
100 feet

**ESTIMATED TIME**
1.5 hours

**MAPS**
USGS Cape May;
Cape May Point State
Park: state.nj.us/dep/
parksandforests/; South
Cape May Meadows:
nature.org/en-us/
get-involved/how-to-help/
places-we-protect/
south-cape-may-meadows/

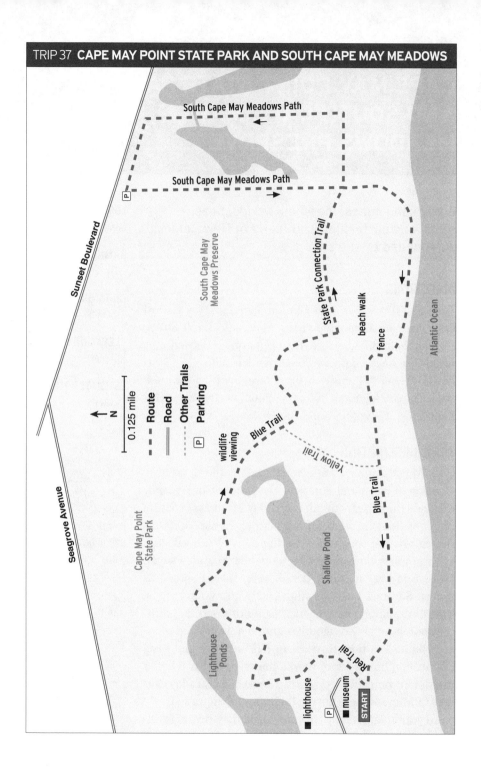

South Cape May Meadows Path

South Cape May Meadows Path

South Cape May
Meadows Preserve

Sunset Boulevard

State Park Connection Trail

beach walk

fence

Atlantic Ocean

N

0.125 mile

- - - Route
——— Road
······· Other Trails
P Parking

wildlife
viewing

Blue Trail

Yellow Trail

Blue Trail

Seagrove Avenue

Cape May Point
State Park

Shallow Pond

Lighthouse
Ponds

Red Trail

lighthouse

P

museum

START

beach walk past a World War II bunker before heading back to the parking lot with bird observation deck and lighthouse.

Get started from the Cape May Lighthouse parking lot. (*Note:* In summer, the lot fills quickly, so get there early.) The 157-foot-tall lighthouse, with 199 steps, is open seasonally ($8 for adults, $5 for children ages 3 to 12, and free for children younger than 3). Parts of the trail are exposed to sun, so you may want to bring a hat for added sun protection. In summer, bring bug spray, and remember to apply the spray to your feet to guard against chigger bites. (Chiggers are tiny red mites that bite and cause maddening skin irritation.)

Stop at the visitor center for maps and other information. Flush toilets are available here. Walk to the end of the parking lot, toward the evergreens, and go straight onto the combined red-, yellow-, and blue-blazed trails (Duck Pond, Monarch, and Plover trails, respectively). Cross the raised boardwalk through cedars and a pretty foliage archway, stopping to read the nature signs about the great blue heron, great-horned owl, muskrat, and more. Get your bearings on the comfortable bench, noting the decorative reeds and plants, such as shadbush and pitch pines. Then get up and take a left onto red-blazed Duck Pond Trail, universally accessible, toward a pond with ducks, swans, and perhaps an osprey.

A bird blind on your right may or may not be open, depending on the season. The pitch pines are impressive and shady. Note the sassafras trees, red-leaved in fall, and eastern red cedars. Lighthouse Pond quickly comes into view; take advantage of the observation deck for a close-up look at the swans. The trail splits into three (0.3 mile); turn left on the combined blue- and yellow-blazed trails (Plover and Monarch) away from the parking lot. Still on a boardwalk, observe the different kinds of trees: black gum, with deep-red leaves in fall; persimmon (uncommon in New Jersey); and sweet gum, with its star-shaped leaves. Cross a bridge with a pretty view of the pond to the left. Benches afford a comfortable view of the water and a big field.

Past the pond, the boardwalk turns to a dirt path. Stay on the combined Plover and Monarch trails. Garter snakes may twist through the dirt in front of you. Enter an open area featuring a pond, wetlands, and ducks. Cross it on a boardwalk onto a dirt path again. On the right, the shallow pond shimmers in the sun; a cozy thicket is on the left as you walk this fun, narrow route. When you reach the upcoming woods of white oak and black gum, take a seat on the convenient bench for an excellent view of the pond and lighthouse. At the intersection, climb the wildlife viewing platform to watch swans eat, preen, and swim (0.8 mile).

Return to the intersection and turn left onto blue-blazed Plover Trail. After about 200 yards, go over the bridge. Take the boardwalk through an open marsh, turning around to orient yourself to the ever-present lighthouse. Head into the woods, looking for persimmon trees, and at the intersection with an unnamed dirt road (1.1 miles), turn to the right. Continue on Plover Trail, over another bridge with another excellent view of the lighthouse. Go left through a gap in the

The crashing waves of the Atlantic Ocean are hard to resist. Cool your hike-weary feet in the surf.

fence at the large sign for the 0.25-mile State Park Connection Trail, also blazed blue (1.2 miles); you are now entering South Cape May Meadows, a nature preserve and migratory bird refuge, via the State Park Connection Trail. (*Note:* This trail is not on the state park map.) Head to the pond for more ducks (mallards, American black ducks and wigeons, gadwalls, and shovelers), and enjoy the sugar-sand trail through an open field.

At the next fence, go straight to explore South Cape May Meadows. (A right turn here leads to the beach.) You are now on South Cape May Meadows Path. Keep the fence on your right. At the next intersection, go left (the path sports a brown blaze here). In late summer and early fall, enjoy the monarch butterflies floating about, part of their annual migration toward central Mexico, more than 2,000 miles away. You'll see a pond on the right with houses in the distance.

Stroll a bit farther to some benches and an observation deck (1.7 miles). Look in the sky for turkey vultures and raptors such as eagles, ospreys, falcons, and hawks. Scan the meadow for songbirds—warblers, wrens, and sparrows subsist here. Look at the water's edge for great egrets and terns feeding in the shallows. Swans and ducks float farther out. Listen to the roar of the ocean nearby and smell the salty breeze.

Refreshed, begin walking on a bridge between two ponds. This ordinary-looking footbridge covers an important water control structure that can change water levels in the wetlands during storms or drought. Employees use two special hooks to add or remove boards that raise or lower water levels on either side of the bridge. Lowering the levels during Hurricane Sandy handily absorbed 10 inches of rain. Manipulation during migration or nesting facilitates the survival of waterfowl. Take a moment to check out this marvel of water control and watch a turtle or two.

At the gate and paved road (Sunset Boulevard, 1.9 miles), turn left onto a gravel path that parallels the road and you'll encounter The Nature Conservancy's large parking lot. Don't enter the lot, but turn left to reach the conservancy's kiosks and building with a mossy "living roof." Check the posted schedule for programs. Take a left staying on South Cape May Meadows (blazed white here, 2.0 miles), heading into the sun toward the birdhouses and over another water management bridge on a long, straight, exposed path. Stop on the bridge and watch snapping turtles navigate the water control boards beneath.

At the next intersection (Dune Trail, 2.4 miles), keep straight to head to the Atlantic Ocean. The ocean pops up beyond the hill, shimmering and salty. Stroll down the fenced path and turn right onto the sand, toward the lighthouse, keeping an eye out for your return path on the right. In summer, piping plovers, with their black-banded necks and plaintive calls, skitter on the sands, searching for mollusks. During nesting season in spring, be careful of their eggs, laid in shallow depressions in the sand, because the federal government now classifies piping plovers as an endangered species. Enjoy the ocean, pausing to dip your toes in the water.

At the split rail fence, you'll see a sign for Cape May Point State Park. (2.7 miles). Leave the beach and follow it. At the next intersection, go left (2.8 miles) on the blue-blazed Plover Trail that will eventually return you to Cape May Point State Park. You'll pass a pond to the right, where you can enjoy more bird-watching. If you look left at about 3.1 miles, out to the Atlantic Ocean, you will see a World War II bunker, built in 1942 when the park was a military base. At low tide, the gun turrets at the front are visible. The sea will eventually claim the bunker, which was once 900 feet inland. If you'd like to take a path through the dunes to check out the bunker, before it disappears, now is your chance.

Otherwise, head toward the lighthouse. Tall bushes on either side of the trail provide shade and puddle ducks paddle in a pond to your right. Follow Plover Trail into the lighthouse parking lot, stopping to climb the wooden hawk-watching platform, where 30,000 raptors pass annually, and read the informative signs about the plants, mammals, bats, and birds of the coastal dunes.

## DID YOU KNOW?

Storms in the twentieth century eventually washed away most of the Victorian-style resort town of Cape May (remnants lie on the ocean floor). Entrepreneurs and conservation groups began to rebuild at the end of the century. Cape May Point has beautiful quartz pebbles (commonly called "Cape May diamonds") created by thousands of years of waves—search for them in the sands.

## OTHER ACTIVITIES

Hike the 2.5-mile Diamond Beach Trail at West Cape May's Higbee Beach Wildlife Management Area (west end of New England Road). Chill at Cape May Point's Sunset Beach, and watch for dolphins around a submerged concrete ship (502 Sunset Boulevard). To the north lie short trails at Lizard Tail Swamp Preserve (406 Courthouse–South Dennis Road, Cape May Courthouse, 08210) and Eldora Nature Preserve, which includes a boardwalk (2350 NJ 47, also called Delsea Drive, Delmont, 08314). Shoppers, historians, and foodies will enjoy the Victorian charm of restored Cape May.

## MORE INFORMATION

Cape May Point State Park is open dawn to dusk. Mailing address: P.O. Box 107, Cape May Point, NJ 08212; 609-884-2159; state.nj.us/dep/parksandforests/parks/capemay.html. South Cape May Meadows is open dawn to dusk. (*Note:* The beach is open for nature viewing only from March 15 through August 31.) The Nature Conservancy, 692 Sunset Boulevard, Cape May, NJ 08204; 908-879-7262; nature.org/ourinitiatives/regions/northamerica/unitedstates/newjersey/index.htm.

# 38

# MAURICE RIVER BLUFFS PRESERVE

Rugged, watery beauty awaits on this hike, which loops through forested wetlands and along the bluffs of the Maurice River.

## DIRECTIONS

Get onto NJ 42 from I-76 East. After 1.5 miles, merge onto NJ 55 via Exit 13 toward Glassboro/Vineland. After 33.0 miles, merge onto NJ 47 (North Second Street) via Exit 27 toward Millville. After about 2 miles, turn right onto East Vine Street. In 0.2 mile, turn slightly left onto North Brandriff Avenue. In 0.5 mile, stay straight to go onto County Highway 555 (South Race Street). In 1.10 miles, County Highway 555 becomes Silver Run Road (County Road 627). In 1.61 miles, turn left at the the large green-and-white sign for Maurice River Bluffs Preserve and you will reach the parking lot, which is on the right at 1200 Silver Run Road. The parking lot holds about 50 cars. There are no bathroom facilities. *GPS coordinates:* 39° 21.207' N, 75° 02.009' W.

## TRAIL DESCRIPTION

This 525-acre preserve nestles along 34.5-mile-long Maurice River, an important watershed that includes some the state's largest contiguous wild rice marshes. You'll find no shortage of birds in this habitat for nesting ospreys, bald eagles, songbirds, and waterfowl. Look for the freshwater odonates (carnivorous insects, such as dragonflies and damselflies). You'll hike through oak-pine forests, fields, and freshwater marshes, and alongside the river. You may see red foxes, river otters, or muskrat.

This is a perimeter hike around the entire preserve on the Blue, Orange, Red, White, and Yellow trails, starting and ending at the explanatory kiosk in the parking lot. Read the kiosk map, and consider taking a picture of it for

**LOCATION**
Millville

**RATING**
Moderate

**DISTANCE**
5.5 miles

**ELEVATION GAIN**
400 feet

**ESTIMATED TIME**
3 hours

**MAPS**
USGS Dividing Creek; njhiking.com/nj-hiking -maps/maurice-river-bluffs/ Maurice-Bluffs-Trail-Map .pdf

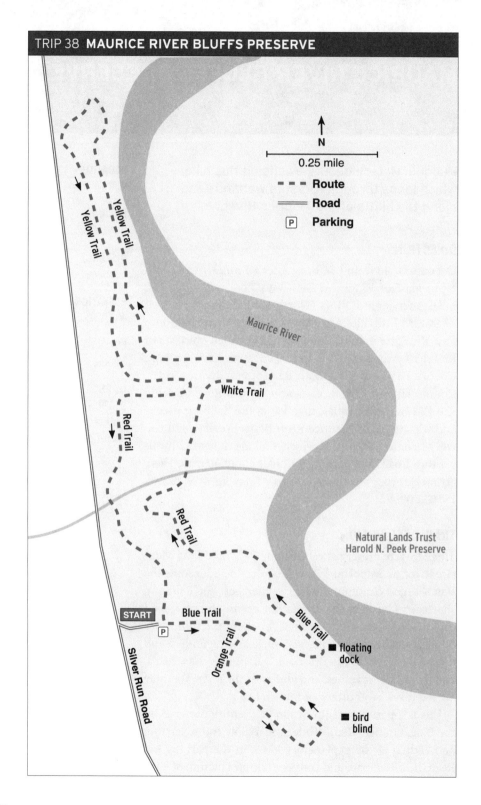

N

0.25 mile

- - - Route

Road

P  Parking

Maurice River

Yellow Trail

Yellow Trail

White Trail

Red Trail

Red Trail

Natural Lands Trust
Harold N. Peek Preserve

START

Blue Trail

Blue Trail

P

Orange Trail

Silver Run Road

floating
dock

bird
blind

reference. (*Note:* The kiosk map has the Orange Trail on it and the online map does not.) In general, the route is well marked, with many wooden steps, but some parts loop creatively; you may be confused, but follow the markings and you won't get lost.

From the map kiosk in the parking lot, take a right onto the Blue Trail. Enjoy the woods on a narrow, rooty path with a steep dropoff to the left. At the T intersection, make a quick left onto a wider path, still the Blue Trail. The pines make a tunnel above a flat, sandy path. At the next intersection, turn right at the arrow onto the Orange Trail (0.2 mile). A charming picnic table sits beneath a tree. Just beyond the table, go right at the fork.

A narrow, grassy path offers no shade until it enters a grove of fragrant cedars and pines. At the T intersection, go right at the orange marker among twisted trees and down a small ravine. Soon, a rope-railing bridge appears, crossing a deep ravine. Pass it and go right at the orange markers toward the bird-blind loop.

A narrow trail leads down a rooty bank into a charming hollow that makes you feel splendidly isolated. Turn left to go uphill and then down six wooden steps. Take a side trip to the bench to admire the marshy area.

Back on the Orange Trail, go down two sets of wooden steps. Linger at the covered bird blind on the right, complete with seats, overlooking the marshy river (0.6 mile). Go uphill eight steps and rest at the picnic table with a view of the marsh. Keep walking, and at the map and direction arrows, go right at the fork (still on the Orange Trail; left leads to the rope-railed bridge). The path narrows through twisted trees. Take a left at the T intersection, away from the parking sign. The grassy path leads through quiet pines. At the next Y intersection (0.9 miles) turn right toward the bird blind. Keep following the Orange Trail loop until it intersects the Blue Trail; turn right onto the Blue Trail, away from the parking sign and the Orange Trail loop (1.1 miles). (*Note:* From January through July, the Blue Trail is sometimes closed to protect nesting bald eagles. You can use the Alternate Blue Trail, accessed by heading straight across the intersection onto the faint connector path through the pines—blue trail markings are visible once you enter the pines and the map posted in the park shows the path.)

This section of the Blue Trail is delightfully wide and sandy. Note the birdhouse or bat house sitting on a pole to the right. You will reach the ruins of an old concrete building on your right. At the next Y intersection, the river shines in front of you. Go left here, following the blue marker. (*Note:* Stay off the private property to the right.) Sit at a picnic table atop the hill to enjoy the river and dock (1.3 miles). Then take the concrete steps down the steep bank and walk on the large large floating dock you just saw, with benches to contemplate river life; look for eagle's nests.

The trail continues along the water's edge and a pretty beach. (*Caution:* This part of the hike is very rooty.) Follow a series of steps for fine views of the river. Stay on the Blue Trail as you climb up and down the river banks on a series of steep steps.

Many steps and bridges help ease the ups and downs on this hike.

The Blue Trail narrows through the woods, with gentle ups and down and a calming river view from the bluff sections. At the T intersection at a kiosk, go left, staying on the Blue Trail for some steep ups and downs. Go up seven steps and turn left to descend the trail. At the next intersection, turn right at the trail signs and map to follow the Red Trail (1.8 miles), with the river on your right. Note the large sand mining pit on the left. At the bank, turn left and take the gently sloped path down. Turn right to continue on the Red Trail.

Cross a small wooden footbridge, welcome in this swampy area. Go left at the Y intersection up a bank. At the left-pointing arrow on the Red Trail sign, turn right, *away* from the Red Trail; you will soon see a White Trail marker at a posted map; turn right onto the white-blazed White Trail (2.3 miles). Where the trail meets the marsh, look for small "haystacks" signaling a muskrat's home. Via a rooty, uphill jaunt, you'll reach a land point with excellent views of the river.

At the next white blaze, take a left downhill to continue the river walk and explore the sandy crescent beach. Follow the white blazes uphill to a picnic table high on the bluffs overlooking the river. Continue on the White Trail loop, with the river on both sides, onto a narrow peninsula. Carefully navigate the steep chute between banks to explore remains of an old dock.

Turn left at the marker to continue on the White Trail and take an almost immediate right onto the narrow Yellow Trail (2.7 miles), which curves through the woods, with two large concrete cisterns on the right (you'll loop back to them). With high banks to the left and the river to the right, this section feels wild and isolated. The path curves sharply to the right, down steps. (*Caution:* In late fall, leaves make the steps slippery.) Pass the remains of four concrete columns on the right and a big concrete slab on the left, and then climb some steps uphill for an excellent river view.

At the Y intersection, take the Yellow Trail to the right, up and down steep steps. Follow the Yellow Trail, enjoying another excellent river view at the bottom of more steps, until you reach a sandy four-way intersection; go straight. As you walk the flat Yellow Trail through the forest, you'll hear the cars on Silver Run Road.

At a four-way intersection, the Yellow Trail curves to the left up a steep bank. In late fall, the ground is covered with blooming club moss—these plants are actually tiny evergreens. Walk a charming, narrow, elevated path above two small valleys, then go down a steep bank to flat terrain. Take a quick right at the concrete cisterns, head to the four-way intersection, and go right, toward a posted map. Here, you've completed the loop (4.4 miles).

To return to your car, take a right at the Y intersection immediately past the map to get onto the Red Trail (marsh on your left). Stay on the Red Trail and go right at the Y intersection, through the woods. Take a left on the Red Trail at the next junction, with signs and three wooden posts (*don't* go straight on red here, even though you could). Pass the sand mining pit and deep ravine from before. Take a right at the Y intersection to go downhill toward the bridge. Cross the marshy area on a footbridge; turn right at the Red Trail sign. Steep banks close in on either side. Go up a hill and straight, toward a posted map. At the next intersection, go right on the Blue Trail toward the sign for the parking area (5.0 miles), enjoying the narrow up-and-down path.

## DID YOU KNOW?

The Maurice River is a critical link between the Delaware Estuary and the Pinelands National Reserve (see page 148). There's a functioning drive-in theater at the Delsea Drive-In (2203 S. Delsea Drive, Vineland). Glassblowers await at Wheaton Arts and Cultural Center in Millville (1000 Village Drive).

## OTHER ACTIVITIES

Explore two peaceful Natural Lands Trust sites in Millville that have raptors and Atlantic white cedar bogs: Harold N. Peek Preserve, across the Maurice River (2100 S. Second Street), and Buckshutem Wildlife Management Area on Route 49. Don't miss the 5-mile wetlands walk and museum at Bayshore Center at Bivalve (see Trip 40). Drive to the virtually abandoned town of Sea Breeze, once a thriving resort (take Route 601 and turn left when the road splits).

## MORE INFORMATION

Open 6 A.M. to 7 P.M. (Gate is locked at closing time.) The Nature Conservancy, 200 Pottersville Road, Chester, NJ 07930; 908-879-7262; nature.org/en-us/ get-involved/how-to-help/places-we-protect/delaware-bayshores-maurice -river-bluffs-preserve//.

## 39

# GLADES WILDLIFE REFUGE

The New Jersey Pine Barrens meets the Delaware Bayshore habitat in old-growth forest and sandy beaches, complete with bald eagles.

## DIRECTIONS

On NJ 55 South, take Exit 27 toward Millville. Merge onto NJ 47 South (North Second Street). After 2.5 miles, turn right onto County Highway 555 (East Main Street). In 0.3 mile, turn left on Cedar Street to follow County Highway 555. In 0.25 mile, turn left onto South Race Street to continue following County Highway 555. In 7.0 miles, turn right onto Railroad Avenue. Cross the tracks near an industrial sand mining plant, and continue on Railroad Avenue to where it intersects with CR 718 (Ackley Road). Turn left onto CR 718 and travel for 0.33 miles. The trailhead is on the left. It will be marked by a chain in a white plastic pipe, stretched between two posts, a white blaze on a tree, and a white metal sign for Natural Lands Trust (NLT). Park on the shoulder of the road. *GPS coordinates: 39° 18.425′ N, 75° 08.160′ W.*

## TRAIL DESCRIPTION

The largest of the NLT preserves, this 6,765-acre refuge is also a National Audubon Society Important Bird Area and has reared and released at least 45 bald eagles from its "hacking boxes," boxes mounted on a high tower and used to safely rear eaglets. The preserve covers tidal marshes, forested swamps, wooded uplands, beaches along Delaware Bay, and an outstanding old-growth forest.

This hike is a special blend of scenery through woods, lakes, and marsh to the refuge's old-growth forest and the sugar-sand beach at a 1,000-acre lake. Seeing eagles is a strong possibility here. The refuge has about 120 acres of old-growth forest, and trees up to 400 years old. Winter is

**LOCATION**
Port Norris

**RATING**
Moderate

**DISTANCE**
5.2 miles

**ELEVATION GAIN**
200 feet

**ESTIMATED TIME**
2.5 hours

**MAPS**
USGS Cedarville, USGS Dividing Creek; natlands .org/glades-wildlife-refuge; ExploreNLT app

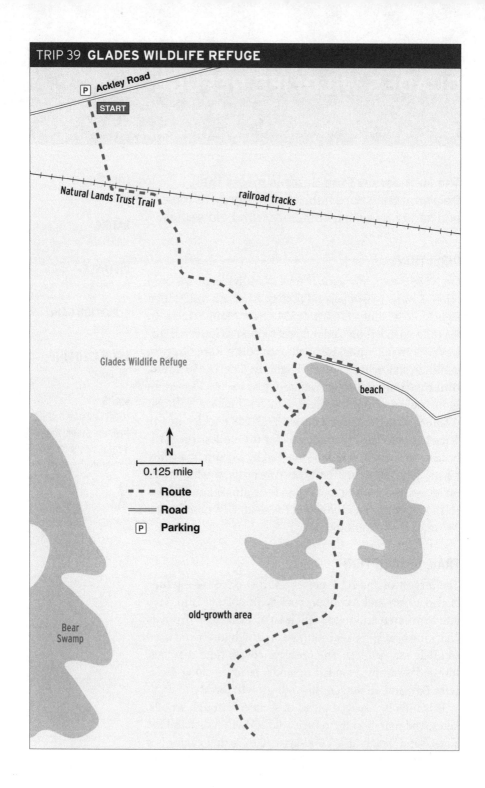

TRIP 39 **GLADES WILDLIFE REFUGE**

P Ackley Road

START

Natural Lands Trust Trail

railroad tracks

Glades Wildlife Refuge

beach

N

0.125 mile

- - - **Route**
===== **Road**
P **Parking**

old-growth area

Bear
Swamp

prime time to spot bald and golden eagles, rough-legged hawks, and short-eared owls. Spring brings a chorus of frogs and songbirds. Diamondback terrapins are active in summer. Fall blazes with color.

You'll follow an area informally referred to by a local Natural Lands Trust employee and trail guide as "the spoil"—the area of material discarded when companies mined this area for sand and gravel to make glass and building materials—and "the lakes." The Natural Lands Trust route isn't particularly well marked, except with a few white signs, some random blue blazes, and some plastic surveyor's ties. But the lakes will keep you anchored, so don't be afraid of getting lost.

The white-signed Natural Lands Trust Trail to an old-growth forest starts flat and leafstrewn as you enter a tunnel of pine trees. In 0.2 mile, cross the defunct railroad tracks at the white blaze, turn left, and walk down the tracks a short distance (stay to the middle; the rails are slippery), keeping an eye out for the white NLT sign on the right (0.3 mile), at which point you leave the tracks and turn right into the woods onto a faint trail. Pink plastic surveyor ties on skinny trees mark the way to sour gums, sweet gums, holly trees, pitch pines, sweetbay magnolias, and, uncommon in New Jersey, swamp chestnut oaks.

NLT markers guide the way through a row of immense White Atlantic cedar trees, probably planted to preserve a long-ago boundary line. Enjoy the rarity of this string of cedars. Walk through an enchanted forest of tulip poplars and highbush blueberries, and then take the path, brown with fallen leaves in December, to a footbridge over a stream that disappears into gravel and pops out again.

Follow the path deeper into the spoil area, going straight over a bridge and up a hill created by past mining activity. Go down the hill and turn right at the bottom of the hill onto a wide path, an old logging road (0.9 miles). To the left is an inland lake, courtesy of a mining pit. Follow the banks of the lake through lumpy, human-made hills and veer left toward the end of the lake. Cross a footbridge over a creek, which eventually grades out to Delaware Bay. Go straight, up and down more mining humps. Then head down to the left, toward the lake, before taking a right (1.2 miles) as the trail straightens out, following the banks of the lake once more. Look for eagles roosting in trees around the water.

Some dark-blue blazes appear, either vestiges from an earlier trail or the beginnings of a new one being built. Follow them slightly uphill and then down a steep incline, keeping the lake on your left. The NLT path begins to veer right, away from the lake into the woods. (Or if your sense of adventure has been met, retrace your steps to the road where your car awaits.) Pink plastic survey markers continue to show the route. The lake is to the right; keep watch for eagles.

The NLT Trail itself becomes a bit nebulous now. But it's worth exploring in order to reach the ancient trees. Walk through a basin of land and up to a rim road. Take a right, keeping the lake on your left. Walk on the raised rim path through the forest, following the lake. A sunken path appears soon on your right; walk down to it. Now you're in the presence of old-growth trees—admire

Sand appears snow-like in the former mining pit overlooking Inner Lake.

the sour gums and black gums with bark four inches thick, like roofing shingles. These trees are 250 to 300 years old and are very slow-growing. Some of the branches are severely angled because of wind pruning and breaks from mistletoe, which especially loves sour gums. Many old-growth trees are hollow. Also note the unusually tall swamp magnolias in this area.

Continue on the sunken path. Take a right into the woods to see balls of mistletoe atop a 400-year-old sour gum, whose leaves shine burgundy in the fall.

Make your way back to the sunken path and cross a root bridge over a stream, with the lake still on your left. To your right is a 400- to 500-year-old sour gum, perched on a mound (no one knows why). Past the tree, the faint path turns right, into the woods to a small stream. Look for barn owls and red-shouldered hawks here.

Be careful around the thorns of the smilax, also called catbrier or greenbrier. (*Note:* The smilax plant is edible and tastes like asparagus.) As you round the lake over small mining humps, note the "princess tree," or royal paulownia. You'll also see a large, dying sour gum, bark hanging in shreds. Note the abundance of old holly trees, survivors because their wood is hard to split.

It's time to turn around (2.3 miles). Walk back toward the lake, up the raised rim path, and then turn left to retrace your steps. The lake is on your right now. At 3.3 miles, where you first encountered the lake, continue straight, heading toward the other side of the lake. Old metal oil tanks are to your left. The path levels out. Turn right onto a large white-sand beach area (3.6 miles). An oversize human-made dune (remnants of the sand quarry) affords a high, comfy perch from which to gaze at the amazing 1,000-acre lake. Ramble to the water's edge and search the sand for animal tracks.

Leave the beach and take a left into the woods. Soon you are back to where you first encountered the lake (4.1 miles). Take a right, then a left to go over the footbridge to the railroad tracks (4.7 miles). Turn left on the tracks, and after you pass two NLT signs on the right, the obvious NLT path appears on the right (4.8 miles). Take it into the woods, following the white blazes. Soon you'll be back at your car.

## DID YOU KNOW?

In winter, frogs burrow into leaves and hibernate: Their breathing and heartbeat stops, ice crystals form in their bodies, and they produce "antifreeze" to keep their cells from freezing. Frogs love seasonal vernal pools; at the refuge, "ditch plugs" slow the pools' drainage.

## OTHER ACTIVITIES

Hike at 5-mile Shaws Mill Pond, where you can enjoy the tree frog symphony in June and look for eels in the pristine 28-acre pond (Railroad Road/Ackley Road over railroad tracks to intersection with Shaws Mill; park entrance beyond). Experience the 1.5-mile Maurice River Bicycle & Walking Trail over six bridges in the heart of Millville (to access the trail, take Waltman Park east to Sharp Street). Visit Egg Island Wildlife Management Area, near Fortescue (County Road 553, left on Maple Street).

Check out the four other hiking trails at Glades: Warfle Farm Trail, access at Turkey Point Road and Hickman Avenue (0.5 mile round-trip); Maple Street Trail, access at Maple Street and Turkey Point Road (4.0 miles round-trip); Bald Eagle Trail, access at Turkey Point Road in Downe Township (1.5 miles round-trip); and Tat Starr Trail, access on Route 637, also called Fortesque Road (2.0 miles round-trip, and most people's favorite). Explore these on your own, starting at the Maple Street trailhead to pick up a copy of a map.

## MORE INFORMATION

Open sunrise to sunset. Trail maps at kiosks. Main information kiosk is at Turkey Point Road and Maple Street. Natural Lands Trust, New Jersey Field Office, 2100 S. Second Street, Millville, NJ 08332; 856-825-9952; natlands.org/glades-wildlife-refuge.

# 40

# BIVALVE WETLANDS WALK

New Jersey's coastal salt marshes teem with wildlife. The walkways and nature signage in Bivalve make this an easy exploration. Bring your binoculars.

## DIRECTIONS

Take I-295 South toward NJ 42 South/Delaware Memorial Bridge/Atlantic City. Merge onto NJ 42 South/North via the exit on the left toward Atlantic City. Merge onto NJ 55 South via Exit 13 toward Glassboro/Vineland, and stay on NJ 55 for 41.0 miles. Stay straight to go onto Route 47/NJ 47. After 3 miles, turn right onto County Highway 670 (Mauricetown Crossway Road). After 1.52 miles, stay straight to go on County Highway 649 (Mauricetown Bypass). In 2.0 miles, turn left onto County Highway 649 (now North Avenue). In 2.5 miles, turn right onto Main Street (County Highway 553). In 0.5 mile, take the third left onto High Street. In less than 1.0 mile, the trailhead is on the right, at a bike trail sign, across from Bayshore Center at Bivalve. There is parking in the paved parking lot at the trailhead for about ten cars, and more ample parking across the road at the center (30 cars). *GPS coordinates:* 39° 14.003′ N, 75° 02.089′ W.

## TRAIL DESCRIPTION

Here's a chance to see a New Jersey coastal salt marsh the easy way: on a (mostly) elevated, flat boardwalk. Come early in the morning or late in the day to catch the stunning sunrise or sunset. Birds love salt marshes (largely because of the insects), so look for long-tailed ducks, red-winged blackbirds, green-winged teals, starlings, seagulls, bald eagles, ospreys, snowy egrets, and more. The reeds, water, and mud are favorite incubators and playgrounds for fish, shellfish (including crustaceans), mammals,

**LOCATION**
Port Norris

**RATING**
Easy

**DISTANCE**
3.8 miles

**ELEVATION GAIN**
50 feet

**ESTIMATED TIME**
2 hours

**MAPS**
USGS Port Norris;
Maps available at trailhead kiosk

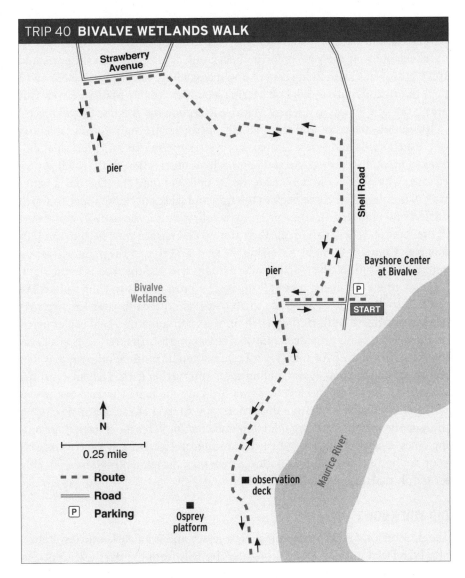

insects, and diamondback terrapins. Spring and fall bring flocks of migratory birds. Summer is buggy and best avoided. Winter is starkly beautiful.

(Salt marshes protect the mainland from erosion and floods and purify water. See page 208.) Rutgers University has a lab a mile away, the Haskin Shellfish Research Laboratory, that supports aquaculture research.

Park at the paved parking lot at the trailhead with the bike trail sign. The Bayshore Center at Bivalve is across the street, and its museum provides an excellent education on the local oyster industry. Head up the wooden ramp as the reeds sway at shoulder height. Take a left, then a quick right onto the 180-foot pier stretching over the marsh (0.1 mile); many avian friends will accompany you. Search the water for muskrat and diamondback terrapins, and enjoy the sweeping marsh vistas, which are especially lovely at sunset. This walk is part of the New Jersey Coastal Heritage Trail (see page 170).

Take a right off the pier onto the boardwalk where smooth cordgrass and spike-grass wave like a living carpet. You'll pass a huge pile of oyster shells and a flock of ravenous gulls at Sail Loft Marina on the left, next to Maurice River. This area is actually an estuary, where Maurice River and the Atlantic Ocean meet.

The boardwalk ends, and the trail becomes a surprisingly comfortable mix of crushed shells and grass. Snowy egrets stalk the marsh on either side; red-winged blackbirds swoop. As you approach an observation deck, you'll spy an elevated osprey nest, often with an osprey in it. Go onto the deck for a better look (0.6 mile). Then come back to the trail and walk out to the water to watch anglers and crabbers. In late April, tiny wildflowers dot the path. The first part of the route ends here (0.8 mile). Turn around and retrace your steps to the 180-foot pier. Continue straight, following the trail, and go past the point where you entered it (1.4 miles). The marshy water is to the left, and the road is to the right.

Go around a red metal gate (1.9 miles). An open field is to your right. Take the trail to your left, which leads to an observation area to your left. Striking dead trees (snags) jut from the marsh on your left; sometime bald eagles perch on them. Evergreens provide an unusual color contrast. The trail ends at a parking lot at Strawberry Avenue (2.4 miles), but you'll continue onto an 820-foot pier traversing the marsh and ending at an observation deck. Lichens crust the wooden railings. Indigo-blue swallows flit; look for marsh wrens. See if you can spot a muskrat or diamondback terrapin. Marvel at the channels cutting through the marsh, restoring tidal flow and creating acres more habitat, including miles of new tributaries. When you are sated, retrace your steps to go back to your car, noting the ingenious pulley system on a cluster of birdhouses, possibly for purple martins, on a tall pole.

## DID YOU KNOW?

The *AJ Meerwald* is the state ship of New Jersey and is an authentic restoration of a 1928 Delaware Bay oyster schooner. She sails from the Bayshore Center at Bivalve. Educational, public, and charter sales are available; you can even train to sail a tall ship. Call 856-785-2060, extension 107, for information. Bivalve once claimed the title "Oyster Capital of the World," and Bayshore Center's indoor museum showcases this unique culture. More exhibits on the history of the oyster industry are at the rear of the museum, under the large boating shed, and can be visited any time, even when the indoor museum is closed.

## OTHER ACTIVITIES

A famous pile of conch shells is less than a mile away in Shellpile: Take a left from the trailhead parking lot, a quick right onto Miller Avenue, and then left to the shells, next to the New Jersey State Police marine station. Visit Thompson's

Oyster shells make a fitting trail on this level walk through the marshes of Bivalve Wetlands.

Beach and Moore's Beach (see Trip 36). Hike several wildlife management areas: Heislerville to the south (7,467 acres), Dennis Creek and Corson to the south (more than 8,000 acres), and Edward G. Bevan to the north, in Millville (more than 16,000 acres).

## MORE INFORMATION

The trail is open year-round, dawn to dusk. The museum (ADA accessible) and café are open Wednesday through Sunday from 11 A.M. to 3 P.M., but call ahead, because weather affects openings. Bayshore Center at Bivalve, 2800 High Street, Port Norris, NJ 08349; 856-785-2060; bayshorecenter.org. Estuary Enhancement Program, Public Service Electric and Gas, Nuclear LLC (PSEG); 888-MARSHES (627-7437); corporate.pseg.com/corporatecitizenship/environmentalpolicyandinitiatives/estuaryenhancementprogram.

# DELAWARE RIVER

The Delaware River region represents a balanced mix of rural and urban, with cities, forests, wooded stretches, and a plenitude of waterways—the queen of which, in this region, is the Delaware River.

The Delaware forms the entire boundary between New Jersey and Pennsylvania and parts of the river are designated a Wild and Scenic River by Congress. The Delaware River is the longest free-flowing river in the eastern United States, running 330 miles from New York through Pennsylvania, New Jersey, and Delaware on its way to the Atlantic Ocean. The Delaware River flows past forests, farmlands, villages, and cities, and it links some of the most densely populated sections of the United States.

Most counties in the Delaware River region are also linked by a well-developed transportation system, NJ Transit, enabling travel and commuting to work in nearby Philadelphia. You'll find overlapping loyalties to sport teams here, as well as to recreational and historical subjects. For instance, the site where General George Washington crossed the Delaware River on December 25, 1776, lies in both New Jersey and Pennsylvania (see Trip 45). The canal that opened up this area to trade in the 1800s runs along both sides of the Delaware River. On the New Jersey (eastern) side, it stretches 70 miles, from Milford to New Brunswick, and is called the Delaware and Raritan Canal (see page 40). On the Pennsylvania (western) side, it runs 60 miles, from Easton to Bristol, and is called the Delaware and Lehigh Canal.

This region is also the home of Princeton University, Rowan University, and New Jersey's state capital of Trenton.

Physiographically speaking, the Delaware River region falls into the Inner and Outer Coastal Plains. A narrow strip on the western side of the region lies in the Inner Coastal Plain. The Inner Coastal Plain is relatively flat, with many meandering rivers. Pleasantly wooded, the northern part has forests of mixed oak, upland pine, beech oak, and red maple–sweet gum. The southern part segues to

Facing page: One of Parvin State Park's floating docks makes paddling an appealing alternative to hiking.

Virginia pine, white cedar swamps, hardwood swamps, and marshes. The Inner Coastal Plain occupies about 14 percent of the area of New Jersey and contains about 14 percent of the state's population.

The narrow strip in the Inner Coastal Plain is separated from the Outer Coastal Plain by a low ridge with bumpy hills, called "cuestas." The Outer Coastal Plain occupies the remaining portion of the Delaware River region and is also relatively flat. The forest communities consist of southern mixed oak, upland pine and oak, red maple–sweet gum, and Virginia pine. Nearer the coasts and in the Pinelands, the mix shifts to coastal white cedar swamps, pitch pine lowland forests, hardwood swamps, Pine Barrens shrub swamps, and marshes.

The Pinelands creep into the western sections of Gloucester, Camden, and Burlington counties. In fact, Black Run Preserve (Trip 47) in Burlington County calls itself "the Gateway to the Pinelands."

Each county in the Delaware River region has a wealth of waterways, beyond the Delaware River. Camden County has the urban Cooper River. The more remote Salem County boasts Alloway Creek, Cohansey River, Salem River, Maurice River, and Parvin Lake (see Trip 46). Bustling Burlington County enjoys Mullica River (see Trip 42), Rancocas Creek, and Assiscunk Creek. Mercer County, the site of Princeton University, benefits from Assunpink Creek and Crosswicks Creek. Raccoon River lies in Gloucester County. Gloucester and Salem counties share Oldman's Creek. The waterways spill over into a cooling network of creeks and streams, nestled deep in the woods.

Dozens and dozens of national parks, state parks, forests, and recreation areas lie in the five counties that make up the Delaware River region. Spring brings showy displays of wildflowers and blooming shrubs and trees. Raspberries, blackberries, and blueberries ripen in the summer. Fall shines with colored leaves against the October sky, and migratory songbirds, swans, and ducks abound. In winter, trails beg to be skied and bare branches expose striking vistas. Forests hide beaver, deer, groundhogs, foxes, raccoons, and more.

The Delaware River region has something for everyone, from secluded rambles to urban adventures (see outdoors.org/DEriver for more information).

# 41

# TED STILES PRESERVE AT BALDPATE MOUNTAIN

Enjoy an aerobic workout in a wooded bird haven, stewarded meadow, and native plant preserve with views of Philadelphia's skyline and the Delaware River.

## DIRECTIONS

From I-95, take Exit 1 for NJ 29 North/River Road. Travel on NJ 29 for approximately 4.6 miles to Fiddlers Creek Road. Turn right; the preserve entrance is 0.2 mile on the left (327 Fiddlers Creek Road). The parking lot has space for about 40 cars. *GPS coordinates:* 40° 19.111′ N, 74° 53.400′ W.

## TRAIL DESCRIPTION

This hike is a local favorite for two good reasons: variety and beauty. The weekend rambler as well as the experienced hiker can enjoy more than 12 miles of marked trails that wind and loop through a wildflower meadow, along a flat ridgeline, up and down rugged stretches through mature forests, and past the remains of a nineteenth-century settlement. The route also boasts the highest point in Mercer County at 470 feet. A 40-acre central area showcases open fields undergoing reforestation (some fenced in to protect trees from deer). The Fiddler's Creek ravine on the east side runs from Fiddlers Creek Road roughly south toward the Delaware River. There are three parking lots, allowing for a long, straight hike if you want to use two cars and leave one at your final destination.

Much of the property at this site, formerly known as Kuser Mountain, was once owned by the Kuser family, and many of the original structures remain, including the renovated main house (Strawberry Hill Mansion, available for private events), livestock barns, a guest

**LOCATION**
Titusville

**RATING**
Moderate

**DISTANCE**
9 miles

**ELEVATION GAIN**
450 feet

**ESTIMATED TIME**
4.5 hours

**MAPS**
USGS Lambertville, USGS Pennington; nynjtc.org/map/ted -stiles-preserve-baldpate -mountain-trail-map; *Hiking Atlas*, Sourland Conservancy

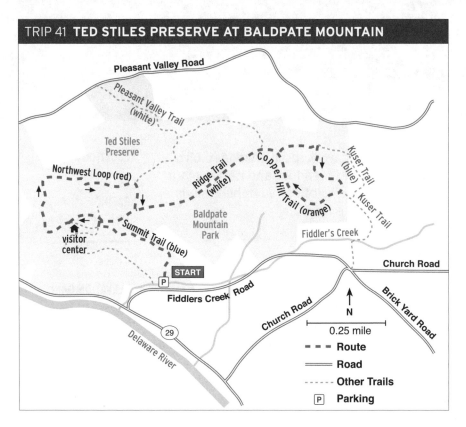

Pleasant Valley Road

Pleasant Valley Trail (white)

Ted Stiles Preserve

Northwest Loop (red)

Ridge Trail (white)

Copper Hill Trail (orange)

Kuser Trail (blue)

Kuser Trail

Baldpate Mountain Park

Fiddler's Creek

visitor center

Summit Trail (blue)

START

Church Road

Fiddlers Creek Road

Church Road

Brick Yard Road

Delaware River

29

N

0.25 mile

- - - Route

Road

Other Trails

P  Parking

lodge, and a springhouse. Protected as open space in 1998 by a consortium of Mercer County, the State of New Jersey, Hopewell Township, and the Friends of Hopewell Valley, the preserve (originally called Baldpate Mountain Preserve) stretches across almost 1,800 acres of a diabase ridge (subvolcanic Jurassic rock) running roughly east to west. Baldpate is part of the Sourland Mountain ecosystem and volcanic Sourland Mountain ridge, and was almost a rock quarry and a luxury housing development. Ted Stiles, a conservationist and Rutgers University professor, devoted ten years working to ensure the protection of this land, and the name of the preserve was changed in 2007 to honor his efforts.

The area is beautiful in all seasons but truly comes alive in spring, with native wildflowers, returning birds, and blooming redbud, dogwood, and tulip poplars. Watch for flying squirrels in summer. Admire migrating hawks in fall in this National Audubon Society Important Bird Area. Winter views and snow-covered ruins are stunning, and blue-blazed Summit Trail to white-blazed Ridge Trail affords challenging snowshoeing.

This hike starts at the main gravel parking lot on 327 Fiddlers Creek Road (big green-and-white sign; no bathrooms). Right behind the kiosk, take blue-blazed Summit Trail. Flat stepping-stones on a well-maintained dirt path lead through sun-dappled woods. You'll meet many families and dogs on this popular trail. A gradual climb through oaks, American beeches, and hickory trees leads to the first of three ascents: This one goes through a boulder field on the rugged stone (diabase) Devil's Staircase. At the junction, go left; the right path leads to a pond.

The meandering route levels off in a few hundred yards at 0.8 mile, where you'll cross a gravel road and continue on Summit Trail beneath a leafy tree tunnel. (If you need a flush toilet, turn left on the gravel road, go past the stop sign, and the dedicated toilet building is on the left just past Strawberry Hill Mansion. Stay and explore the stone terrace and view from renovated Strawberry Hill Mansion.) The trail opens onto a 7-acre stewarded meadow alive with native grasses, black-eyed Susans, mountain mint, wild bergamot, and other native wildflowers. At the picnic tables, turn left onto white-blazed Ridge Trail (1.1 miles), and head for the permanently mounted telescope to peek at Philadelphia and the Delaware River. Enter the shady woods on a dirt-and-gravel path, which can be muddy but is mercifully free from rocks. At 1.3 miles, go right at the junction onto red-blazed Northwest Loop Trail, and enjoy gentle ups and downs for about a mile through the quiet green forest, with bird songs and the occasional bounding deer. Take a right (2.3 miles) at the triangle-shaped junction onto your second ascent, still on the red-blazed trail. After 0.2 mile, you'll reach a gravel road. Turn left here onto white-blazed Ridge Trail (2.5 miles), which becomes pavement, but watch carefully for a small dirt trail on the left where Ridge Trail continues. You can explore the old Welling/Burd farmstead buildings and peaceful, secluded pond to the right, but return and take the dirt trail into the woods.

The up-and-down dirt path passes a white cinder block building on the right. At about 3.2 miles, the unmarked 470-foot Baldpate summit (Mercer County's highest elevation) hides to your left among the trees. Stay on white-blazed Ridge Trail, passing tree-trunk seats and stunning blowdown. Reach the power lines and Pleasant Valley Road parking lot. Follow the fence to the left along the lot, and take a right at 3.8 miles onto orange-blazed Copper Hill Trail, marked with a black "C" on a white wooden sign. The rocky, grassy, narrow trail is secluded; stay on the orange blazes, ignoring the blue- and red-blazed side paths.

Rocky ruins of an old homestead on your right mark the beginning of the third ascent, which rewards you with remains of an old chimney, fireplace, and adjacent cellar hole. Farmers formerly settled in this area, known as Honey Hollow (and bootleggers, too, some say). Look for rock caches—piled-up stones for homes never built. Grasses and bushes comb your legs on the narrow path leading back to the tree-trunk seats. Go left onto Ridge Trail at 4.9 miles.

Stay left at the next fork. Pass the cinder block building again on your left, and continue straight onto a paved road (ignore red-blazed Northwest Loop Trail on right). Follow the tall wire fence (to protect the area undergoing reforestation) on the right as the path broadens. At the fork, the fence ends; stay right on Ridge Trail. Continue to the big meadow and picnic tables. Go back the way you came by taking a left at 6.5 miles on blue-blazed Summit Trail and crossing the gravel road to continue on Summit Trail. Take the trail down the Devil's Staircase to the parking lot (7.6 miles).

Observation binoculars in the meadow reveal views of the Delaware River and Philadelphia.

## DID YOU KNOW?

Northern and southern bird species love Baldpate Mountain because of the location, contiguous forest, and high-quality understory. Here you'll find the highest concentration of nesting Nearctic-neotropical (migratory) birds in New Jersey, plus majestic raptors, including Cooper's hawks. Rare reptiles (eastern box turtle) and amphibians (Fowler's toad) live in this area too.

## OTHER ACTIVITIES

Cross Fiddlers Creek Road at the parking lot, and turn right to walk the shoulder for a few hundred feet. On your left is red-dot-blazed Overlook Trail, which leads to the 121-acre Fiddler's Creek Preserve. Take NJ 29 South to historic Washington Crossing State Park (Trip 45). To the north lies charming Lambertville, where Howell Living History Farm (70 Woodens Lane) has live animals and maple syrup lines (foot access to Ted Stiles Preserve via Hunter Road to Pleasant Valley Road).

## MORE INFORMATION

No fee. Open dawn to dusk daily mid-February to mid-November, and year-round on Sundays, but check web page for hours during hunting season. Mercer County Park Commission, Historic Hunt House, 197 Blackwell Road, Pennington, NJ 08534; 609-303-0700; mercercountyparks.org/#!/parks/baldpate-mountain.

# 42

# MULLICA RIVER TRAIL: ATSION TO QUAKERBRIDGE

Enjoy a lengthy leg-stretching hike along the Mullica River in the flat, preternaturally beautiful, and quiet Pine Barrens of Wharton State Forest.

## DIRECTIONS

Take I-295 South to US 130 via Exit 57B-A toward Bordentown/Burlington. In 0.13 mile, merge onto US 130 North via Exit 57A on the *left* toward Bordentown. In 1.0 mile, turn right onto Farnsworth Avenue (County Highway 545). In 0.25 mile, turn right onto US 206 South. Go 17.5 miles, and then take the second exit of the roundabout to stay on US 206 South. In 11.0 miles, turn left at the big brown sign that says "Wharton State Forest, Atsion Office." (GPS says "Vincentown.") A dirt parking area has room for at least 50 cars. *GPS coordinates:* 39° 44.522′ N, 74° 43.539′ W.

## TRAIL DESCRIPTION

The Mullica River Trail is in the heart of the Pinelands in the 115,000-acre Wharton State Forest, one of four state forests in the Pinelands National Reserve (see page 148). The trail encompasses key aspects of the Pinelands: a river, cedar swamps, pine trees, sand roads, and flat paths. You'll probably have the path mostly to yourself, but there's much to see and hear on this long hike. In spring, tree frogs sing, and mountain laurel, pyxie, and turkey beard bloom. In early summer, note the rare bog asphodel, a lily with small bright-yellow flowers that's found only in the Pine Barrens. Spot red-bellied turtles in the water. Keep a lookout for turkeys and pygmy pines—mature pygmy pines are only 4 to 10 feet high. (*Note:* This area is extremely buggy from May to October.)

**LOCATION**
Shamong

**RATING**
Moderate

**DISTANCE**
9.9 miles

**ELEVATION GAIN**
320 feet

**ESTIMATED TIME**
4.5 hours

**MAPS**
USGS Indian Mills; njparksandforests.com/parks/maps/WhartonAreaMapFinal_reduced.pdf

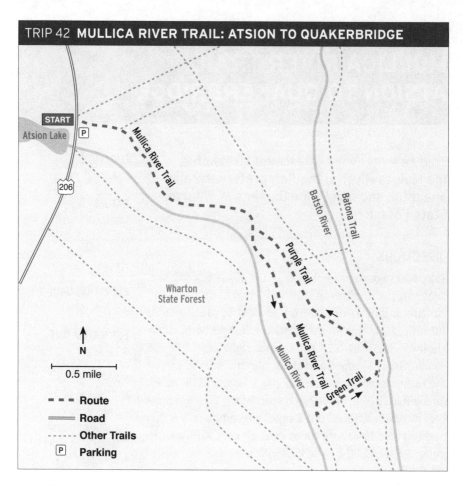

You'll take yellow-blazed Mullica River Trail, purple-blazed Beaver Pond-Quaker Bridge Trail, and green-blazed Wilderness Camps Connector Trail in a lollipop, and then retrace your steps. Some of the turns are tricky because of fire ditches, hunters' roads, and false trails made by ATVs, so be alert. If you don't see a blaze for a while, backtrack. You are walking into the sun, so wear sunglasses.

The yellow-blazed Mullica River Trail begins at the trail sign in front of the ranger's station, which was the Atsion General Store until World War II, when the gasoline scarcity forced it to close. Pick up a map at the trail sign. Take a left on the trail and walk by Atsion Mansion and the building ruins on the left. At a metal post on your right, blazed with yellow, you can go left to visit the composting outhouse. If nature does not call, walk on down the dirt road, past the gun club on the right and the cemetery and historic, still functioning, white church on the left. The graves date back to the late 1800s.

Follow the yellow blazes on short metal posts and turn left into the woods at a double yellow blaze. The path is soft with pine straw. Very soon (0.7 mile), you'll cross yellow-blazed railroad tracks and a wide dirt path, then head toward the "9 miles to Batsto" sign. Continue on the moss-lined path through a pine forest. Mountain laurels hug the edges. At the Y intersection, go right to follow the yellow blazes. At the four-way intersection, go right again, still following yellow blazes. (*Caution:* Do not go straight, which will take you into the woods.) At the next four-way junction, cross the road to follow the yellow-blazed path; soon after, cross another dirt road and go into the woods. At the "8.5 miles to Batsto" sign, turn right. Enjoy the calm pines.

(*Note:* A confusing welter of hunting and ATV roads are coming, so read carefully.) At a T intersection with double yellow blazes, curve right for a few steps on the dirt road, then go straight, keeping the water and sand pit to your right. A Y intersection appears immediately; take the right fork toward the yellow-blazed tree, away from the sand pit. Go right at the next fork; the yellow blaze crops up soon. (If you find yourself at the dirt road for cars, back up and find the yellow blaze.)

The sandy path bumps pleasantly up and down. Cross a dirt road and go into the woods at the yellow blaze. Walk through striking fire-damaged pines. A private property sign appears on the left. Soon you'll reach the "8 miles to Batsto" sign. A very narrow path meanders through the woods, with a spookily picturesque marsh-pond-bog to the left (2.2 miles). The trail comes to a T intersection at a dirt road; go left at double-yellow blazes onto the road. Cross a small bridge. Right after the bridge is a double yellow blaze on a tree. A few yards past that, a yellow blaze on a metal post leads you into the woods to the right.

A stream on the right follows this narrow path. Pass the "7.5 miles to Batsto" sign. In December, bare, white trees are stark against the blue sky. Reach a huge, sandy circle with many spokes. Stay straight, keeping the water on your right. A wide path brings yellow blazes and tall shrubs on the right. At another big intersection with many paths, go straight, toward the yellow blaze. (Do not take side paths into the forest.) The Mullica River curves prettily through the trees to your right, a picture postcard for the Pine Barrens. You might see a red fox.

At the Y intersection (double yellow blazes), turn left, away from the river. In a few hundred yards, turn right at the T intersection toward a yellow blaze that leads you to the right, down a sandy road. At the next Y intersection, go right and again admire the lovely river. Two big wooden signs pop up: "Beaver Pond–Quaker Bridge Trail" and "Mullica River Trail" (3.0 miles). Turn left here (away from the river) to get on the purple-blazed Beaver Pond-Quaker Bridge Trail, heading toward Batona Trail and Lower Forge Camp.

The Purple Trail is a pleasant little path through the woods, very meditative. Keep straight on the purple blazes at all times. You'll cross several fire ditches (trenches dug to stop or slow a wildfire or brushfire, which can devastate, and have devastated, the Pine Barrens). Cross a one-lane dirt road and go into the woods. Keep an eye out for the double green blazes of the Wilderness Camps Connector Trail on the right; they appear within sight of a big open area with

Ghostly bare branches frame a lake in the Pine Barrens at sunset.

sand roads (4.6 miles). (If you reach the open area, backtrack.) Turn right at the green blazes onto a narrow woods path of the Wilderness Camps Connector Trail. Lichens and moss continue to decorate the green trail. Cross a fire ditch and enter a burned area with low shrubs. Cross four more fire ditches. Two big wooden trail signs appear at a three-way intersection; turn right to follow the yellow-blazed Mullica River Trail (5.4 miles). (One of the other paths connects to the Batona Trail—see Trip 49. The third route leads to Batsto Village, a 5-mile journey one way.)

Here the Mullica River Trail is a pretty, moss-lined woods trail, as narrow as a balance beam, and deliciously crowded by pines. Note the reindeer moss. Signs for Atsion appear every 0.5 mile. After the sixth fire ditch, the trail intersects with a big sandy road, with the river gleaming in front. Turn right toward the two big signs for Mullica River Trail and Beaver Pond–Quaker Bridge Trail, which you passed earlier, and go back the way you came. It's a bit tough to follow the signs, but just keep watch for the yellow blazes. At the circle with the trail spokes, take the far left spoke, blazed yellow. At the sand pit and water, go straight. You'll spot a yellow blaze on the left as the road curves right; take that left path into the woods, and keep following yellow blazes to the parking lot.

## DID YOU KNOW?

On the other side of US 206 lies 100-acre Atsion Lake, a recreational facility with swimming, camping, cabins, and more. Nature trails are wheelchair accessible. Per-car fees of $5 to $20 apply. You can tour nearby Atsion Mansion, built in 1868 as a summer home for the ironmaster Samuel Richards; call 609-268-0444 for information.

## OTHER ACTIVITIES

Hike Piper's Corner Preserve, a transitional forest between hardwoods and the Pine Barrens; part of the Rancocas Conservancy. Stroll and visit resident wildlife at Woodford Cedar Run Wildlife Refuge, an environmental education center and rehab facility for injured wildlife; (The refuge is at 4 Sawmill Road in Medford. Call 856-983-3329 for more information.) Many eateries line US 206 North, and there's a winery on US 206 South. Enjoy farmers markets in season and wholesale nurseries.

## MORE INFORMATION

Open dawn to dusk. Wharton State Forest, Atsion Office, 744 US 206, Shamong, NJ 08088; 609-268-0444; state.nj.us/dep/parksandforests/parks/wharton.html.

# 43

# JACOB'S CREEK

This secluded nature hike features masses of wildflowers, easy stream crossings, and the remains of an old dam.

## DIRECTIONS

From I-95 South, take Exit 1 onto NJ 29 toward Lambertville. After a few miles, turn right at the light and bridge onto Washington Crossing–Pennington Road. Go 1.37 miles and turn left onto Bear Tavern Road (County Highway 579). Go 0.4 mile and turn right onto Pennington–Titusville Road. After 0.75 mile, park in the gravel lot on the right at the green trailhead sign, which is located before a concrete bridge. Only four or five cars can park in the tiny lot. *GPS coordinates:* 40° 19.101′ N, 74° 50.294′ W.

## TRAIL DESCRIPTION

This is a darling hike: easy, with water features, stream crossings, and a phalanx of wildflowers in spring, summer, and fall. You'll walk through mature woods, stroll past old farm roads, and visit the remains of an old dam. Nature signs educate you along the way about this lovely section of the Hopewell Valley, which is partially in the Franz Preserve. Stay on the trail; white diamonds and white arrows mark the way. You'll be moving through private property sometimes, using public-access easements obtained by the Friends of Hopewell Valley Open Space. Since you are following a creek, some areas may be slippery and muddy. A boardwalk spans an occasionally marshy portion. (Trekking poles for stream crossings might come in handy.)

There's a pretty southbound spur to the right of the parking lot, which you can hike at the end of this out-and-back trip. For now, read about the trail on the kiosk,

**LOCATION**
Hopewell

**RATING**
Easy

**DISTANCE**
2.7 miles

**ELEVATION GAIN**
250 feet

**ESTIMATED TIME**
1.5 hours

**MAPS**
USGS Pennington; njtrails .org/trail/jacobs-creek-trail

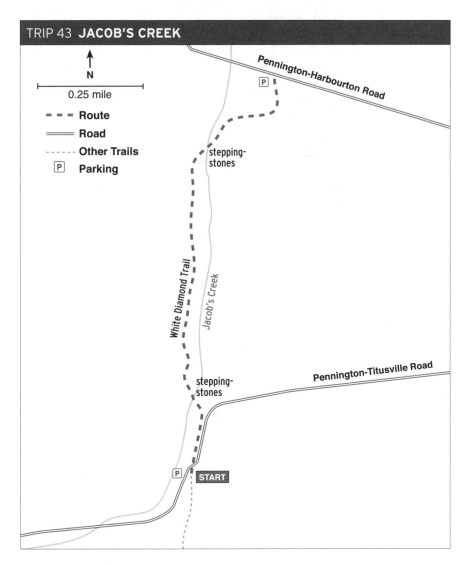

N

0.25 mile

- - - **Route**
=== **Road**
----- **Other Trails**
P **Parking**

Pennington-Harbourton Road

P

stepping-stones

White Diamond Trail

Jacob's Creek

stepping-stones

Pennington-Titusville Road

P START

then cross the road to the Jacob's Creek Trail sign to go north. A grassy path follows Jacob's Creek as it flows to the right. Stepping-stones lead over a creek rivulet (which can be wetter in early spring). In summer, enjoy a forest of 6-foot-tall Queen Anne's lace (wild carrot), spring beauties, and purple dame's rocket. You can hear the cars on the right, but you can't be seen from the road, giving you a wonderful feeling of privacy. Toward the end of the flower field, walk under the lowering branches of some remarkably large spruce trees. You are following the white-blazed White Diamond Trail.

Inhale the sweet smells of nature as you approach what looks like the remains of an old stone wall, framed by blooming blackberry bushes. This is actually a dam that once crossed Jacob's Creek. Hurricane Irene in 2011 destroyed the dam, except for this 5-feet-tall section.

Sturdy boardwalks make crossing wetland areas level and easy.

Carefully tread some stepping-stones over a creek (0.2 mile) and pass through a stand of cedars. There's a red barn uphill to the left. The narrow, leafy dirt path curves to the right, heading slightly uphill. Note the stone cliff on the left and stream on the right. The birds are riotous in the spring. At a clearing, the path again crosses the creek on stepping-stones. Follow the white arrows on metal posts along the well-marked trail. Walk past mounds of oxeye daisies. Veer right at a white arrow for a slight uphill into a forested area. Through the trees on the right, you can see a black iron maple syrup still next to a deer stand as you wind away from creek. (Hunting is allowed from September to February. See "More Information.")

The creek reappears on the right as you go uphill, following white diamond markings. Take a left at a white arrow. Cross a power-line clearing, with showy fields of yellow rocket. Follow a white arrow past more oxeye daisies. Enter the woods again and note another maple syrup still to the left. Pause to sit on a convenient bench and admire the steep ravine below, filled with skunk cabbage and yellow wildflowers in the spring and summer.

Go downhill, crossing a small ditch on stepping-stones. Enjoy a fun boardwalk of a few hundred yards. Pause to look for salamanders in the dark pool of water nestling under the roots of an overturned tree. Cross another stream on stepping-stones (0.8 mile). The narrow dirt path begins to veer away from the stream, and you're engulfed by green, although houses are visible to the left and right. At the clearing, turn left at a white diamond trail marker. (*Caution:* Do not cross the ravine.) Head toward the creek and cross it at the white arrow on a metal sign, using the thoughtfully provided stepping-stones (1.1 miles). Step up a small stream bank, and then turn left.

As you walk the white trail, a house and a metal fence are on the left. The trail briefly follows the fence before ending at paved Pennington–Harbourton Road (1.2 miles). The parking lot at this end of the trail is slightly larger than the first one (holds maybe six cars), but the trail entrance, hidden in the woods, is almost impossible to find (*hint:* look just beyond telephone pole 91). You have reached the end of the hike. Simply turn around and backtrack, hidden from sight in these lovely woods.

When you return to your car (2.4 miles), don't forget to take the pretty 0.3-mile southern spur that runs along the creek. It follows a floodplain and thus is green, gorgeous, and shady, with blooming wildflowers, including purple dame's rocket, phlox, and yellow iris in the spring. You are close to the creek (where birds bathe and ducks float) and get to cross four wooden footbridges. The path ends at a white rectangle on a metal post. Stop and turn around. There's a nice view of the bridge as you walk back to your car.

## DID YOU KNOW?

The Hopewell Valley, bordered on the west by the Delaware River and on the north by the Sourlands region, has 90 miles of hiking trails. Visit the website of Friends of Hopewell Valley Open Space to download *Guide to Walking Trails in the Hopewell Valley*, which contains information on 22 hikes (fohvos.info/wp-content/uploads/2017/11/walkingTrails2015.pdf).

## OTHER ACTIVITIES

Walk Woolsey Brook Trail in Alliger Park (Titusville) on Washington Crossing–Pennington Road (County Road 546), about 0.5 mile west of Scotch Road. Drive northwest about 30 minutes to Stockton to hike secluded Wickecheoke Creek Preserve and see Green Sergeant's Covered Bridge (preserve is at 2–8 Pine Hill Road; bridge is at 707 Rosemont Ringoes Road). Visit Hopewell and Pennington to the northeast: In Hopewell, see the Hopewell Museum, and in Pennington, stop by Hopewell Valley Vineyards and the impressive Watershed Institute at the Stony Brook-Millstone Watershed Reserve.

## MORE INFORMATION

Open dawn to dusk. Hunting is allowed on selected days from early September through mid-February and in some sections from October through February, excluding Sundays. Check the website: Under "Preserves," find "Nexus Preserve." Friends of Hopewell Valley Open Space, P.O. Box 395, Pennington, NJ 08534; 609-730-1560; fohvos.org.

# 44

# LAURIE CHAUNCEY TRAIL

Found by few, this hidden haven, deceivingly placed on the perimenter of a corporate park in Princeton, showcases a creek, rock outcroppings, and an oasis of green.

## DIRECTIONS

On I-95 North, take US 206 North via Exit 7B toward Lawrenceville/Princeton. Go 4.0 miles and turn left onto Province Line Road. Travel to the concrete barrier at the end of the road (about 2 miles) and park along the shoulder. Perhaps five or six cars could park here. *GPS coordinates:* 40° 21.085' N, 74° 42.565' W.

## TRAIL DESCRIPTION

This hike is unusual because it's part of the lunchtime strolling grounds of the Educational Testing Service (ETS), and as such, is not known by many hikers. ETS is the organization that develops and scores academic tests: SAT, GRE, PSAT, and more. Say a friendly hello to those who walk sporting ETS name badges. The trail winds through an abundance of red maples, ashes, and tulip poplars, and partially follows Stony Brook Creek and some impressive granite outcroppings. You'll go through an ecotone (watch for the signs), a transition area between two different ecological communities. Animals like ecotones because of easy access to multiple habitats and food sources. Look for deer; foxes and raccoons come out at dusk.

Spring brings fairy-tale greenery and shade-loving wildflowers. Pick raspberries in summer. Golden leaves float in Stony Brook in the fall. The rocks and leaves can be a bit slippery in winter. A bonus in any season is the rare three-pony bridge you'll see at the end of the hike.

**LOCATION**
Princeton

**RATING**
Easy

**DISTANCE**
2.7 miles

**ELEVATION GAIN**
200 feet

**ESTIMATED TIME**
1.5 hours

**MAPS**
USGS Princeton; njtrails
.org/trail/laurie-chauncey
-trail-at-ets

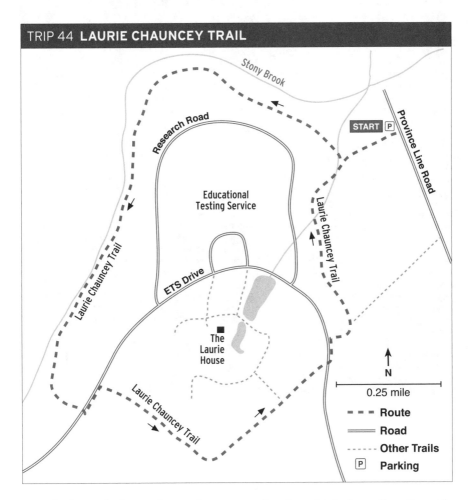

Park alongside the road near the concrete barrier, which closes the other side of the road permanently to traffic (you'll hike it later).

Walk south, away from the barrier, about 275 feet, until you see a marker for Laurie Chauncey Nature Trail on the right. Enter the woods. At the next trail marker, go straight. The dirt path slopes down gently to a bridge on your left. Don't take the bridge; go straight instead, and then follow the trail as it curves to the right.

Now a stream is on your left as the path slopes gently down; be careful on the rocks. Cross a bridge with Stony Brook Creek on your right. Ignore steps to the left—they lead up to the ETS building. The creek is beautiful, and you can linger here next to the impressive rocks that appear on your left. Soon after this, there's a little path on the right where you can walk out onto the rocks in the creek, large enough to perch on without getting wet, and bask in the sun, which plays on branches of overhanging trees. At the junction (0.2 mile), go right following the flat, grassy path along the creek. A road is on your left. Soon two more sets of steps to the ETS building appear on the left; ignore them. Maneuver a stream

The trail winds along Stony Brook, through verdant forest.

crossing on stepping-stones. Go over three bridges on this pretty, winding, narrow dirt path.

Cross another bridge at a tree with carvings—do not take the path to the left. Here, Laurie Chauncey Trail is gorgeous, grassy, and green as it intersects with a series of jogging trails. At a four-way intersection, with a power line above, go straight at the trail marker to stay on the route. Jogging trail 9 is to your right. Walk through a tunnel of bushes. At the next trail marker, go left onto paved ETS Drive (jogging trail 20 is to your right). Cross the road (1.4 miles). In 100 yards, the trail marker leads you right into the woods on a grassy path that turns into a wide dirt one. At the trail junction, go straight, and then follow the trail as it bends to the left onto a grassy boulevard. At the four-way intersection, go straight—jogging trail 2 is to your right. At the three-way intersection (jogging trail 3 to your right), go straight. You'll come onto an open path that leads to the ETS parking lot (1.7 miles). You'll also see a sign explaining what an ecotone is, as well as a real ecotone. Note the mowed swatch of grass (actually a pipeline right-of-way) that neatly divides the woods from a meadow filled with tall mountain mint: a prime example of a transitional area between two communities of plants and animals—and improbably located at the edge of a parking lot.

Walk across the ETS campus to get onto the trail again (don't worry, it's allowed). Head straight across the grass toward the flagpole. When you reach the road (ETS Drive), cross it (2.0 miles). Go left to walk along the shoulder of the road and you'll soon come to a trail marker where Assessment Road (not on map in this book) and ETS Drive meet (2.1 miles). Turn right onto the trail, which is now a wide, mowed grassy path with the Laurie Chauncey Nature Trail sign. A gorgeous field is to the right. At the next trail marker, go left into the shady woods and cross a miniature bridge. At the Y intersection, go straight onto a pebble-and-dirt path with a ditch on the left. Cross two more bridges and go slightly downhill into an area lush with skunk cabbage. At the next Y intersection, go right, still slightly downhill, and cross two more bridges, before going uphill and down on a narrow dirt path. You can see a building to the left through the trees. Cross one final bridge, and at the T intersection, turn right at the trail sign. Go uphill, then turn right at the next trail sign (2.5 miles) to go back to Province Line Road.

*Bonus*: Put your pack in the car. Walk past the concrete barrier, and go about one-eighth of a mile down the closed paved road. Feel free to walk on the yellow line as this road is permanently closed to traffic. You'll come to a rare three-pony-truss bridge over Stony Brook. Pony trusses are not tall enough to be joined together with cross braces on top. The road continues on the other side of the bridge. If you have time, before the bridge there is a trail to the right marked "Stony Brook Trail"—a nice way to extend your hike. (*Note:* On the map, it's labeled Ettl Farm Trail.)

## DID YOU KNOW?

You can buy a local guide to sixteen of the best trails through preserved open spaces in Princeton: *Walk the Trails in and Around Princeton*, by Sophie Glovier (Princeton University Press, revised edition 2017).

## OTHER ACTIVITIES

Carson Road Woods, on Carson Road, has 4.4 miles of trails through a beech forest, with streams and meadows. Explore the Institute Woods at the Institute for Advanced Study, next to the Princeton Battlefield State Park (American Revolution). Hike 48 poems (yes, poems) at the Scott and Hella McVay Poetry Trail on Rosedale Road at the Johnson Education Center (opengreenmap.org/greenmap/new-princeton-green-connections/scott-and-hella-mcvay-poetry-trail-27888).

## MORE INFORMATION

Open dawn to dusk. ETS Corporate Headquarters, 660 Rosedale Road, Princeton, NJ 08541; 609-921-9000. Trail information: njtrails.org/trail/laurie-chauncey-trail-at-ets/.

# 45

# WASHINGTON CROSSING STATE PARK

Enjoy excellent river views where George Washington crossed the Delaware and a stroll on historic Continental Trail Lane on this hike to the park's northern section.

## DIRECTIONS

Take I-95 to Exit 1 toward Lambertville/NJ 29 North. Go left at the fork, merging with River Road (NJ 29). In about 3 miles, turn left at the light (near restaurant and gas station) onto Washington Crossing–Pennington Road and then *immediately* turn right (before the bridge into Pennsylvania) into the spacious parking lot (at least 50 cars). *GPS coordinates:* 40° 17.810′ N, 74° 52.090′ W.

## TRAIL DESCRIPTION

Journey back through time in 3,575-acre Washington Crossing State Park, where the friendly ghosts of American Revolution soldiers speak to you at every turn. You may catch a glimpse of bewigged George Washington himself during the many historical reenactments. Fifteen miles of trails wind through the park. See the spot where General Washington and his soldiers crossed the icy Delaware on the night of December 25, 1776. Walk Continental Lane Trail, the route over which Washington's troops began their march to Trenton and won a morale-boosting battle. (The Trenton Battle Monument is on North Warren Street in Trenton.)

The park is eminently walkable in every season. In fall, the river and canal reflect the shimmer of colorful deciduous trees. Cross-country skiing beckons in winter, as well as the December 25 reenactment of Washington crossing the Delaware. Enjoy historical events and performances at the Open Air Theatre in summer. Wildflowers paint the park in spring. The visitor center, museum, and historic

**LOCATION**
Titusville

**RATING**
Easy

**DISTANCE**
3.9 miles

**ELEVATION GAIN**
350 feet

**ESTIMATED TIME**
2 hours

**MAPS**
USGS Pennington; state.nj.us/dep/ parksandforests/parks/ maps/WashingtonCrossing AreaMapFinalDraft.pdf

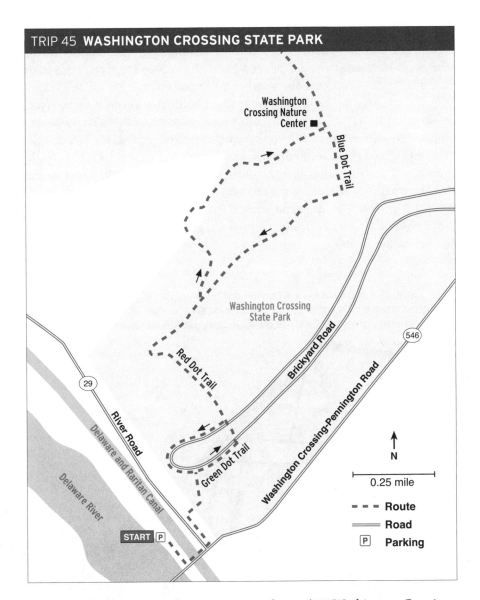

Johnson Ferry House are a few minutes away by car (355 Washington Crossing–Pennington Road). Entrance fees are charged per vehicle from Memorial Day weekend to Labor Day. On weekends, New Jersey residents pay $5 and non-New Jersey residents pay $7. On weekdays, admission is free.

This hike starts briefly on Green Dot Trail, then follows Red Dot Trail up and down, over bridges, and through the forests and fields to reach the natural area and nature center in the remote northern section of the park. The return trip follows Blue Dot Trail to Red Dot Trail.

Leave the parking lot, where Pennsylvania peeps at you across the Delaware River, and walk toward the bridge and historic Nelson House (enter, if it's open).

Follow the red brick path to the left, cross the pedestrian bridge over the picturesque Delaware and Raritan Canal, and turn left onto the paved walkway, which soon becomes the dirt Green Dot Trail. Cross a paved road to stay on this trail. Take a right (0.4 mile) onto the wood-chip Continental Lane Trail, flanked by welcoming woods, which marks a route that Washington's army marched (you are on this historic trail for only 0.1 mile). Turn left onto Red Dot Trail and stay on it, watching junctions and crossings carefully. Cross a paved road (open field to the right), and enter woods through an opening in a fence, walking alongside a meadow. Enter the woods again on the first path on the left. You'll soon see the Red Dot marker on the left. At the junction of Red Dot and Green Dot trails, go straight. The woods are deep and lovely. Cross over Green Dot Trail on the left. (Turn right on Green Dot Trail if you want to go to the picnic/playground area and the visitor center.)

Washington Crossing Bridge marks the area where, on the night of December 25, 1776, George Washington crossed the Delaware River, the first move in a surprise attack organized by Washington against the Hessian forces in Trenton, New Jersey. Photo by John Hoey, Creative Commons on Flickr.

Head downhill through the quiet green woods. At the bottom of the hill lies an impressive sometimes-dry creek bed. Turn left on Red Dot Trail (0.8 mile) and then right to cross the wooden footbridge. Veer right (straight) off the bridge, still on Red Dot Trail (Yellow Dot Trail is to the left), and head up a small hill. Then turn left to stay on Red Dot Trail. At the crossroads with Blue Dot Trail, keep straight on a well-worn, narrow, furrowed path, flanked by sentinel trees.

Cross Blue Dot Trail again and head down a rooty downhill slope. To the left is an open field in the distance. Follow Red Dot Trail across another bridge, and cross the Blue Dot Trail twice more. The Red Dot Trail ends, but keep going straight, past the bench on your right, and turn left onto the paved road (1.9 miles) to visit the nature center's exhibits. Staff members raise bees out back, and there is an outdoor solar dryer. A covered pavilion to the left seats about 30. Retrace your route to Red Dot Trail.

At the first junction, veer left onto Blue Dot Trail (2.3 miles). After a few hundred feet, veer right to stay on the trail. On a gentle downward slope canopied by trees, go toward signs for the nature center's theater. Come out of the woods and take a right on a paved road (2.5 miles). The Open Air Theatre (music and plays in good weather) is about 200 yards to your left, toward the parking lot and bathrooms. Continue straight on Blue Dot Trail, walking across grass now. Turn left on Blue Dot Trail and walk beneath the lacy canopy of trees.

At the trail intersection, take a left onto Red Dot Trail (2.9 miles). Retrace your steps from here, following Red Dot Trail until it reaches Green Dot Trail near the pedestrian bridge. Step to your right to view where George Washington crossed the Delaware in 1776 (sign and monument). Then cross the pedestrian bridge and head back to your car.

## DID YOU KNOW?

An observatory and museum (fee) are in the park. An artist's paradise is 20 minutes away at the beautifully landscaped, nonprofit 43-acre Grounds for Sculpture. 80 Sculptors Way, Hamilton; 609-586-0616.

## OTHER ACTIVITIES

Drive 15 minutes for a 1-mile hike to Goat Hill Overlook (administered by Washington Crossing State Park), with excellent views of the Delaware River and bridges. To visit the museum across the river at Washington Crossing Historic Park in Pennsylvania, 1112 River Road, Washington Crossing, PA, 18977; 215-493-4076.

## MORE INFORMATION

Open 8 A.M. to 7 P.M. Washington Crossing State Park, 355 Washington Crossing–Pennington Road, Titusville, NJ 08560; 609-737-0623; njparksandforests .org/parks/washcros.html.

# 46

# PARVIN STATE PARK

Don't miss the wildflowers and blooming trees and shrubs in spring, the egrets fishing in the lake, and the charm of an isolated swamp trail.

## DIRECTIONS

From Route 55 North or South, take Exit 35 toward Glassboro/Vineland and follow signs to the park (about 30 miles from the exit). The huge parking lot holds at least 50 cars. *GPS coordinates:* 39° 30.658′ N, 75° 07.912′ W.

## TRAIL DESCRIPTION

Parvin is another park built by the Civilian Conservation Corps (CCC), an outgrowth of the New Deal program created by President Franklin D. Roosevelt during the Great Depression. The CCC constructed the main beach complex, a parking lot, campsites, and cabins. In summer, the 2,092-acre park is rich with campers and bird songs. Here at the edge of the Pine Barrens, several miles of trails through cedar swamps, holly groves, pine forests, and laurel thickets delight in all seasons (except perhaps summer, peak bug season). Spring is a heady mix of blooms and perfumes from more than 200 kinds of flowering plants, plus wild azaleas, dogwoods, mountain laurels, and magnolias. You can lounge on the beach and swim in Parvin Lake in season ($2 walk-in entry fee to beach from Memorial Day weekend through Labor Day).

On this hike, start on green-blazed Parvin Lake Trail and wander deep into secluded areas on Parvin Lake Trail, orange-blazed Knoll Trail, brown-blazed Black Oak Trail, red-blazed Long Trail, blue-blazed Forest Loop Trail, and then back to Parvin Lake Trail, getting a good overview both of the swamp hardwood forests and pine forests. Even in the parking lot, you'll hear birds shriek and, in September, see hawks soar. Cross the road to the

**LOCATION**
Elmer

**RATING**
Moderate to Strenuous

**DISTANCE**
9.3 miles

**ELEVATION GAIN**
375 feet

**ESTIMATED TIME**
5 hours

**MAPS**
USGS Elmer; state.nj.us/dep/parksandforests/parks/maps/ParvinFinalDraft2_reduced_Area_broc.pdf

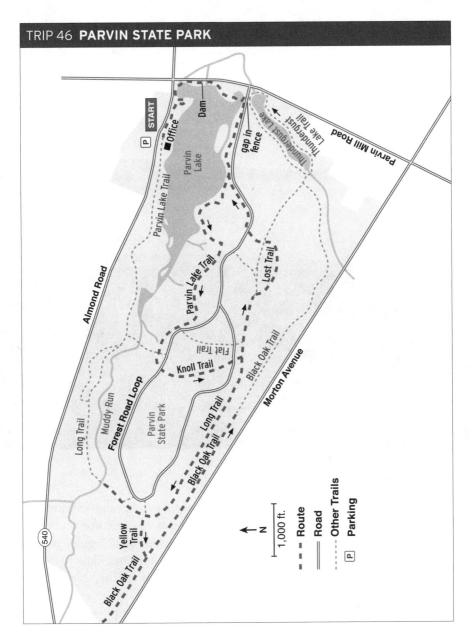

park office in front of the beach and Parvin Lake. Stop in and pick up a map and a guide to birds. Unisex flush toilets are located outside the office.

Facing the lake, turn left onto the red brick trail, which becomes the sandy, flat, green-blazed Parvin Lake Trail (trails are mainly identified by color only). Walk alongside a green metal fence that parallels the road. Then cross a field and go over a footbridge with an inviting pagoda to the left. Cross White Bridge (built by the CCC), and the path changes to dirt as it winds around the lake into the woods. Soon a concrete sidewalk goes past a dam; birds fish here. Head toward

An egret awaits dinner at Parvin Lake dam.

the first floating dock, and stop to rest on perfectly placed benches overlooking the lake. Nature signage makes the trail educational as you continue your hike, walking toward two floating docks separated by a parking lot (0.7 mile at lot).

After enjoying the docks, take a bridge over the lake. At the trail junction with a yellow-blazed connector trail and blue-blazed Forest Loop Trail, stay right on Parvin Lake Trail (0.9 mile). Check out the cabins for rent on the left. The lake narrows to a tributary as the woods encroach and turn swampy. At a four-way trail intersection, at the sign for Island Point picnic area, go straight to continue on green-blazed Parvin Lake Trail.

The lake comes into full view again on the right; lily pads bloom. Note the nature signs that describe the plants along the the hike and the stately column of trees (1.0 mile). Keep on the green-blazed trail, ignoring feeder trails to the left. Intersect a paved road with camping and picnic areas on the right, all part of Jaggers Point camping area (1.4 miles). Fill your water bottle at the red pump to your left. Go right on the paved road and right at the green sign, then make a quick left at the playground. At the next trail junction, stay on the green-blazed trail (do not go left at the campground area). Lake views disappear. At the next trail junction, go left to stay on the green-blazed trail. (*Note:* There is no trail sign.) The path narrows as shrubs encroach and sounds recede. Go more deeply into the quiet woods over a wooden footbridge, and reach the 2-mile green trail marker. Cross a wooden bridge over swampy water. At the paved intersection, go straight—you are now entering orange-blazed Knoll Trail (2.4 miles).

Secluded woods embrace you as the trail narrows, hugged by low shrubs. Watch out for low-hanging branches at the wooden bridge. Cross a paved path, keeping straight on the orange-blazed trail. The woods open up as you cross two more footbridges. At the paved road (which is the blue-blazed trail, 2.8 miles), go straight, still on Knoll Trail. At the next junction, take a right onto red-blazed Long Trail (2.9 miles). Sit on a moss-covered log and have lunch. As you continue on beautiful elevated Long Trail, the atmosphere becomes quieter as you walk the sandy edge of the Pine Barrens; tall, thin pines grow from a crazy jumble of blowdown. Enjoy the peaceful seclusion and red-headed woodpeckers.

At the four-way junction, go left on the yellow-blazed connector trail (3.8 miles) onto a wide, soft path through the forest. At the next junction, take a left (road and houses to the right) onto the brown-blazed Black Oak Trail (4.0 miles). Swampy areas are covered with carefully placed branches to walk on. The brown-blazed trail ends in swamp, with Morton Avenue on the right (4.8 miles). You are alone, a rare occurrence in today's world. Stay a while and enjoy the mysterious solitude. Turn around so that Morton Avenue is now on your left. Walk to the end of the brown-blazed trail going the other way (pass the junction at 5.6 miles). Expect some intricate spiderwebs, as no one walks here. Black Oak Trail dead-ends at houses and private property (5.9 miles). Backtrack to the junction with the yellow-blazed connector trail and go left onto the connector trail (6.2 miles). At the junction of the yellow-blazed connector trail and the red-blazed trail, go right onto the red-blazed trail (6.6 miles).

Soon you walk over plank footbridges, and the path becomes sandy. At the junction, go right onto the red-blazed trail (orange-blazed trail is to the left). Cross a dirt road—keep straight on the red-blazed trail. Pass a pink-blazed connector trail to your left (7.5 miles). The trail becomes wide and flat. You will see light-orange-blazed Lost Trail to your right, but keep straight on the red-blazed trail. At the next junction, take a right on the red-blazed trail as it narrows. Observe odd-shaped blowdown.

At a four-way intersection, take the light-orange-blazed Lost Trail on the left because the red-blazed trail was closed as of September 2016 due to storm damage. Then go right at the split, toward the paved road. A sign for Jaggers Point campground is to your left. Go right on the paved road, which is blue-blazed Forest Loop Trail (8.2 miles). Pass a forest regeneration area sign on the right. Soon on the left is the familiar, civilized green-blazed trail. Take a left onto it (8.8 miles). Go down a short hill and turn right at the path; the hike is now a retrace on green-blazed Parvin Lake Trail.

Along the way, enjoy the highbush blueberries and the plop-plop of frogs in the lake. Pause at the large root ball (mass of exposed roots and dirt) of an uprooted tree; fish jump in the branches that sprawl across the lake. Watch the sunset and egrets fishing at the dam before you cross the road and return to your car.

## DID YOU KNOW?

Parvin State Park was a camp for German prisoners of war and a summer camp for children of displaced Japanese Americans. Remains of Native American encampments dot the area. Hike around the other lake in the park, Thundergust Lake, on the yellow-blazed Thundergust Trail.

## OTHER ACTIVITIES

Explore the eighteenth- and nineteenth-century sawmill and gristmill and the former homes of mill workers at Fries Mill Ruins in the Manumuskin River Preserve near Millville. In Millville, explore 5,000-acre Union Lake Wildlife Management Area (County Road 552).

## MORE INFORMATION

Open sunrise to sunset. There is a $2 beach fee from Memorial Day weekend through Labor Day. A snack bar is open in season. Parvin State Park, 701 Almond Road, Pittsgrove, NJ 08318-3928; 856-358-8616; state.nj.us/dep/parksandforests/parks/parvin.html.

# 47

# BLACK RUN PRESERVE

Find quiet in the heart of a thriving metropolitan area in this pristine and eerily calm far north-western corner of the Pinelands National Reserve.

## DIRECTIONS

Take I-295 South to Exit 36A toward Berlin onto NJ 73 North/South. Go 7.0 miles and turn left onto Braddock Mill Road. Go 0.66 mile and turn right onto Tomlinson Mill Road. Go 0.07 mile and take the second left onto Braddock Mill Road. Go 0.62 mile and keep left at the fork to continue on Braddock Mill Road. Go 0.02 mile and turn left onto Kettle Run at the stop sign; 179 Kettle Run is on the left, *past* the larger parking lot (20 cars) for the Black Run Trail on the right. The dirt lot accommodates about 12 cars. *GPS coordinates: 39° 50.757′ N, 74° 53.991′ W.*

## TRAIL DESCRIPTION

This island of undeveloped watershed is set in the hugely urban area of Marlton, with every amenity known to man on NJ 70 and NJ 73. But you would never know this oasis was here unless you looked. The site of a former cranberry farm, Black Run Preserve somehow escaped development. The open savannas and ponds and the biodiversity are delightfully startling in an area just 15 miles from Phil-adelphia, and the preserve's pristine habitats support spe-cies native to the Pine Barrens, such as the carnivorous sundew plant, green frogs, and sunfish. Located in the northwestern corner of the Pinelands National Reserve, this 1,300-acre area of the Pine Barrens is billed as "the Gateway to the Pinelands."

The very active group Friends of the Black Run Preserve (FBRP) makes improvements constantly, so some of the trail colors and names may have changed. But the trail

**LOCATION**
Marlton

**RATING**
Easy

**DISTANCE**
3.2 miles

**ELEVATION GAIN**
100 feet

**ESTIMATED TIME**
1.5 hours

**MAPS**
USGS Clementon; blackrun.org/wp-content/uploads/2016/01/BlackRunMapJune2017.pdf; interactive map: blackrun.org/map

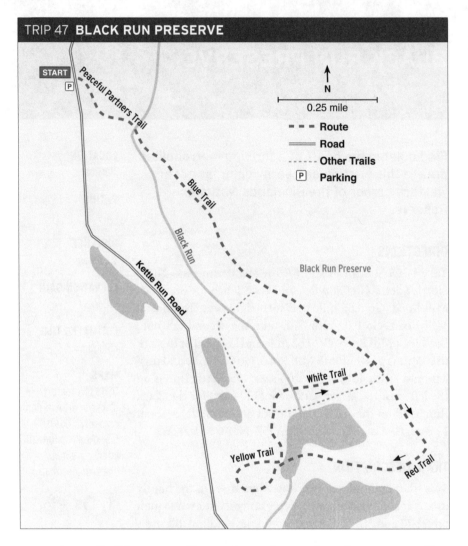

system is very flexible, so you will get a nice workout and good scenery regardless of any layout or color changes. With luck and funding, the Peace Bridge, a bridge to connect the west side of the preserve to the east, will now be complete. A flood in 2004 breached a dike, cutting off access to the west side. Locals improvised what they called a "shaky bridge" to connect east and west, but then a family of beavers built a five-foot-tall dam on top. The Peace Bridge will honor a culture of respect, especially the historical relationship between the Lenni-Lenape people and the Quakers.

Early spring brings a myriad of blooming wildflowers and aquatic plants but can be wet. Summer is buggy. Fall and winter accentuate the Pine Barrens' eerie beauty.

Carry a cell phone to scan the downloadable maps at information posts throughout the park (although cell coverage can be iffy in this area). As of 2018, there were 12 miles of trails. You'll take green/blue-blazed trails to a red-blazed trail to a funky yellow/white/red/blue-blazed loop and then back all the way on blue blazes.

Begin on Peaceful Partners Trail (which may start out green-blazed before turning blue-blazed) at the parking lot, near the informational kiosk (chemical toilet here also). Take time to read about the Pine Barrens (see also page 148). The first trail marker has a smartphone QR code to download a map. At the fence, go straight, following the green and blue blazes (0.3 mile). (The orange-blazed Nature Trail goes to the right and leads to a former cranberry bog.)

Immediately, you'll cross an impressive bridge over peaty, piney water, with the melody of frog song. Walk the flat cinder path. At the Y intersection after the bridge, turn right to stay on the blue-blazed trail (the red-blazed Long Path Trail goes to the left), a soft dirt path lined with pine straw. Mosey off to the right to get a good look at the bog with waterlilies. In spring, scan the water for the yellow spikes of blooming golden club, or check the woods for blooming white turkey beard. (*Caution:* Be careful not to turn off on the many faint rogue trails.) Keep going straight past the path on the right on this nice shady walk. Stop off at a sign about carnivorous plants, and see if you can spot any sundews or pitcher plants as you walk on a short, wooden viewing station. Soon, there is another short nature trail to your right—explore it for a few minutes, looking and listening for chickadees, tree swallows, and eastern bluebirds, and perhaps noticing the fluffy white blooms of turkey beard in spring. Then return to the Blue Trail.

At the next Y intersection, turn left to stay on the blue-blazed trail (Long Path Trail goes to the right). Admire the pretty bog to the right. The path turns into Pine Barrens sugar-sand.

At the second Y intersection, stay right on the blue-blazed trail (white-blazed Kettle Trail goes to the left). Fantastically shaped pines are all around, lining the pancake-flat, sandy pine straw path. At the third Y intersection, go straight to stay on the blue-blazed trail (white-blazed trail goes to the right). Steep banks frame the sandy path. At the fourth Y intersection, stay straight on the blue-blazed trail (white-blazed trail goes to the left).

Soon the path splits; take the left fork. Check out the open savanna, which is somewhat lower than the path, patterned with grasses, pitch pines, and pygmy pines. At a four-way intersection that looks like a sand pit (1.3 miles), take a right onto the red-blazed Long Trail (red-blazed Long Trail goes to the left also).

Cross the observation planks over a bog on the right; this black water is very acidic, which gives rise to the unique flora of the Pine Barrens. Turn onto a narrow strip of the red-blazed trail, which cuts between two bogs—a unique experience. You'll pass several wooden-and-metal boxes on the edges of the lake, remnants of the cranberry industry no doubt. The rolling path is carpeted with pine straw, going past fantastically shaped blowdown. In April, frogs croak. At the Y intersection, go left onto an unnamed yellow connector trail (1.7 miles).

Remnants of former cranberry farming can still be seen in Black Run Preserve.

At the next Y intersection, turn right. There's an abandoned car on the left with a "for sale" sign (1 cent). Despite that amusing sight, you're in a very atmospheric place, otherworldly and peaceful. Cross a peaty stream with beautiful grasses to the left. It's quite pleasant walking on a carpet of pine straw.

The red trail ends in a T intersection with a wide path. You are heading into the funky but rewarding loop. Turn right onto the white-blazed trail (1.8 miles). A Y intersection comes up quickly. Turn right at the arrow that says "start." The path becomes a yellow connector trail and leads to a footbridge at a four-way intersection (1.9 miles). Take the far left path onto the red-blazed trail—a large, fantastically twisted downed tree is to the left. Walk under trees that lean across the path. At the next intersection, take a left to get back onto the white-blazed trail; a field is to the right with a watery bog where frogs jump. A birdhouse is on the left. Keep going straight on the white-blazed trail at the next intersection. At the following intersection, turn left onto the sandy blue-blazed trail (2.3 miles) with a pine straw path and pleasant woods. You've completed the loop. Go straight at the Y intersection onto the blue-blazed trail, noting an interesting bog on your left. At the next intersection, go straight to stay on the blue-blazed trail. The path is wide, and another bog is on your left. Turn left to cross a bridge at the next intersection, and you are back at the parking lot.

## DID YOU KNOW?

Founded in 1676, Marlton is one of the oldest cities in the country. The Garden State Discovery Museum, for children 10 and younger, is northwest of the preserve, in Cherry Hill (2040 Springdale Road, Suite 100, 856-424-1233).

## OTHER ACTIVITIES

To hike the bogs of Black Run Trail, take a right out of the parking lot and an almost immediate left at the sign down a pitted dirt road to a 20-car parking lot. Explore the far west side of the preserve from the parking lot at 500 Tomlinson Mill Road. Access the preserve from the northwest side by parking at the Links Golf Club (you must sign up for a free social membership at the clubhouse).

## MORE INFORMATION

Friends of the Black Run Preserve, 123 E. Main St., P.O. Box 1124, Marlton, NJ 08053; 609-451-0580; blackrun.org.

# 48

# COOPER RIVER PARK LOOP

Stretch your legs on an urban and suburban adventure over bridges, past playgrounds and woods, and through neighborhoods.

## DIRECTIONS

From I-295, take Exit 34B for Marlton Pike/Route 70 West. After 3.9 miles, take the second exit on the right for Cuthbert Boulevard South. Make the first right onto North Park Boulevard. After 0.5 mile, turn left into the parking area for Cooper River Park. The large lot probably has 200 spaces. *GPS coordinates:* 39° 55.660' N, 75° 03.964' W.

**Public transportation:** Take PATCO trains to Collingswood, Westmont, or Haddonfield; see area map for walking directions. Take NJ Transit bus routes 406, 413, 450, or 451.

## TRAIL DESCRIPTION

Cooper River Park epitomizes New Jersey: urban and suburban living side by side. Where else can you see a juvenile hawk drying his wings on someone's freshly mowed front lawn? Other contrasts meet the eye as you walk the loop around Cooper River and wind through the pretty streets of Haddon Township, passing a yacht club, an outdoor carnival, miniature golf, food trucks, playgrounds, private homes, war memorials, large auto dealerships, and more. The 346-acre park in Camden County is truly an urban adventure that spans several municipalities (Cherry Hill, Collingswood, Pennsauken, and Haddon Township) and boasts eight parking lots. It's also part of the Camden GreenWay, a network of thirteen trails that, when complete, will link communities throughout the Camden County area to Philadelphia.

The park is bounded by North and South Park drives, Route 130, and Grove Street. The loop trail is mainly

**LOCATION**
Cherry Hill

**RATING**
Easy

**DISTANCE**
7.8 miles

**ELEVATION GAIN**
200 feet

**ESTIMATED TIME**
3.5 hours

**MAPS**
USGS Camden; camdencounty.com/wp-content/uploads/2017/07/COOPER-RIVER-3-23-16.pdf; pecpa.org/wp-content/uploads/12-Trail-Itineraroes-Brochure1.pdf

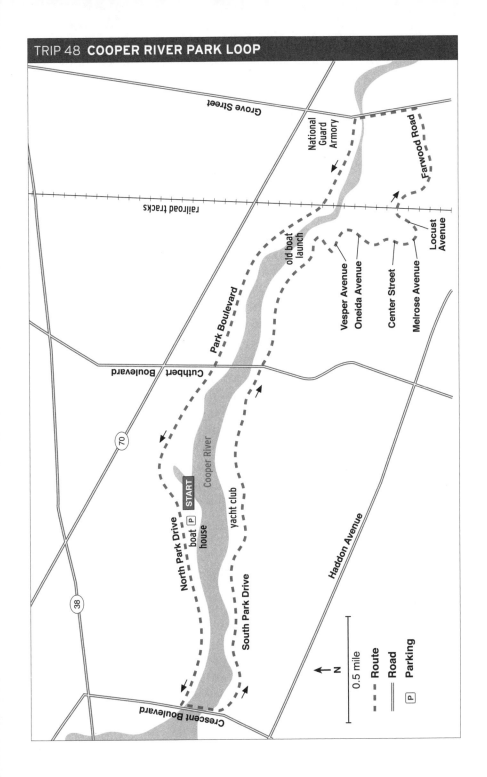

TRIP 48 **COOPER RIVER PARK LOOP**

Grove Street

National Guard Armory

Farwood Road

railroad tracks

Locust Avenue

old boat launch

Vesper Avenue

Oneida Avenue

Center Street

Melrose Avenue

Park Boulevard

Cuthbert Boulevard

70

Cooper River

START

boat house

North Park Drive

yacht club

South Park Drive

Haddon Avenue

38

Crescent Boulevard

N

0.5 mile

- - - Route
═══ Road
P Parking

asphalt and parallels the road (North Park and South Park drives), except for the residential jaunt, which extends the mileage, through Haddonfield. The park itself is a swath of green between the trail and the river.

You'll start at the Cherry Hill parking lot, which has a restaurant with a beer garden. Head west on the asphalt trail (the river will be on your left), following the green-and-purple "Enjoy Camden County" banners. You can stop at any point and walk down to the generous river or take advantage of the park's many amenities: playgrounds, boat rentals, running tracks, volleyball courts, pavilions, picnic tables, and more. Ground-up tires make the surface of the playground area soft and eco-friendly.

As you head past the benches that conveniently dot the trail, be mindful of bicyclists. Cooper River shimmers to the left past a series of stone steps leading down to a soccer field. Trees line the route for a while, as you pass portable toilets, food trucks, and boat and kayak rentals, but soon you'll need your hat for protection from the sun. The impressive, orange-colored Camden County Boathouse, home to several New Jersey rowing clubs and available for party rentals, is on your left (0.4 mile). Walk around the building for a lovely river view and a stroll on the docks.

Back on the trail, commercial buildings line North Park Drive on your right, a wonderful urban contrast to the dewy green of the park. Stroll down the brick path to your left to admire a unique memorial for victims of terrorism. Picnic tables rest under 100-year-old trees. Look straight down North Park Drive at the Oz-like Philadelphia skyline shimmering in the distance. Follow the path over the Cooper River Bridge (1.1 miles), where NJ 30 and NJ 130 meet, but pause to take a left down the stone staircase to visit the Polish war memorials. When you cross the bridge, stop in the middle for a moment to drink in the river view. The sign for Camden city limits is on the other side of the bridge. Veer left once you cross the bridge, staying on the asphalt path, which winds past a pavilion and viewing tower toward the river. At the parking lot, turn left. You are now walking east on South Park Drive.

South Park Drive, technically in Collingswood, is a very pretty residential street. Soon, on your left, is a mowed path around tall greenery. Follow the path to a hidden wooden bridge and pond: a cool, shady reprieve (1.1 miles). The semicircular path curves back to the trail. Admire a dolphin statue and several others in an outdoor sculpture park (2.3 miles). In the parking lot for the Cooper River Yacht Club rests a huge old anchor. A sweet little park building, Hopkins House, is next (250 South Park Drive). Walk around back and admire the view, the wide, green expanse, and giant trees leading to the river. Take advantage of the picnic tables and trees. A bit farther along you'll see a breathtakingly big weeping willow and a mimosa tree at the water's edge. At the traffic light, take the crosswalk over across Cuthbert Boulevard (3.0 miles) to continue on South Park Drive. More residential areas are to the right. The trail is quieter and more peaceful here, the river narrower and wooded. You may see a hawk or an eagle.

Cooper River is perfect for boating, an adventure to keep in mind for your next visit.

Cross to the circular stone platform on your left, walk down the short dirt path, and you'll be in a meadow the length of several football fields. The river, which seems to disappear, is through the trees ahead. Explore here if you'd like, otherwise, return to the asphalt trail.

The trail curves generously left at a large yellow arrow. Here at the arrow, make a side trip to a meadow by taking the dirt path on your left (3.8 miles), which veers left to the huge meadow, a surprising find in this urban setting. Walk the meadow, keeping slightly to your left so that you will see a barely visible path through the woods. Take the path and be rewarded by solitude and peace at an old stone boat launch on the sleepy river. Retrace your steps to the yellow arrow and turn left. In a few hundred yards you'll reach Vesper Avenue, where the residential part of the loop begins, on sidewalks.

Turn left on Vesper Avenue, then curve right as Vesper changes to Oneida, where you continue on the sidewalk. At a T intersection, go left on Utica, then take the first right onto Center Street. After two blocks, go left on Melrose (4.4 miles). At a T intersection, head left onto Toledo Street, which curves and becomes Elgin (the river is to your left, but you can't see it yet). At another T intersection, turn left onto Locust. Then turn right onto Utica (4.8 miles) and carefully cross the still-active railroad tracks. Cross Coles Mill/Windsor Road (the street has two names and the street signs change from red to white). The road curves to the right and becomes Farwood Road—stay on this road. Do not take Farwood Circle. The neighborhoods are delightfully varied; some houses have solar panels on the rooftops.

Cross Longwood Street and Cedar Street. At the T intersection, turn left onto Grove Street (5.4 miles). The purple-and-green banners resume. Cross the river on the bridge. Steps offer a shady spot for a snack or rest. Past the steps, turn left onto the asphalt trail again (5.7 miles) and walk behind the National Guard Armory along the river. Go under a picturesque railroad bridge (6.1 miles). A parking lot and a dog park (Pooch Park) appear soon. Commercial businesses line the road on the right, and the wide river flows on your left. Cross Cuthbert Boulevard (7.1 miles)—you are 0.7 mile from your car. Boat rentals and an attractive viewing area pop up on the left; cross a stone bridge, where you might spot a white heron. Pass war memorials, modern sculpture, a pavilion, and statue of Christopher Columbus before reaching the parking lot.

## DID YOU KNOW?

Petty's Island floats in the Delaware River between Camden and Philadelphia. The Natural Lands Trust is cleaning up this former CITGO Petroleum Corporation facility, now home to rare plants and eagles, hawks, falcons, and more. Public access is planned for 2021, but you can tour now through the New Jersey Audubon Society.

## OTHER ACTIVITIES

Visit Dinosaur Discovery Park in nearby Haddonfield, where the world's first nearly complete dinosaur skeleton was excavated (dead end of Maple Avenue, just off Grove Street). Hike adjacent Pennypacker Park. Stroll the Camden waterfront to see the Battleship New Jersey Museum and Memorial, Adventure Aquarium, Camden's Children Garden, and the marina promenade. There are many places to eat on NJ 73. Thirty minutes northwest lies 250-acre Palmyra Cove Nature Park (1335 NJ 73, Palmyra).

## MORE INFORMATION

Open dawn to dusk. Camden County Board of Freeholders, Office of Constituent Services, Courthouse, Suite 306, 520 Market St., Camden, NJ 08102; 866-226-3362; camdencounty.com/service/parks/cooper-river-park.

## 49

# CARRANZA MEMORIAL TO APPLE PIE HILL TO ROUTE 72

This car shuttle hike in the Pine Barrens wonderland features black-tea-colored streams, cobalt blue lakes, Atlantic white cedar swamps, and the highest elevation in the Pine Barrens.

**LOCATION**
Tabernacle

**RATING**
Moderate

**DISTANCE**
12.3 miles

**ELEVATION GAIN**
500 feet

**ESTIMATED TIME**
5 to 6 hours

**MAPS**
USGS Indian Mills; njconservation.org/ documents/ BatonaTrailReroute Map.pdf; state.nj.us/dep/ parksandforests/parks/ docs/batona14web.pdf

## DIRECTIONS

Take US 206 South to 72 East. In about 2.5 miles, 72 crosses County Road 563. After 1.0 mile, look for a narrow roadside dirt lot on the right; it holds about ten cars. *GPS coordinates for dirt lot*: 39° 51.904′ N, 74° 31.703′ W.

This is a "car shuttle" hike, meaning that two drivers and two cars are needed for this hike. Both drivers should begin at the dirt lot listed above. One driver leaves a car at the dirt lot. The other driver will shuttle both hikers south 15 to 20 minutes to 163 Carranza Road. The hike starts here at Carranza Road, goes north, and ends at the dirt lot where the car is. You will need to drive back to Carranza Road to pick up the second car. Car shuttle directions to Carranza Road are as follows: Take 72 North, then turn left on 70 West, left on New Road, right on County Road 532, and right onto Carranza Road (County Road 648). Follow Carranza Road for about 1 mile; almost immediately after Carranza Road changes to a dirt road, look for a Batona camping area sign on the left and turn right onto the dirt road directly opposite the sign. The road quickly forks to the right; go right and park in the large dirt lot that holds about twenty cars. *GPS coordinates for Carranza Road lot*: 39° 46.608′ N, 74° 37.945′ W.

## TRAIL DESCRIPTION

You are about to hike a section (known as Section 3) of the famous Batona Trail. "Batona" is an acronym for BAck TO NAture and was coined by the Batona Hiking Club, which built the trail in 1961 and maintained it until

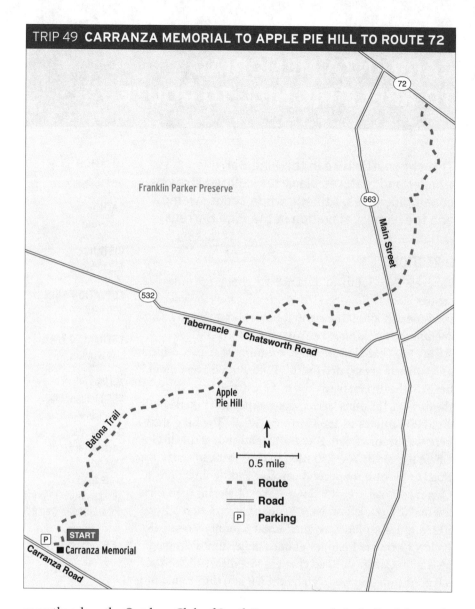

recently, when the Outdoor Club of South Jersey assumed the bulk of the work. The Batona Trail is 53.5 miles long and runs through the heart of the Pine Barrens (see page 148), cutting through Bass River State Forest, Wharton State Forest, Franklin Parker Preserve, and Brendan T. Byrne State Forest. The entire trail can be hiked in a minimum of three days, either by backpacking or car shuttling.

If you like pine trees, you'll adore this trip. Pine trees love the sandy, nutrient-poor soil here. Pitch pines, short-leaf pines, white pines, loblolly pines, pygmy pines, and Virginia pines render the surroundings green in winter, a good time to visit to avoid the bugs for which the Pine Barrens is infamous. Summer brings wild edibles, such as blueberries and huckleberries, but also brings chiggers. (*Note:* Coat your feet with repellent before you put on your socks.) Early spring, before the heat, showcases wildflowers, including carnivorous plants and wild orchids. In fall, the sedges, shrubs, and grasses mellow into color until the understory looks afire.

The hike travels south to north on Section 3 of the pink-blazed Batona Trail, heading in an easterly direction so the sun is at your back and not in your face. (Starting the hike by 10 A.M. or later will ensure this convenience.) This 12.3-mile section includes Wharton State Forest; an improved reroute through Franklin Parker Preserve, a former cranberry farm; and the southern tip of Brendan T. Byrne State Forest. (By going through Franklin Parker Preserve, hikers no longer have to walk along highway shoulders and through residential neighborhoods.) Be aware there are many footbridges, some a bit tricky. You'll travel only one trail—the pink-blazed Batona Trail, with many, many turns—all the way from the Carranza Memorial to Route 72. This involves a car shuttle. (See "Directions" section above for details.) Of course, if you don't want to use two cars, you can adjust the hike accordingly.

After you have reached the parking lot on Carranza Road, walk a few yards down the parking lot road and turn right toward the wooden barriers and the Carranza Memorial. Captain Emilio Carranza Rodriguez, the "Lindbergh of Mexico," crashed his plane here in 1928 during a thunderstorm. Walk past the memorial to the paved park road and turn right onto the road. (If you need a toilet, cross the road and enter the campground; a pit toilet is on the right.) Keep walking on the road, past the sign on the left for the Batona camping area, and after about one-eighth of a mile, look for a pink-blazed tree on the left. Pink blazes and wooden arrows mark the twisting, turning Batona Trail, so look closely for them. Turn left at the pink-blazed tree, go straight at an intersection, and follow the pink blazes. If you started at 10 A.M. or later you will keep the bright sun at your back, not in your eyes, because you are walking east.

Starkly beautiful Beaver Lodge Pond appears on the left. Take time to search for beaver dams; you may see a muskrat. Follow the pink blazes for two left turns, over white sand and into the woods. Note the mile markers every 0.5 mile to pace yourself. After the 32-mile marker, turn left at the pink blaze and cross a bridge. Turn right into the woods almost immediately after the bridge—tricky turn! You are headed to Apple Pie Hill, considered a high elevation (205 feet) in the Pine Barrens. Note the beautiful Atlantic white cedar swamp on the right. At the 32.5-mile marker, cross one of many picturesque but narrow footbridges. After you "summit" Tea Time Hill (see teapot sign), head toward the 60-foot fire tower (4.2 miles). A locked fence keeps out vandals, but the tower is open if staffed (call 609-726-9010 to find out beforehand). From the tower, you can see Philadelphia's skyline shimmering to the west and Atlantic City's to the south. Franklin Preserve (where you are heading) is east, and Fort Dix and the Lebanon fire tower are north.

Descend the tower, walk past it, and turn left, then right at the pink blaze, going into the woods again. At mile marker 35, turn right onto a road cover with deep sugar-sand. Turn left at the next pink blaze, then right near mile marker 36. Cross paved Tabernacle Chatsworth Road (County Road 532) into the woods (5.3 miles). You are now in the heart of Franklin Parker Preserve. Thank the New Jersey Conservation Foundation for purchasing this property and allowing public access. Listen for barred owls and tree frogs. Go right at the fork and check the nearby mailbox for a "Batona Trail Re-route" map. Then cross paved Russ Anderson Road (6.1 miles) into the woods. Follow the pink blazes to a fence delineating private property; go right here, then straight. The trail and footbridges bypass boggy, swampy areas. Look for carnivorous vegetation, such as sundews and pitcher plants.

Cross a dirt road and head toward the azure lake for a lunch break; this is the most peaceful place to linger. After you eat, follow the blazes over an interesting dirt-and-log path beside the lake, but be careful—it can be rooty and wet. Hike on a spine (an old cranberry/blueberry dike) between the lake on the left

**A still night at Franklin Parker Preserve; the Batona Trail runs through four preserves on this hike. Photo by Richard Lewis, AMC Photo Contest.**

and a bog on the right, a unique experience. Soon you'll cross County Road 563 (8.7 miles). Follow the blazes on a pretty rolling path over tannic streams to another pure lake. Head right around the lake, and take a rest on a convenient bench to admire the view. Then continue to follow the pink blazes. Be sure to turn right at the double blaze near the 40.5-mile marker, and take the footbridge. Rolling terrain begins, courtesy of former ATV trails. Go straight at a clearing with a trail mailbox, and cross paved Laurel Lane (11.1 miles). Navigate roots and footbridges, and cross another paved road, watching carefully for pink blazes. At about the 43.5-mile marker, there are wobbly footbridges over a rooty, seasonally wet swamp: It's fun, and a favorite part of the hike, but be careful. You'll soon see your car on Route 72.

## DID YOU KNOW?

The Carranza Memorial marks the site of the aviator's crash on July 12, 1928, during a historic goodwill flight from New York City to Mexico City. In New York City, 200,000 people lined the road to view his coffin. Mexican schoolchildren donated pennies to fund the memorial, made from granite near Carranza's home.

## OTHER ACTIVITIES

On the west side of Wharton State Forest lies one-mile Tom's Pond Trail and 15.5-mile Goshen Pond Trail. In the southern section, take the Batona Trail east about 6 miles to the ghost town of Martha, passing interesting ruins along the way. Go crazy and hike the entire Batona Trail north to south, from Ong's Hat to Coal Road (car shuttle or backpack). Take advantage of the famous New Jersey diners and other eateries on US 206 and NJ 72.

## MORE INFORMATION

The Batona Trail is maintained by the Batona Hiking Club (batona.wildapricot .org), the Outdoor Club of South Jersey (ocsj.org/hiking.html), and the New Jersey State Park Service at Wharton State Forest, 31 Batsto Road, Hammonton, NJ 08037; 609-561-0024; state.nj.us/dep/parksandforests/parks/wharton .html#trails.

# 50

# BRENDAN T. BYRNE STATE FOREST

Enjoy sandy, offbeat beauty as you hike past flooded and reclaimed cranberry bogs, floating tundra swans, and historic Whitesbog Village.

## DIRECTIONS

From the New Jersey Turnpike, take Exit 7 and follow US 206 South to NJ 70 East. Make a left onto CR 530 West. Pass a sign for Brendan T. Byrne State Forest, and turn right onto Whitesbog Road. Take a left into the Whitesbog Village visitor parking lot before the T intersection and general store. The dirt lot holds about 40 cars. *GPS coordinates: 39° 57.541' N, 74° 30.582' W.*

## TRAIL DESCRIPTION

Brendan T. Byrne State Forest (formerly Lebanon State Forest) is a 37,242-acre forest in the Pine Barrens. The Lebanon Glass Works operated here (lured by the sand) from 1851 to 1867. In 1908, the state acquired the land and began reforestation. Today, white cedars, pines, woodpeckers, and turkeys enliven the area. The white-sand trails dissecting the pure waters of flooded cranberry bogs (some of which are still farmed) provide a beauty like no other.

There are many trails available, but this hike is an easy, attractive one through the heart of the forest. Wooden markers with numbers 1 through 8 marked in red guide visitors through a birders' paradise: bluebirds, goldfinches, scarlet tanagers, pine warblers, and more. In the winter, graceful white tundra swans live here, taking a break from their home in the Arctic tundra. These shy birds are also called "whistling swans" because of their high-pitched honks. As with most hikes in the Pine Barrens, the trail is best from October through May, after chigger and bug season. Blueberry bushes and false heather color the

**LOCATION**
Browns Mills

**RATING**
Easy

**DISTANCE**
6.8 miles

**ELEVATION GAIN**
160 feet

**ESTIMATED TIME**
3 hours

**MAPS**
USGS Browns Mills;
njparksandforests.org/
parks/byrne.html

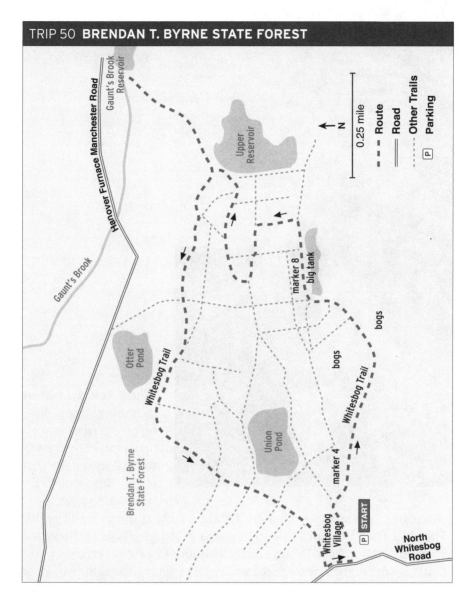

understory in fall, and you may spot a bald eagle. Early spring brings flowering gentian, leatherleaf, aster, and more.

From the parking lot, head over the wooden bridge toward the general store (stop in to pick up a Whitesbog hiking map), and turn right onto the Whitesbog Trail, which is a dirt path throughout the hike, at red marker 1. Admire the historical houses on the left and right as you approach red marker 2. Take a right at the fork to follow the Whitesbog Trail as it winds through the blueberry fields/ cranberry bogs. Admire the sphagnum moss bog. (Sphagnum moss can hold many times its weight in water and is excellent at preventing soil erosion.) At the New Jersey Women's Heritage Trail marker, read about Elizabeth Coleman

The classic sugar-sand of the Pine Barrens skirts the edges of former cranberry bogs.

White, best known for cultivating the blueberry. A true agricultural pioneer, White was the first female member of the American Cranberry Association.

Keep going straight to red marker 4. Take a right at the fork, still on the Whitesbog Trail, a dirt path, and continue to go straight. Take a left onto the Whitesbog Trail at the red arrow and red state forest sign at the cranberry bog. In winter, admire the artistry of the ice crystals webbing across the surface of the flooded bog. Now the soft, sandy path swallows your feet and rolls your ankles; be sure to wear shoes with good support. Go straight at the aqua-blue (not red, for unknown reasons) arrow, then turn right at the intersection to stay on Whitesbog Trail. Take some time to look around: You are walking a narrow strip of land between two flooded bogs, shining like diamonds in the sun. After red marker 8, turn left (1.9 miles).

At the next intersection, turn left to continue on the Whitesbog Trail. Enjoy the eerie, beautiful bogs; watch for Jersey Devil tracks in the sand (see page 189). Geese make arrows in the sky against the clouds. Take a right at the fork, and another right at the next fork. Enjoy the pitch pines, pygmy pines, and cedar trees. Keep going straight.

Take a left at the next fork (at Upper Reservoir). Look and listen for the visiting white tundra swans (November through March) clustered along the shore. Listen for their high-pitched, three-syllable *wow-wow-wow*. Look for houses for bluebirds. Keep straight at a three-way intersection with two unnamed trails. Go over a bridge and take a right. Then veer left to a lovely lunch stop at the faded, stenciled state forest sign, surrounded on three sides by Gaunt's Brook Reservoir. You can hear traffic from the highway, but you are hidden by the pines (3.7 miles).

Turn around and go back on the Whitesbog Trail the way you came until you reach the three-way intersection (4.3 miles). Take the middle trail and follow the double red arrows. Go left at a fork, then right at the next fork onto a fragrant pine straw–strewn path. Continue straight as the surface of the Whitesbog Trail becomes packed sand. Take the middle path when the trail splits, and keep going straight, over a wooden bridge. Ignore the first left after the bridge, but take the second left turn at the fork (5.6 miles). Keep going straight for 1.2 miles on the Whitesbog Trail, stopping to admire a beaver dam on your left. Note the huge, open sand area, like an inland beach, and enjoy the sparse beauty of sand, pine trees, bogs. The emptiness of the Pine Barrens is one of its main attractions. Go straight over hard, flat sand, with bird songs overhead. You'll see the homes of Whitesbog Village on the left; turn left on the path at the houses, and you are back to where you started.

## DID YOU KNOW?

New Jersey is the third-largest cranberry-producing state, and nearly all the berries are produced in the Pine Barrens. Prime harvesting season is mid-September through mid-November. You can book a cranberry bog tour in October from Pine Barrens Native Fruits (888-272-6264). Sand from the Pine Barrens was used in Ipana toothpaste, popular in the 1950s.

## OTHER ACTIVITIES

Tour the 36-building Whitesbog Village, once the family farm of J.H. White and now managed by the Whitesbog Preservation Trust. The White family began growing cranberries here in 1857. Pick up a map from the still-operating general store. Hike the popular Mount Misery and Pakim Pond trails in the state forest. At the far southwestern corner of the park lies Ong's Hat trailhead, considered to be the beginning access point to the 53.5-mile-long Batona Trail. Don't try to hike it all in one day! state.nj.us/dep/parksandforests/parks/docs/batona14web.pdf.

## MORE INFORMATION

New Jersey State Park Service at Brendan T. Byrne State Forest, P.O. Box 215, New Lisbon, NJ 08064; 609-726-1191; njparksandforests.org/parks/byrne.html.

# APPENDIX
# OTHER HIKES IN NEW JERSEY

Briefly listed below, by region and county, are some hike-worthy trails not included in this book due to space constraints or extensive coverage in other publications. Research these gems on your own; maps are readily available from land managers' websites. Happy trails!

## SKYLANDS
## MORRIS COUNTY

**Black River County Park (Chester):** Four trails wind through this pretty 858-acre park. Take the popular 2.3-mile Black River Trail along the Black River and past the Cooper gristmill.

**Farney State Park (Rockaway):** Hike a portion of the 10.4-mile Four Birds Trail on a 7-mile moderate loop hike to Indian Cliffs. Check out the bat-viewing platform at Hibernia Mine in the 4,866-acre park. On Split Rock Road across the Splitrock Reservoir Dam.

**Hacklebarney State Park (Long Valley):** This 1,186-acre park is home to the hemlock ravines and the Black River. Hike 9 rugged but short trails, totaling 5 miles. Try the 0.1 mile waterfall trail. The park is known for brilliant foliage in the fall. 119 Hacklebarney Road.

**Pyramid Mountain National Historic Area (Montville):** A moderate hike to Tripod Rock (a 180-ton boulder balanced on three smaller boulders) on the 3-mile loop hike via Mennen Trail is a must in this 1,534-acre area. Thirty miles of trails include a waterfall hike on the 5.2-mile Turkey Mountain loop hike. 472 Boonton Avenue.

## HUNTERDON COUNTY

**Allamuchy Mountain State Park (Hackettstown):** The Musconetcong River winds through this 9,092-acre park, which is divided into the southern Allamuchy Natural area (14 miles of marked trails) and the northern section of the park (20 miles of unmarked trails). Three miles north of Hackettstown between Willow Grove/ Waterloo Road (Route 604) on the east, Route 517 on the west, and Cranberry Lake (Route 206) on the north.

**Ken Lockwood Gorge Wildlife Management Area (Annandale):** Walk the unpaved road (closed to cars) that parallels the South Branch of the Raritan River through a deep gorge. This 498-acre preserve is one of New Jersey's most picturesque wildlife management areas. Also try the Columbia Trail. 203 Raritan River Road.

**Musconetcong Gorge Preserve (Bloomsbury):** Take the moderate-to-strenuous Ridge and Highlands trails (views of the gorge) and Waterfall Trail in this 523-acre preserve. 182 Dennis Road.

**Spruce Run Recreation Area (Clinton):** Spruce Run Reservoir is the third largest reservoir in the state and 15 miles of recreational shoreline grace this park. All trails are easy to moderate, including 2.6 miles of the Highlands Trail. 68 Van Sycel's Road.

**Stephens State Park (Hackettstown):** Follow an easy but rocky path along the Musconetcong River, which flows through this 805-acre park. Choose among six marked trails, ranging from flat to steep and rocky; includes 2 miles of the Highlands Trail. 800 Willow Grove Street.

**Voorhees State Park (Glen Gardner):** The Civilian Conservation Corps (CCC) built many trails and structures in this 1,336 acre-park. Twelve easy-to-moderate trails crisscross the park, including 2.3 miles of the Highlands Trail. 251 County Road (Route 513).

**Wickecheoke Creek Preserve (Stockton):** Ramble along the creek on easy Wickecheoke Trail in this 4,000-acre preserve. Wear waterproof boots because the creek can get high after periods of rain. In the middle of the Wickecheoke Creek Preserve you can find New Jersey's only covered bridge. Built circa 1860, the Green Sergeant's Covered Bridge crosses the creek at County Road 604. 24 Risler Street.

## WARREN COUNTY

**White Lake Natural Resource Area (Hardwick):** A moderate yellow-blazed trail and a blue-blazed trail take you past 69-acre, spring-fed White Lake, with its chalky marl bottom composed of freshwater mollusk shells and clay. "Marl" is sedimentary rock or soil consisting of clay and lime, formerly used as fertilizer. Walk past ruins of a marl processing factory and lime kilns in the 394-acre park. Entrance on Stillwater Road (CR 521).

## SUSSEX COUNTY

**Janet Van Gelder Wildlife Sanctuary (Sussex):** Enjoy two rugged trails (each 3 miles or less) marked by white blazes and red plastic ties in this 221-acre sanctuary. Look for red-tailed hawks and search for Chewbacca's grave (a dog, one hopes). Take CR 515 to Lounsberry Hollow Road.

## SOMERSET COUNTY

**Lord Stirling Park (Basking Ridge):** Adjacent to the Great Swamp National Wildlife Refuge, this 425-acre park has 8 miles of hiking trails, which include 3 miles of ADA-accessible boardwalk through a sensitive marsh landscape. Former estate of William Alexander (who was never recognized as a Lord by Parliament). 190 Lord Stirling Road.

**Washington Valley Park (North Branch):** Find easy hiking around the 21-acre reservoir on Red Reservoir Trail. Enjoy hawk migration in fall. This 719-acre park is at the geographic center of Somerset County. Entrances on Miller Lane (hawk-watching) and Newman's Lane (reservoir).

## GATEWAY
## PASSAIC COUNTY

**Apshawa Preserve (West Milford):** Five miles of easy trails in the heart of the Highlands of northern New Jersey. 4 Northwood Drive.

**Franklin Lakes Nature Preserve (Franklin Lakes):** Take an easy stroll around a 75-acre lake. A universally accessible trail runs along part of the waterfront. 1 Nature Preserve Way.

**High Mountain Park Preserve (Wayne):** Challenge yourself on 11.5 miles of trail in this 1,300-acre preserve. Try the 4-mile summit hike on Summit Trail. This is the Preakness Range of the Watchung Mountains. 100 University Drive.

**Pequannock Watershed (Newfoundland):** Clear streams, ponds, and dramatic rock outcroppings invite hiking in this 151,847-acre watershed. Try moderate Bearfort Ridge, Hanks Pond, and Firetower hikes. Permit required and fee charged. 167–127 Echo Lake Road.

**Wawayanda State Park (Milford and Hewitt):** Challenge yourself with 60 miles of trails in a 34,500-acre park. Walk a suspension bridge. Hike to Terrace Pond at 1,380 feet. Explore Bearfort Mountain Natural Area. Twenty miles of the Appalachian Trail run through this park. Main entrance is on 885 Warwick Turnpike, Hewitt.

## HUDSON COUNTY

**Stephen R. Gregg Park (Bayonne):** Stroll this 100-acre park, named after a World War II hero. A half-mile promenade offers dramatic waterfront views along Newark Bay. John Fitzgerald Boulevard off of I-78 (Bergen County).

**Hackensack River Greenway (Teaneck):** Travel 3.5 miles along Hackensack River (the Continental Army crossed here: "a bridge that saved the nation"). There are several public access points, including this one from Andreas Park: From Route 4 East, take the River Road/Teaneck/Bogota/New Milford exit on right. Follow the signs for River Road at the bottom of the ramp. Turn left for the section of the Greenway heading north, and right for its southern section. To begin a hike at Andreas Park travel 0.5 mile north on River Road from the Route 4 off-ramp to Grenville Avenue and turn left.

**Historic New Bridge Landing (River Edge):** Stop at Bergen County Historical Society for this walking tour covering the American Revolution. New Bridge served as a battleground, fort, encampment ground, military headquarters, and intelligence-gathering post in every year of the American Revolution. 1201 Main Street.

**Ramapo Valley County Reservation (Mahwah):** A 4,000-acre park where you can exercise your dog around Scarlet Oak Pond as well as take moderate-to-strenuous hikes such as the 3.75-mile Vista Loop and the 3-mile Ridge Loop. 608 Ramapo Valley Road (Route 202).

**Ringwood State Park (Ringwood):** Trails are moderate in this 4,444-acre park. Visit New Jersey Botanical Garden, Shepherd Lake, and Ringwood Manor, a mansion with relics from the iron-making days. 1304 Sloatsburg Road.

**Saddle River County Park (Saddle Brook):** Enjoy easy, urban hiking along a stream in the 577-acre park. 1417 Saddle River Road.

**Tenafly Nature Center (Tenafly):** Seven marked trails and a butterfly house grace this 400-acre center. Try yellow-blazed Pfister's Pond Trail. 313 Hudson Avenue.

## UNION COUNTY

**Rahway River Park (Clark):** Hike a 4-mile urban trail along the Rahway River. St. George Avenue off of I-95.

## ESSEX COUNTY

**Eagle Rock Reservation (West Orange):** Enjoy 400 acres along the Watchung Mountain ridge. The easy Lenape Trail (see Trip 17) skirts the eastern edge of the park. Visit the Essex County 9/11 Memorial with extraordinary views of the New York City skyline. The main entrance to the park is located on Eagle Rock Avenue, between Prospect and Mountain avenues.

**Hilltop Reservation (Verona):** Short, easy trails take you along a preserved ridge-line located on the second Watchung Mountain. Try 1.3-mile Peace Trail and 0.3-mile More Peace Trail in the 282-acre park. Eastern entrance on Fairview Road between Valley View and Bolton roads.

**South Mountain Reservation (West Orange):** Hike six marked trails in the 2,110-acre reservation. Six miles of the moderate Lenape Trail (see Trip 17) run through here, and lead to waterfalls. Easy and pretty fall hike from Tulip Springs parking area along Glen Avenue in the town of Millburn takes you along Rahway River to Hemlock Falls. Cherry Lane, off of I-78.

## JERSEY SHORE
## MONMOUTH COUNTY

**Allaire State Park (Wall Township):** Enjoy 20 miles of trails in this 3,205-acre park. Park on Route 524 (Atlantic Avenue) in the large, multiuse Edgar Felix Memorial Bikeway and the Freehold and Jamesburg Railroad Trail parking lot, or at the park entrance. 4625 Atlantic Avenue.

**Huber Woods Park (Locust):** Use 8 miles of hiking trails in this 367-acre woods, which includes an environmental center and reptile house. 25 Brown's Dock Road.

**Manasquan Reservoir (Howell):** Enjoy 1,205 acres of popular woods and wetlands. Hike 5 miles around the reservoir or walk the 1.1-mile Cove Trail for wildlife viewing and to visit the environmental center. 311 Windeler Road.

**Monmouth Battlefield State Park (Manalapan):** Wander a 1,818-acre American Revolution battlefield (excellent visitor center). 16 Business Route 33.

**Perrineville Lake Park (Millstone):** Wander 5 miles of easy trails in this 1,239-acre park with several entrances. Take 1.5-mile Lakeview Loop Trail. 23 Agress Road.

**Turkey Swamp Park (Freehold):** This is the largest park in the county at 2,261 acres, with a 17-acre lake and 9 miles of easy trails. 200 Georgia Road.

## OCEAN COUNTY

**Bass River State Forest (Tuckerton):** Hike 23 miles of trails, including a white pine plantation planted in 1928; Joe's Trail and Absegami Trail are popular; part of the 53.5-mile-long Batona Trail also runs through here. 762 Stage Road.

**Cattus Island County Park (Toms River):** Take easy strolls on 6.9 miles of well-marked trails on 500 acres, enjoying Barnegat Bay views. Visit Cooper Environmental Center. 1170 Cattus Island Boulevard.

**Cloverdale Farm County Park (Barnegat):** Stroll a 1.4-mile nature trail on a 90-acre working cranberry farm rich in history. 34 Cloverdale Road.

**Double Trouble State Park (Bayville):** Walk 8 flat miles in this 8,495-acre park in the Pine Barrens, which includes a historic district and cranberry bogs; an extensive trail guide is available online. 81 Pinewald Kewsick Road (County Route 618).

**Jakes Branch County Park (Beachwood):** The hangar where the Hindenburg was kept is visible in the distance. Hike 8.6 miles of easy trails in this 400-acre park billed as the "Gateway to the Pinelands." There's a five-story observation deck. 1100 Double Trouble Road.

**Lochiel Creek County Park (Barnegat):** An easy 1.75-mile trail in a 177-acre park in freshwater wetlands and pin oak uplands includes a connector to the longer, flat Barnegat Branch Trail (Trip 28). 950 Barnegat Boulevard North.

# GREATER ATLANTIC CITY
## ATLANTIC COUNTY

**Cedar Lake Wildlife Management Area (Williamstown/Buena Vista):** The sandy trails of the Pine Barrens surround a beautiful natural lake. In winter, walk 0.2 mile north of the dam on the left side of Jackson Road, then cross a dike to the back of the lake to spot bald eagles. 117 Jackson Road in Williamstown.

**Clarks Landing Preserve (Port Republic):** This is a destination for nature lovers (especially those who love pitcher plants and bald eagles). The trails in this 654-acre preserve (administered by the New Jersey Natural Lands Trust) are not particularly well-marked, but a short, sandy path follows Mullica River. From the intersection of Route 30 and Route 50 in Egg Harbor City, continue West on Route 30/White Horse Pike. After 3.1 miles, turn left on Leipzig Avenue. After 5 miles, continue across Clarks Landing Road into the roadside parking area for Clarks Landing Preserve on Clarks Landing Road.

**Hammonton Creek Wildlife Management Area (Hammonton):** The trails at this 4,852-acre expanse are not well-marked, but this is the former site of a large World War I ammunition company. Also thrilling are the remnants of a 1.5-mile-long elevated wooden racetrack loop, built by the Atlantic City Motor Speedway. (Please respect the private property boundaries.) From the intersection of Route 30 and Route 206 in Hammonton, continue East on Route 30/White Horse Pike. After 2.3 miles, turn left onto Moss Mill Road. After 1.5 miles, turn left onto a sand road just before the sign for Hammonton.

**Hammonton Lake Park (Hammonton):** This park (part of the Pine Barrens) has flat terrain, a lake, and wildlife (turtles are especially lively in spring). Hammonton is also the self-proclaimed blueberry capital of the world. You can manage a 2- to 3-mile hike if you combine Hammonton with the adjacent Smith Conservation Area. 100 Sports Drive.

**KEEP Conservation Preserve (Port Republic):** This little-known local nonprofit preserve of 83 acres of woodlands and wetlands lies along Nacote Creek. See Great Horned Owls, egrets, osprey, and bald eagles. On Chestnut Neck Road off Route 9 (New York Road).

**Lakes Bay Preserve (Pleasantville):** This secluded 24-acre peninsula (administered by the New Jersey Conservation Foundation) juts southward into the bay. Enjoy a marsh and share a half-mile strip of sandy beach with pelicans and sea lavender. Strong, steady winds make it a great spot to watch wind surfers. The bay was named after Simon Lake, a Pleasantville native, who invented the submarine in 1894. Public access is by foot only. Lakes Bay Preserve is at the end of Baypoint Drive off the Black Horse Pike, West Atlantic City.

**Weymouth Furnace Park and John's Woods Preserve (Weymouth):** There are no marked trails, but industrial history buffs can wander the ruins of an 1800s furnace, forge, and paper mill. To make this a nature hike (and see more ruins), cross County Route 559 (Weymouth Road), and walk the trails of 202-acre John's Woods Preserve, administered by the New Jersey Natural Lands Trust. 2050 Weymouth Road.

## SOUTHERN SHORE
## CAPE MAY COUNTY

**Cape May National Wildlife Refuge (Cape May Court House):** Four easy trails cover about 3 miles through marshes and forests. Look for piping plovers. 24 Kimbles Beach Road.

**Corson's Inlet State Park (Ocean City):** Enjoy undeveloped land along the oceanfront. Four trails, each less than 1 mile, feature sand dunes and bird-watching. County Highway 619.

**Higbee Beach Wildlife Management Area (Cape May):** Trails in this serene spot lead to a 1.5-mile beach at the tip of Cape Island along Delaware Bay. The six sites in this more than 1,000-acre wildlife management area are Signal Hill, Davey's Lake, Pond Creek, Sassafras Island, Hidden Valley, and the magnesite plant. Take Route 626 to New England Road (County Route 641). After 1.5 miles, the road dead-ends at the beach on New England Road.

**Lizard Tail Swamp Preserve (Cape May Court House):** Hike 3 easy miles within the Cape May Forest on trails created by The Nature Conservancy. 460 Court House–South Dennis Road.

## CUMBERLAND COUNTY

**Egg Island Wildlife Management Area (Fortescue):** The hikes are short and easy on a quiet beach, past salt marshes and tidal creeks, in this 6,714-acre expanse with diamondback terrapins and horseshoe crabs. Take County Route 553 to Maple Street.

**Eldora Nature Preserve (Delmont):** Hike 5 miles of marshes, swamps, and woodlands on three trails. A boardwalk overlooks West Creek and a marsh. The preserve is on the southern end of the Pine Barrens and is the site of The Nature Conservancy New Jersey Chapter's Southern Field Office, established expressly for the protection of rare moths. 2350 NJ 47.

**Harold N. Peek Preserve (Millville):** Hike wetlands around the Maurice River and observe a wild rice marsh in this 344-acre preserve. As you roam 3 miles of easy trails, you may spot an eagle. 2100 South Second Street.

## DELAWARE RIVER
## MERCER COUNTY

**Abbott Marshlands (Bordentown):** Tidal freshwater wetlands can be found in the congested Trenton-Hamilton-Bordentown area, amazingly enough. Several trails are in Abbott Marshlands. Bordentown Bluffs Trail is of moderate difficulty and is part of Delaware and Raritan Canal State Park. Pretty and wooded, it follows Crosswicks Creek. Easy trails include Roebling Park Trail in Spring Lake, Tidal Water Trail, and Towpath Trail. The Bordentown Bluffs Trail entrance is at 180 Orchard Ave.

**Institute Woods and Rogers Refuge (Princeton):** Find 13 miles of easy trails and great bird-watching on protected land and a refuge adjacent to Princeton Battlefield State Park. For Rogers Refuge, take Alexander Street toward Route 1, and turn right onto West Drive just before the Stony Brook Bridge. After 0.25 mile, park on West Drive, or turn left onto the gravel driveway and park in the small lot next to the first viewing platform. 10 West Drive.

**Princeton Battlefield State Park (Princeton):** Hike the suspension bridge. This loop is less than 1 mile through the woods but very rewarding. The park is 1.5 miles south of Princeton University and 3.8 miles north of Interstate 295/95. Mercer Road (Princeton Pike).

**Stony Brook-Millstone Watershed Association (Pennington):** Hike 3 to 5 easy miles past a farm, meadows, and a pond. This sometimes-whimsical trail features a Haiku Station, a Hobbit Tree, and a Lonely Tree. 31 Titus Mill Road.

## BURLINGTON COUNTY

**Crystal Lake Park (Bordentown):** This 370-acre park includes 8 miles of moderate trails through woods and past wetlands and a lake. 2401 Axe Factory Road.

**Historic Smithville Park (Easthampton):** Hike about 4 miles of easy trails (one of them floats) past Smith Mansion and an old factory complex. 801 Smithville Road.

**Rancocas State Park (Hainesport):** This 1,252-acre park offers about 8 miles of easy trails in a 58-acre natural area of forests with an extensive freshwater tidal marsh. Enter on Rancocas Road or Deacon Road.

## CAMDEN COUNTY

**Pennypacker Park (Haddonfield):** Hike lovely, easy, wooded trails near Cooper River, Hopkins Pond, and Driscoll Pond. Search for the commemorative stone that marks where William Foulke discovered the first nearly complete dinosaur skeleton in 1858. Pennypacker Park is bounded by Kings Highway, Park Boulevard, and Grove Street.

**Winslow Fish and Wildlife Management Area (Hammonton):** Go through calm, peaceful hardwood and upland forests, fields, swamps, and past a section of the Great Egg Harbor River. There is a 1.6-mile round-trip hike that follows the Blue Hole Trail (blazed with a blue dot on a white dot). Blue Holes are rumored to be dark-blue, deep hangouts for the Jersey Devil, who will pull you to the bottom in a flash if you so much as dip a toe. It's a fun place to wander and eat blueberries. Take US 322 to Piney Hollow Road; go west on Inskip Road off Piney Hollow Road. Trail entrance is behind an archery range.

## GLOUCESTER COUNTY

**Piney Hollow Preservation Area (Newfield):** In this space right next to Unexpected Wildlife Refuge (see below), visitors can hike several miles of moderately difficult trails through woods and over bogs, dikes, and swamps. 1394–1526 Piney Hollow Winslow Road.

**Tranquility Trail (Woolrich Township):** Take an hour-long hike through wildflowers and fields, with brief woods, to a vista of Raccoon Creek. The name of the trail was chosen from hundreds of student projects from the township's schools. 300–331 High Hill Road.

**Unexpected Wildlife Refuge (Newfield):** Explore and observe nature and swamps in about 10 miles of moderately difficult trails (tricky bridges, blowdown). All visitors must make an appointment (call 856-697-3541). 110 Unexpected Road.

**Woods of Wenonah (Wenonah):** Walk 6 miles of easy trails, marked by wooden trail signs, and traverse 40 bridges! Railroad tracks bisect the woods, so the trails run on both the east and the west sides of the railroad tracks. North Jefferson Avenue.

## SALEM COUNTY

**Elephant Swamp Trail (Elk Township):** A 12-mile out-and-back hike travels along an old railroad line, built in 1978 and demolished in the 1990s. Features include farmland, swamps, Atlantic white cedars, and open fields, with some nature signage. Legend has it that when a circus was traveling by train through Elk Township in the 1800s, an elephant escaped. The elephant got loose in the swamp and was never seen again. From Route 55, take exit 45, and head South on CR 553 (Bucks Road). Turn right at the first light onto Route 538/Elk Road. After 1.4 miles, turn left into the parking area on Elk Road.

**Fort Mott State Park (Pennsville):** A post–Civil War fort offers easy trails (less than 2 miles). 454 Fort Mott Road.

**Supawna Meadows National Wildlife Refuge (Pennsville):** In spring, hike the short Forest Habitat Trail through a forest and around a pond to hear a symphony of spring peepers and southern leopard frogs. Grassland Trail is good for viewing northern harriers and American kestrels in winter; an observation platform overlooks a finger of tidal marsh. The refuge is supported by the Friends of Supawna Meadows National Wildlife Refuge. 197 Lighthouse Road.

# INDEX

# ABOUT THE AUTHOR

Priscilla Estes, the former chair of AMC's Delaware Valley Chapter, has been leading hikes since 1996. In 2012, she summited Kilimanjaro at the age of 56. After years of editing medical books and writing magazine features and a novel, she now hikes, writes, teaches yoga, and plays the gong; visit priscillaestes.com.

# AMC BOOK UPDATES

At AMC Books, we keep our guidebooks as up-to-date as possible to help you plan safe and enjoyable adventures. After publishing a book, if we learn that trails have been relocated, or that route or contact information has changed, we will post an update online. Before you hit the trail, check outdoors.org/bookupdates.

While hiking or paddling, if you notice discrepancies with a trip description or map, or if you find any other errors in the book, please submit them by email to amcbookupdates@outdoors.org or by letter to Books Editor, c/o AMC, 10 City Square, Boston, MA 02129. We will verify all submissions and post key updates each month. We are dedicated to making AMC Books a recognized leader in outdoor publishing. Thank you for your participation.

# ABOUT AMC IN NEW JERSEY

## AMC's Delaware Valley Chapter

The Appalachian Mountain Club's Delaware Valley Chapter offers a wide variety of hiking, backpacking, climbing, paddling, bicycling, snowshoeing, and skiing trips each year, as well as social, family, and young member programs and instructional workshops. The chapter also maintains a 15-mile section of the Appalachian Trail between Wind Gap and Little Gap, as well as trails at Valley Forge National Historical Park. The Delaware Water Gap is also home to AMC's Mohican Outdoor Center, a frequent base for AMC's outdoor leadership workshops. A 90-minute drive from New York City, Mohican offers front-porch access to the Delaware Water Gap, with self-service cabins, comfortable bunkrooms, and the river, wetlands, and Appalachian Trail a stroll away.

To view a list of AMC activities in Pennsylvania, central and south New Jersey, northern Delaware, and other parts of the Northeast and Mid-Atlantic, visit outdoors.org/activities.

## AMC's New York–North Jersey Chapter

The New York–North Jersey Chapter of the Appalachian Mountain Club hosts more than 2,000 outdoor recreation activities per year. With more than 12,000 members, the New York–North Jersey Chapter is the second largest of the twelve regional chapters of the Appalachian Mountain Club. The chapter offers its members more than 20 outdoor events on most weekends, many for beginners.

The New York–North Jersey Chapter of the Appalachian Mountain Club celebrated its 100th Anniversary in 2012, and was the first AMC chapter to be formed. Members come from the New York City metro area, southeastern New York, and northeastern New Jersey area. To view a list of AMC activities in the New York–North Jersey region, visit outdoors.org/activities.

## BE OUTDOORS

**Since 1876**, the Appalachian Mountain Club has channeled your enthusiasm for the outdoors into everything we do and everywhere we work to protect. We're inspired by people exploring the natural world and deepening their appreciation of it.

With AMC chapters from Maine to Washington, D.C., including groups in Boston, New York City, and Philadelphia, you can enjoy activities like hiking, paddling, cycling, and skiing, and learn new outdoor skills. We offer advice, guidebooks, maps, and unique eco-lodges and huts to inspire your next outing.

Your visits, purchases, and donations also support conservation advocacy and research, youth programming, and caring for more than 1,800 miles of trails.

**Join us!**
outdoors.org/join

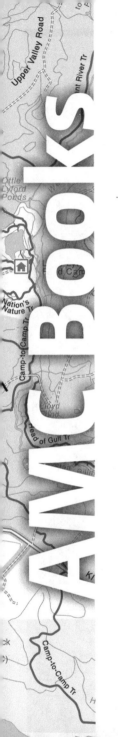